How to Keep Your
Muscle Car Alive

How to Keep Your
Muscle Car Alive

Harvey White, Jr.

This book is dedicated to all of the performance-car owners who strive to create a
true daily driver and then live with it each and every day. It is also dedicated to my understanding and loving wife.

First published in 2009 by Motorbooks, an imprint of MBI Publishing Company, 400 First Avenue North, Suite 300, Minneapolis, MN 55401 USA

Motorbooks titles are also available at discounts in bulk quantity for industrial or sales-promotional use. For details write to Special Sales Manager at MBI Publishing Company, 400 First Avenue North, Suite 300, Minneapolis, MN 55401 USA.

To find out more about our books, visit us online at www.motorbooks.com.

ISBN-13: 978-0-7603-3546-8

On the cover: Big block Hemi or small block wedge, manual or automatic transmission, points or electronic ignition—the technology your muscle car relies on might be forty years old, but you can still count on it to get you down the road today.

On the title pages: Whether it's a MoPar, Ford, or General Motors product, any muscle car can be a reliable daily driver. All it takes is a little effort.

On the back cover: Rear axles need love, too. And, if you know what you're doing, they're easy to work on.

About the author:
Author Harvey White has always appreciated muscle cars. He was fortunate enough to be a teenager in the 1970s when muscle cars were plentiful and inexpensive. While he was still in high school he purchased his first muscle car, a 1969 Olds 442, from its original owner for $500. He has owned and driven a muscle car ever since. His current car is a 1968 Oldsmobile 442 convertible. It's been his daily driver for the past 23 years. Harvey works as an engineering manager in the computer industry. Previously, he owned an automotive service shop that specialized in automotive wiring, fuel injection, and carburetion. He decided to write this book to pass on what he has learned through years of experience keeping muscle cars alive.

Editor: James Manning Michels
Designer: Mandy Iverson

Printed in Singapore

CONTENTS

INTRODUCTION

This book is a practical, real-world guide to driving your three- or four-decade-old vehicle every day. The book ties together many lesser-known tips and tricks and focuses on the more unusual problems the owner of a car this old will face.

The engineers who designed your muscle car did not even begin to consider what it would take to make a vehicle that would last 30 to 40 years or more. This does not mean that your old muscle car cannot be reliable; with a little work from you it can be.

Note that this book is not a how-to-hot-rod guide, as there are several books out there that focus on increasing horsepower and upgrading suspensions and so on.

Bear in mind that years of repair and modification can result in incorrect parts being used, or mismatched combinations of parts, either of which can result in a vehicle that is no longer enjoyable or reliable, and therefore cannot realistically be driven on a regular basis. This book offers tips to help sort out and correct past mistakes. For example, most muscle cars did not come with disc brakes. It is relatively easy to bolt on some calipers, and, presto, now the car has disc brakes. But what about the master cylinder and the brake valves? If these are not also updated, the brakes will not function properly.

This book also focuses on some aspects of vehicle repair that are not common on newer front-wheel-drive vehicles. For example, rear axle service. Remember, if you choose not to service your rear axle yourself and wonder who could do it for you, find a four-wheel-drive truck specialist. They will know how to properly set up your rear axle, or diagnose a driveline vibration that may have been the result of a past transmission swap.

This book is not intended to be a replacement for factory service manuals (which every car owner should have) nor for detailed how-to books that focus on specific components, such as an automatic transmission manual. Instead, this book is intended to be a supplement and an overall guide to help you sort though the various systems on your muscle car.

Finally, you don't have to perform all of the work on your vehicle in order to benefit from this book. Reading this book can be helpful when working with your mechanic. The information can be used to familiarize yourself with some of the considerations that need to be made when making a change, no matter who does the actual wrenching.

CHAPTER 1
WHAT IS A MUSCLE CAR?

As far as this book is concerned, a muscle car is any American-built performance car. I know that some will disagree, as there are those who define a muscle car as a 1964–1971 American-built intermediate model. This book includes all classic American performance cars. Late-model muscle cars such as the Camaro SS, Firebird Trans-Am, or Mustang GT are capable performance cars but are not included in this because they are already reliable daily drivers. This book will focus on what it takes to turn your classic performance vehicle into a reliable, fun car that can be driven daily.

Detroit auto manufacturers created early muscle cars by adding high-performance components to existing models. These components were offered as a package, and this combination of components defined the muscle car. The package included a high-performance big-block engine, heavy-duty transmission, heavy-duty rear axle, upgraded cooling system, and some sort of trim to identify the model. Most muscle car packages also included larger tires. Surprisingly, most muscle car packages in the 1960s and early 1970s did not include a limited-slip rear axle as standard equipment. Factory gauges were also not normally standard equipment.

The big-block engine was one of the key elements that defined a muscle car. Each manufacturer, or for GM, each division, had engine variations that defined the performance level of the car, but generally the vast majority of muscle cars came with the same basic big-block engine as that manufacturer's big luxury cars. For example, Chevrolet produced the Caprice and the Impala, and these could be had with big-block power. In order to create the Chevelle SS, the 396 engine that was available for the large cars was installed in the midsize Chevy. These engines were then usually set up with hydraulic lifters and a four-barrel carburetor. The cam-lobe profile was more aggressive than the standard passenger car offering, but still very streetable. This yielded a very reliable car with moderate performance. Most of these cars in stock tune were capable of low- to mid-14-second quarter-mile times. Note that these realistic performance numbers are a far cry from the 11-second stories everyone likes to remember.

Each division also had one or more premium muscle cars. This was typically the very same car as the base-model muscle car, but with an engine in a more aggressive state of tune. The performance upgrades usually included a higher-performance camshaft (some with solid lifters) and a larger carburetor—or even multiple carburetors, like the Mopar Six Pack cars. Most muscle cars did not have headers, but some of the ultra-high-performance models came with headers in the trunk for the owner to install. Several of these high-performance packages also included a cold air induction system and a limited-slip rear axle. These premium versions are rare; most muscle cars were sold as base models.

Muscle cars were derived from standard passenger vehicles, so it makes sense that they can be just as reliable as a standard passenger car. In fact, many of the performance options added by the manufacturer, such as heavy-duty rear axles and transmissions, were intended to reduce warranty claims.

If you own a muscle car, chances are that it is one of the base models. If performance is your goal, don't fret, as the car's componentry provides a strong foundation upon which you can build a reliable performance machine.

Some enthusiasts believe a muscle car should be restored and not driven. I feel that these cars should be driven. If no one drives these cars, then younger generations will never know what a muscle car really is. How else can someone truly experience a muscle car unless they get to drive or ride in one?

Another topic covered by this book is how to diagnose and repair problems that typically arise with muscle cars. I'll focus on teaching you to think like a true mechanic. There are lots of parts changers out there, but a true mechanic diagnoses the problem and then corrects it. Most mechanics don't work this way; they have a suspicion of what is wrong and then they replace parts until the vehicle is operating correctly. This will not work with an older car that might previously have undergone questionable repairs. The problem might be that the wrong part is on the car.

This is true for every system on the car, so before you begin, you will need to find out if this is how the car came from the factory, or if someone performed a modification. If the offending system was modified, did it subsequently perform as expected? Answer these questions and then you can determine what is really wrong before you start replacing parts.

Another area in which this book will help is proper carburetor tuning. Modern computer-controlled fuel-injection systems have been around for so long that they have all but eliminated mechanics who are capable of properly rebuilding a carburetor, or even performing simple adjustments. If, for example, you need to make jetting changes or other carburetor modifications to properly support a long-duration camshaft, this book will be useful.

FACTORY MANUALS

It is a good idea to obtain a factory service manual. Reprints are available for most muscle cars from companies that specialize in selling reproduction parts. These manuals can prove invaluable when attempting to figure out what parts were installed on the car. Also, if you are running aftermarket parts or want to work on a specific component, obtain a good how-to book for that particular component. Even if you don't do the repair or modification yourself, understanding what should be done will be beneficial.

All the repair sequences described in this book will be explained assuming you have a service manual to guide you through the specifics of each procedure.

Take your time and enjoy working on your car. Take the time to figure out how the system or device that you are getting ready to work on or replace really works and what is going wrong or why it is not fulfilling its purpose. Also, as your vehicle deviates from stock, keep a log that lists what is not stock and where to get replacement parts or what vehicle the assembly that has been installed came from. For example, if the rear axle is replaced, note in the log what year and model car or which aftermarket supplier the rear axle came from. This can be invaluable if you need, for example, a rear axle bearing.

Finally, don't think that a classic car can be driven for years with only standard maintenance. This is simply not true. This is an old machine, and each part has a limited lifespan. Even if you replace and rebuild the entire car all at once, parts will occasionally need to be replaced and rebuilt. This is why I recommend a maintenance schedule.

STREETWORTHY AND RELIABLE

You cannot expect to be able to truly enjoy your muscle car unless it is streetworthy and reliable. But what exactly does streetworthy mean, and what defines reliable? There is much conjecture regarding these two terms, and the real answer will depend on you. Each one of us is different, and we each have certain expectations that a vehicle must fulfill, as well as quirks that we will overlook. A lot of the definition also stems from the capabilities of the vehicle. The owner of a Hemi Road Runner that runs 11-second quarter-mile times will most likely put up with more quirks than if the car had the base-level 383 and ran in the 14s.

It is up to you to set realistic expectations on what is streetworthy and what kind of reliability you expect from your vehicles. It should come as no surprise that I define a reliable vehicle, regardless of performance capabilities, as one that will start every time, and get me to and from work with no failures. That statement is easy to say and a little tougher to accomplish, as most of the vehicles this book pertains to are at least 35 years old. One key to reliability is scheduled maintenance. Another is careful component selection, especially during modification.

Modern technology has helped move the current generation of automobiles to new levels of reliability. This means two things to the muscle car driver: first, there are new advances that can really benefit your early model car, and also that the bar has been raised regarding drivability and performance. There are a few modern cars that are capable of 13-second quarter-mile times or are better right from the factory. These cars have factory air conditioning and premium sound systems. Several of these also get better than 20 miles per gallon on the highway. These cars also behave when stuck in traffic, with no overheating or stalling. Now add in the handling and braking performance; most muscle cars do not even begin to approach these levels of braking and turning performance.

But all is not lost. This book offers sound, realistic advice on how to turn your muscle car into a truly reliable performance machine. Improving the vehicle is part of the fun of owning a muscle car. Choosing components that enhance performance while also preserving reliability and drivability can prove to be a real challenge. Breaking down is frustrating, but even worse is suffering a failure as the result of a modification you made. Careful component selection can avoid this.

Another point to consider is that you will be happier if you keep the car balanced. As you modify one system, it will affect other systems in the vehicle. This may require you to make changes to what you thought was an unrelated system so it can keep up. For example, if you improve handling, you may have to improve the oiling system so the engine is not starved for oil during hard cornering. For me, this is part of the fun: making the whole car better while preserving reliability.

CHAPTER 2
MAINTENANCE

Proper maintenance is the cornerstone of reliability. You cannot expect to take a 35-year-old car and rely on it every day without maintaining it. Maintenance falls into two categories. The first is standard maintenance, which includes fluid changes and tune-ups. The second includes inspections of all stressed components. If this is beginning to sound like a lot of work, it is. But it is not that bad, and personally, I find it enjoyable.

Older cars break down. Most drivers will not put up with a vehicle that has stranded them, especially if it happens more than once. Performing preventive maintenance is the best way to prevent, or at least limit, these types of failures.

Don't get discouraged if you have a breakdown. A car is just a machine, and sooner or later something will break. When a component breaks, analyze the failure to determine what happened. Was the component overstressed? Was the component the wrong part for the intended use, such as an electric fuel pump designed for racing being used every day? Was the part defective? Or was the part neglected until it finally wore out and failed? Once you know what went wrong, you can correct the problem with confidence that that particular failure will not strand you again.

Standard maintenance is the scheduled replacement of lubricants and wear items. Note that replacing lubricants means changing more than just the engine oil. In addition to wear items, such as brake pads, you'll need to concern yourself with all the car's vital fluids. When was the last time you changed the rear axle fluid, or the steering system fluid? If you own a 35-year-old car, these fluids could also be 35 years old if the previous owners never changed them. I have discovered rear end fluid that looked like lumpy tar.

See Table 1 for the fluid change maintenance schedule I developed for my 4-4-2. The intervals apply to any muscle car of the era. Note that lubricant technology has advanced significantly in the last 35 years. You should create a similar table for your car. For this table, change the fluid at either the time or distance, whichever occurs first.

CHOOSING OILS

Lubrication technology has improved greatly since your muscle car was built. This will make a huge difference in how long your engine will last. But what oil should you use? There are several types—standard, synthetic, and synthetic blends. Also, what viscosity should you use? Are multi-viscosity oils safe to use? The answers to these questions depend on how you use your vehicle and what modifications have been made to it.

To select the appropriate oil, you must first understand the differences between what is available. For starters, synthetic, synthetic blend, or conventional: what is the difference? Sure, synthetics cost two to three times as much as conventional oils, but are they worth it?

Another item that needs to be understood is viscosity. This is simply how thick the oil is. This is important, as viscosity is what gives an oil its ability to withstand the shear loads from rotating and sliding surfaces and still provide lubrication. Remember, all oils lubricate by preventing contact between the moving surfaces—it stays between them. Viscosity gives oil the ability to perform this task.

TABLE 1: OLDSMOBILE 442 FLUID CHANGE INTERVALS

Fluid	Mileage	Time (months)	Notes
Engine oil and filter	3,000	3	Synthetic
Transmission and filter	15,000	12	Synthetic
Rear axle	30,000	24	Use synthetic gear lube. Change every 15,000 if equipped with an anti-slip differential.
Coolant	30,000	24	Use extended-life antifreeze.
Steering box	30,000	24	Use the recommended fluid.
Front wheel bearing grease	60,000	48	Do every second front brake job.

You will note that my standard tune-up and oil change interval is every three months or 3,000 miles. Even though I run synthetic motor oil, I still change the oil and filter every 3,000 miles. All other times are based on a 15,000-mile year. The service is performed at either the time or mileage, whichever occurs first.

There are oils out there that do have the correct amount of zinc for your flat tappet camshaft engine. This Castrol synthetic is one that does.

So if viscosity is a good thing, why not pick the highest number, like 50W, or even 90W gear oil? The problem with viscosity is that, if the oil is too thick, it will not be able to get between the surfaces you are trying to protect. Also, the pumping losses will be severe, as it is too hard to circulate through the engine. Finally, cold startups will result in the engine running "dry" while the oil slowly travels through the oil passages. You have to run the lowest viscosity oil that your engine will safely tolerate.

Conventional oil is made from crude oil. This oil or base stock is then treated to an additive package. For example, detergents help prevent varnish and sludge buildup, zinc helps protect high-pressure wear points such as camshaft lobes, and other additives keep the oil from foaming. When the base stock is refined from the crude oil, it is separated by viscosity. All oils get thinner (flow easier) as they warm up. So at 300 degrees F in the bearing, a 10-weight oil will be like water.

If it is a multigrade, like 10W-40, the base stock is oil with a viscosity of 10. Multigrade oils are created by adding polymers to the base stock. These polymers help prevent the oil from thinning down as quickly when it is hot. In theory a 10W-40 will behave like a 10-weight oil when cold, but will resist thinning and behave like a 40 weight when hot. In other words, this oil's viscosity or thickness will remain relatively unchanged over a wide temperature range. The "W" in the nomenclature indicates that the oil meets the specifications for that viscosity at 0 degrees F, and therefore is suitable for winter use.

What really happens is not quite what is expected. When you add the rotating and sliding shear forces inside the engine to the operating temperature, oil viscosity falls off and does not maintain the suggested high-temperature rating. Also, the plastic polymers suffer from thermal cracking when subjected to the high temperatures normally seen in an engine. Besides the loss of high-temperature viscous stability, this also results in varnish deposits in the engine. 10W-40 and 5W-30 oils require a lot of these polymers. Most new cars no longer recommend conventional 10W-40 oils, and some manufacturers even threaten to void your warranty if these oils are used!

Synthetics are different. For starters, they are manufactured and therefore do not have the same limitations as conventional motor oil. Several 5W-30 and 10W-30 synthetics do not have any polymers to maintain viscosity as the temperature increases. Furthermore, since little or no polymers are required, the oil maintains its viscosity better when subjected to the shear forces inside a running engine. For this reason, a 30-weight synthetic will usually provide better lubrication than a 40-weight conventional oil. Another benefit of oil that contains fewer polymers is that its service life is greatly extended.

New car owners need to follow the manufacturer's recommendations. Owners of older cars should use a synthetic 10W-40 if the car is powered by a stock or mildly modified engine. If you prefer conventional oil, do not use 10W-40, as the high amount of polymers is not good for the engine; instead consider a 20W-40. For higher-output big blocks, a 15W-50 synthetic should be used. Supercharged and turbocharged engines should only use a synthetic, due to the extreme thermal stress that is placed on the oil.

Climate is just as important when selecting an oil. During the winter, or if you live where the summer temperature is not too hot, use a 10W-40 synthetic. For warmer climates consider a 15W-50 synthetic for big blocks, especially if you do any extended freeway driving or spend a lot of time stuck in traffic. If you use a good oil cooler, 10W-40 synthetic will be fine for big blocks.

Also, for engines with flat tappet (nonroller) lifters, the amount of zinc in the oil is important. You need 0.10 percent by weight or more zinc in the oil to help protect the camshaft lobes. Engines that use roller lifters do not need the added zinc protection. Most motor oils have reduced zinc content for emission purposes.

CHANGING AUTOMATIC TRANSMISSION FLUID

Most fluids are easy to change—just find the drain plug and you are good to go. Changing automatic transmission fluid is a little tougher, as most automatic transmissions on classic muscle cars did not come with a drain plug. You have to remove the pan to drain the fluid. The best way is to loosen all of the bolts, then remove all except two on one side and one in the center of an opposing side. Now, while supporting the pan, and with the 8-quart (or larger) drain pan centered under the side with only one bolt, remove the one bolt while supporting the pan with your other hand. Gently lower the pan and loosen the two remaining bolts as required to allow the pan to tilt. Once the pan is hanging at a 45-degree angle and has stopped draining fluid, push it back up and remove the remaining two bolts and remove the pan and dump the remaining fluid in the drain pan.

With the pan out of the way, remove and change the filter. At this time, you should consider either installing a drain plug kit or a replacement pan that has a drain plug. You will still have to remove the pan to change the filter, but the draining process is much easier, and less messy.

Be sure to use the recommended fluid type. You can substitute a synthetic, but make sure that the fluid is listed as a recommended replacement automatic transmission fluid for your transmission. This is important for two reasons. The first is that the friction material used on the clutch plates and the bands needs the correct type of fluid to prevent excessive slippage. Second, the wrong fluid can degrade the internal and external seals in the transmission and clutch.

CHANGING POWER STEERING FLUID

Changing power steering fluid is simple: use a suction gun to extract the fluid from the reservoir. Refill the reservoir and turn the wheels lock to lock a few times. Repeat the extraction and replacement procedure, as there is as much fluid in the steering box as is there is in the reservoir. Do not remove the return line or run the engine until no fluid flows, since the vanes in the pump will be damaged as soon as the reservoir runs dry.

MAINTENANCE ITEMS

Scheduled maintenance includes more than just replacing fluids, as several components are designed to wear during normal use. These components need to be replaced before they wear to the point of failure. You can either wait to change these parts until they are worn out, or you can put them on a scheduled maintenance plan. I have found that most wear components have a normal expected lifespan. I prefer to change them at the set maintenance date, as this avoids surprise repair work, or worse, an unexpected failure.

See Table 2 for the maintenance plan that I use for my 4-4-2.

Changing a few known components, such as the water pump and fuel pump, can also avoid unexpected failures. The key is to identify what items on your vehicle are known life expectancy parts, and change

them before they fail. This can easily be taken to the extreme and then the car is no longer fun to drive because you are continuously changing parts. The key is to find the proper balance, and to end up with a reliable car and a realistic maintenance schedule.

To make things simpler, create a maintenance log that lists the service procedures performed.

TABLE 2:
COMPONENT REPLACEMENT INTERVALS

Item	Mileage	Time (months)	Notes
Points	3,000	3	Electronic ignition is more reliable.
Ignition module	60,000	48	A lot better than points, but should be changed to prevent surprise failure.
PCV valve	3,000	3	Check.
Air filter	3,000	3	Inspect and replace if dirty.
Timing	3,000	3	Check and set.
Idle mixture	3,000	3	Check and set.
Idle speed	3,000	3	Check and set.
Cap and rotor	15,000	12	Clean every 6,000 miles.
Plugs	15,000	12	Inspect and clean (or replace) every 6,000 miles.
Belts	30,000	24	Inspect every 3,000 miles.
Hoses	30,000	24	Inspect every 3,000 miles.
Front brakes	30,000	24	Adjust and bleed rear brakes.
Rear brakes	60,000	48	Every second front brake job. Change brake fluid at the same time.
Suspension parts	120,000	8	Ball joints, bushings, tie rod ends, center link, idler arm, and springs.

To make the situation easier, you can replace the maintenance items in groups, like the water pump, starter, alternator, and fuel pump. The goal is to keep the work to a minimum, both scheduled and unscheduled. You will develop a feel for how long certain items last, and then you can group items together for maintenance replacement.

Don't forget to list the car's mileage and the date of the repair. By doing this, you will develop a log that shows how long components last. Fluid changes are shown on Table 1. As you replace components, you can then add the mileage (or time) and know the next anticipated replacement date for that component. See Table 2 for an example of a maintenance chart.

THE TUNE-UP

The tune-up is something that a modern car owner cannot really appreciate. Most of what is occurring in a tune-up is performed by the computer on a modern car. For your muscle car, the tune-up is vital in ensuring that it is performing properly. I perform a tune-up once every 3,000 miles, or once every three months. I perform the tune-up at the same time as the oil change. This is also a good time to inspect various components for any signs of wear or damage.

The tune-up begins with a spark plug inspection (or change at one year or 15,000 miles). The plugs are cleaned, and the gaps are set. Inspect the plugs for signs of improper operation. The following illustrations will show some examples of spark plugs. If your plugs are in good shape, they can be cleaned and re-installed (under 12,000 miles) or new plugs of the same heat rating can be installed. If the plugs are not in the OK range, troubleshoot and correct the problem. This is why I start with the spark plugs—they will steer you to any potential trouble spots. If oil fouling is detected, this indicates a more serious problem.

Reading your spark plugs is the best way to tell what is happening inside your engine's combustion chamber. The color of the burn on the electrode and the firing ring is a good indication of your engine's state of tune and mechanical health. Note that you will not be able to ascertain if your tune is correct for wide-open throttle (or any other single mode of operation) this way.

For a street-driven car, the used plugs should have a very thin, fluffy, dry coating that is light gray to light tan in color. Darker deposits indicate a richer fuel mixture. If the plugs have a lighter or white appearance, this indicates a leaner mixture. In all cases, the plug ground strap and porcelain center

Gap the plugs before installing them. This includes plugs pulled for inspection and deemed worthy to re-install. As for gaps, use the factory recommended gap unless running an aftermarket ignition, in which case you should use the value recommended by the ignition manufacturer. Wider gaps will help fire a lean mixture.

should appear mechanically sound, with no signs of damage, blistering, or bubbling.

If one (or more) of your removed plugs do not match the description above, you can interpret what is wrong based on how the plug looks. Check their color. If the plug is dark or black, with a medium to heavy flaky deposit, the engine is running too rich. If the deposit on the plug is dark and wet, this is an indication that oil is getting inside the combustion chamber. Oil fouling usually results in a damp, heavy coating on the plug.

The plugs should also read similarly for all cylinders. Remove each plug, and place or label it so you know what cylinder it is from. To actually examine each plug, an illuminated plug inspection viewer is handy. Now look at each plug, noting the type of deposits and color. Also verify that the electrode and center porcelain insulator are not blistered or broken.

If all of your plugs appear normal, then exchange them for new plugs and you are done. But if they do not fall into the normal range, ascertain what is wrong and correct the problem. Also, do not read plugs from a vehicle that has been stored and only run for short intervals, unless you gave the vehicle a good long drive prior to reading the plugs. A vehicle that has been excessively idled, or one that is started and run for short periods, can show darker than normal plug colors, as the combustion temperature is low when idling.

If you have removed your plugs, and one or more of them does not read correctly, here is what you need to do. First, is the cylinder that is reading wrong producing power? If the plugs that are reading wrong are too light in color, you may be running too lean. If too dark, you may be too rich. And if the plug shows signs of blistering, or the electrode is melting away or missing, these can be indications of preignition or detonation.

PLUGS READ LEAN

If the plugs have a very light or white coating, this indicates a lean condition. This could be caused by a vacuum leak. Check the carburetor and also look for vacuum leaks around the carburetor base or intake manifold. Also check for leaks in the vacuum hoses or any vacuum-operated accessories, such as the power brake booster or the heater. If one or only a few plugs are reading lean, pay particular attention to the vacuum lines that are attached to the intake manifold near or on the runners that feed the lean cylinder.

If no air leak is found, the lean condition is probably carburetor-related. Check the idle mixture screws. Raise the engine rpm to 1,500–1,800 rpm and listen for smooth operation. If a light miss is detected, the engine may be too lean at cruise or off-idle operation. Check the power valve to see that it is not stuck closed. A smog test machine can really help here. You can also install an oxygen sensor to aid with tuning.

PLUGS READ RICH

Dark plugs indicate a rich condition. The first place to look when you discover this is the carburetor. Watch for a stuck or slow choke. Also check the choke heat source to verify that, as the engine warms up, the choke is fully off. If the choke does not fully open until the engine is at operating temperature, it is closed, or, in other words, operating too long. The choke must be fully off once the engine warms up a little bit. The choke pull-off is a vacuum-operated device that partially opens the choke as soon as the engine starts. If it is not operating or set properly, it will cause the engine to run rich. Also check for signs of flooding, especially at idle. A weak needle and seat valve, or excessive fuel pressure, can lead to nozzle drip at idle and low speeds. And of course, check for proper power valve operation (this is especially true for Holley carburetors).

FOULED PLUGS

Oil fouling is the condition no one wants to see on their plugs. But before you panic, determine the cause. A compression check will tell you if the cylinder is holding pressure. Compare this cylinder to the others. If it is reading low, or if all of them read

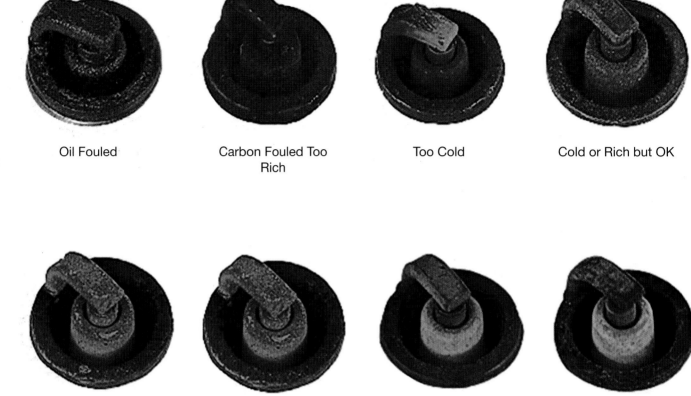

Oil Fouled

Carbon Fouled Too Rich

Too Cold

Cold or Rich but OK

A Touch Cold but OK

Good

Good

Real Good

low (below 120 pounds), you have a ring or valve sealing problem. If the pressure is adequate, then the oil is either coming from a valve oil seal or a leaking intake manifold gasket. If you suspect an intake manifold gasket leak, remove the PCV valve, and seal the crankcase breathers. Now place your finger over the PCV grommet on the engine; if the intake manifold is leaking inside the engine, you will usually be able to detect a slight draw of air into the engine through the breather ports.

PLUGS SHOW DETONATION OR PREIGNITION

If the plug electrode is blistered, melted, or missing, these can be indications of preignition or detonation. The first thing to check is the engine timing. Don't forget to check the high-rpm timing as well the timing at idle. Most cars use a vacuum advance with centrifugal weights for rpm advance; both of these must be checked for proper operation. Ford vehicles used a distributor with both vacuum advance and retard. If the vacuum lines are improperly connected, the timing will be wrong. Don't treat detonation or preignition lightly; the extreme stress will damage internal engine components.

PLUG HEAT RANGE

Plugs with the wrong heat range for the engine can read incorrectly. If a plug that is too cold is used, the plug may read dark or rich. If the plug is too cold, the deposits are typically coarser, and not the fine, smooth, light powdery deposit found on a normal plug. Plugs that are too hot will usually

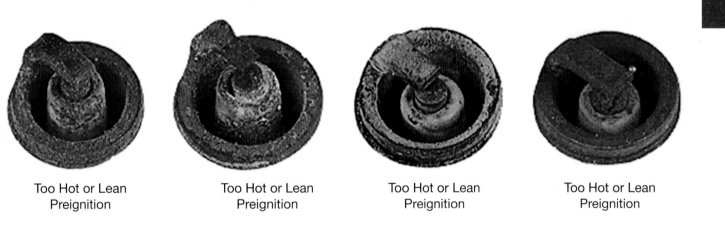

| Best | Good | A Little Hot but OK | Hot or Lean Marginal |

| Too Hot or Lean Preignition | Too Hot or Lean Preignition | Too Hot or Lean Preignition | Too Hot or Lean Preignition |

read lean, and may exhibit signs of overheating, such as blistering on the ceramic insulator.

Make sure that the recommended plug is installed in your engine. Check that all of the numbers and letters match precisely. If the number does not match, the plug heat range is not the same. A lower number is a colder plug, and a higher number is a hotter plug. Hotter plugs do not increase power! Hotter plugs do a better job of resisting fouling, but at the expense of increased susceptibility to overheating or preignition. High-performance engines usually require colder plugs.

BREAKER POINT MAINTENANCE

Once the spark plugs are sorted out, the next step in your tune-up is to set the dwell. If your car still has breaker points, remove and clean the contacts. Replace the points and condenser once a year, or every 15,000 miles. After the points are clean (I use emery cloth), inspect them for signs of pitting, and if any is found, replace the points and condenser (a weak condenser will cause pitting). Once the points are installed, set the dwell. For Ford and Chrysler engines, the gap is set with a feeler gauge. Points on GM engines can be set with a dwell meter, but the points gap must first be roughly set with a feeler gauge so the car will start. I recommend that you set a .017-inch gap for GM cars before you start the engine, then fine-tune the setting with the dwell meter.

For all cars, to properly set the gap, rotate the engine until the points rubbing block is exactly on the high point of one of the distributor cam lobes. Now set the points gap to the manufacturer's recommended clearance using the feeler gauge. The blade should slide with some resistance, but should not open the gap when inserted. Set the dwell to the middle of the specification. Make sure that you place a light amount of distributor grease on the cam. Now install the rotor and cap.

Start the engine and check the dwell with a meter. You want 29 degrees of dwell. If it is too low, you are not allowing sufficient time for the coil to dump at high rpm, and if the dwell is set too high, you are not allowing sufficient time for the coil to charge at high rpm.

For GM owners, this part is simple, as the running dwell can be adjusted and monitored on the meter. For Ford and Chrysler, you will have to shut off the engine, remove the cap, and re-adjust the points. If the dwell is too low, increase the point gap. If the dwell is too high, decrease the point gap.

TIMING ADJUSTMENT

Once the points are cleaned and the dwell is set, the timing can be adjusted. Remember, setting dwell will change the timing. First, connect your timing light to the battery and the number one plug. Disconnect and plug the vacuum advance hose on GM and Chrysler vehicles. For Fords, check the service manual, as you may have a distributor with both vacuum advance and retard. Clean off the timing indicator and the balancer so the markings will be clearly visible. Start the engine and verify the idle timing setting. Loosen the distributor lock-down bolt and turn the distributor to get the correct idle timing.

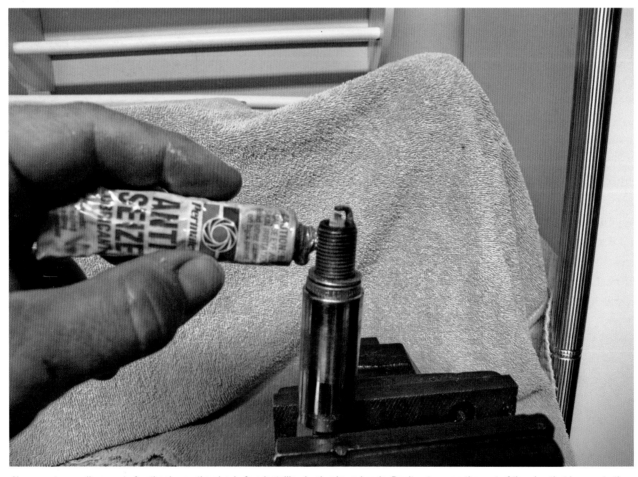

Always put a small amount of anti-seize on the plug before installing in aluminum heads. Don't get any on the part of the plug that is open to the chamber.

Here are the condenser and points for a GM-style distributor.
Don't use cheap points; always use a good performance set.
Not shown is the felt pad that goes on the arm of the points that
holds the grease.

Using the throttle linkage, increase the rpm to 3,000 and note the timing. A dial-back timing light or a degreed balancer will be required. Your timing should be 34–38 degrees. If it is not, the distributor mechanical advance will need to be inspected (see the ignition section). Reset the proper idle speed and turn off the engine. Now reconnect the vacuum advance and restart the car. Depending on whether or not you have ported idle spark advance, your vacuum advance will advance the timing from 5 to 15 degrees either at idle or just above idle. Check for this with your timing light. If the vacuum advance is not functioning properly (no advance), this will result in reduced gas mileage.

CARBURETOR TUNE-UP

Another important part of a tune-up is adjusting the carburetor. First remove the air cleaner and inspect the filter element. Replace if it is dirty. Check for this by comparing the carburetor side to the air inlet side; if the air inlet side is noticeably darker in color, replace the filter.

Before setting the carburetor, inspect the PCV valve. Remove the valve and gently shake it back and forth. A rattling sound should be heard. If not, replace the valve. Make sure you get the correct replacement, as a PCV valve is nothing more than a calibrated air leak. The wrong PCV valve can cause the mixture to be lean or rich. Also check all of the vacuum hoses for brittleness, cracks, or breaks. Replace any that are bad.

Adjust the carburetor next. Warm the engine up to operating temperature. Set the idle speed to the recommended rpm. Adjust the mixture screws. I prefer to slowly turn each screw in until the engine begins to falter, then back out 1/4 turn. Repeat for each screw, then reset the idle speed and re-adjust the mixture screws. This may sound repetitive, but if you had to reset the idle speed, you changed the idle mixture. Re-install the air cleaner and verify that the idle speed does not change.

One final note: before you close the hood, check the brake fluid, engine oil, transmission fluid, and power steering fluid. The radiator fluid level needs to be checked also, but do not remove the radiator cap until the engine has cooled. Check all belts and hoses for signs of wear, and replace anything you find that needs attention. This is also a good time to check for oil and other fluid leaks. This entire process should not take more than 90 minutes at an easy pace.

CHAPTER 3
BRAKES

Along with the suspension and steering systems, brakes are the most important components on the vehicle. No vehicle, of any type, should be operated unless the suspension, steering, and braking systems are functioning properly. Driving a vehicle with substandard suspension, steering, or brakes is not only foolish, but downright dangerous.

Fortunately, these systems are relatively simple, and replacement components are available for almost any vehicle imaginable. I highly recommend refurbishing these systems immediately after obtaining a vehicle, and then monitO-ring them with a time-based maintenance plan. This will result in a vehicle that is both fun and safe to drive.

BRAKE MAINTENANCE

I recommend servicing the brakes on a schedule. On my car, I change the front disc brake pads and inspect the rotors for thickness, warpage, cracks, and other surface irregularities every 30,000 miles. I service the rear brakes every 60,000 miles, inspecting the drums, replacing the brake shoes, brake pad return springs, and mounting hardware, and rebuilding or replacing the wheel slave cylinders. Also, at every other front brake job, the front calipers are rebuilt and the front wheel bearings are repacked. This results in brakes that always work as they should, with no surprise failures.

Also plan on replacing the brake hoses every 120,000 miles, or once every eight to ten years. The master cylinder should be rebuilt or replaced every 120,000 miles, and the power booster should be replaced with the master cylinder. Fortunately, the brake system is one of the easiest and least expensive systems on a car to maintain.

When selecting components for your brake system, use only premium parts. There is usually not much of a difference in price between the "house brand" and the premium components. I get my brake pads, shoes, and hardware at the local auto parts store, but I specify the premium or best parts. For most muscle cars, use premium semi-metallic pads.

Don't skimp on the brake fluid either. When selecting brake fluid, use DOT 4 brake fluid. It has a higher boiling point than DOT 3. I do not recommend silicone brake fluid (DOT 5), as any moisture that gets into the system will not mix with the fluid but will create bubbles of water. When the brakes heat up, perhaps due to aggressive driving, it can cause water in the brake system to boil and turn to steam. Since steam is compressible, this results in a spongy brake pedal and a loss in brake performance. Ultimately, the brake pedal will travel all the way to the floor with no effect. Use only brake fluid from a new, unopened container. Brake fluid attracts moisture, so once the bottle is opened, use what you need, then discard the remaining fluid.

Whenever you service the brakes, even for a simple pad change, bleed the system. While it might seem unnecessary, the bleeding procedure can help extend component life by flushing out old brake fluid. Collect the used brake fluid, and, along with any remaining unused new fluid, dispose of it at an appropriate facility along with your used motor oil, transmission fluid, radiator fluid, and any other waste fluids you accumulate during maintenance procedures.

The easiest way to bleed brakes is with a hand-operated vacuum pump. This can be purchased at your local auto parts store, and it is valuable for

Bleeding with a vacuum pump. Notice that the wrench is left on the bleeder screw so that the bleeder can be closed. Carefully watch the fluid as it travels out of the bleeder. Once it is clean fluid with no bubbles, the bleeding is finished.

troubleshooting heating and air conditioning control valves as well. Get one that has a brake bleeding kit and comes with a catch container so you don't draw brake fluid into the pump.

Begin by placing the appropriately sized wrench on the bleeder valve. Break the bleeder valve loose and then just snug it back tight. Leave the wrench on the bleeder and attach the hose. Crack the bleeder valve loose again about 1/4 turn and begin squeezing the vacuum pump. Watch the fluid as it comes out of the bleeder. When the fluid flow is smooth, clean, and free of bubbles, close the bleeder screw.

Important: It's easy to get too focused on the pumping process. Pay very, very careful attention to

the fluid level in the master cylinder. Don't let the master cylinder fluid level get low enough to draw air into the line, or you'll have to bleed the entire system from the beginning. Always keep the level at least a quarter inch above the drain hole.

REBUILDING DRUM BRAKES

The following procedure is the same for the front and rear wheels. The only difference is that when servicing rear drum brakes, the parking brake hardware must be removed and re-installed. Start by removing the front wheels. Then remove the brake drums. Usually they can be pulled off by hand; refer to the service manual for direction. If a brake drum will not come off, try loosening its adjustor. This can be done using two screwdrivers, one to hold the adjustor lever away from the adjustor wheel and the other to turn the adjustor wheel.

After the drum is removed, clean the drum and measure the inside diameter. Verify that the inside diameter is smaller than the size stamped on the drum. Also verify that the drum is round. This can be done by measuring the inside diameter at different locations around the drum; if all of the measurements match, the drum is round. If the drum is over the indicated size, or if the drum is out of round, the drum must be replaced.

Check the inside of the drum for scoring. If the drum is smooth, sand the inside of the drum with 100-grit sandpaper, the same type you would use for sanding wood. If the drum is scored, the drum must be turned or replaced. You can have the drum turned at your local auto parts store. After turning, verify that the drum is at or below the maximum inside diameter.

Finally, inspect the drum for signs of cracking or other flaws. If you see any cracking or damage, the drum must be replaced.

When servicing drum brakes, you should always replace the brake hardware. Inexpensive kits are usually available that contain all of the necessary springs and shoe-mounting hardware. Check to see if your kit contains the brake adjusters. If it does not, you can reuse the old adjusters as long as they still operate properly and are not otherwise damaged. Replacing the hardware ensures that the springs and brake shoe mounting hardware are up to specification, ensuring that the brakes function as intended.

WHY DRUM BRAKES SQUEAL

If the inside diameter of the drum is too big, drum brakes can squeal. With modern nonasbestos pads, drum brakes can squeal as loudly as disc brakes, although at a lower frequency.

If the shoe arc does not mach the inside diameter of the drum, the brake shoes can chatter, which results in a squeal. Shoes are designed and built to conform to the inside diameter of stock drums. Turning a drum makes it bigger inside. If the drum gets turned past its maximum specified inside diameter, the brake shoe, having been designed to nestle into a smaller-diameter drum, will not make full contact with the drum surface, and will most certainly squeal.

REBUILDING WHEEL (SLAVE) BRAKE CYLINDERS

When rebuilding drum brakes, you should always rebuild or replace the wheel, or slave cylinders as well.

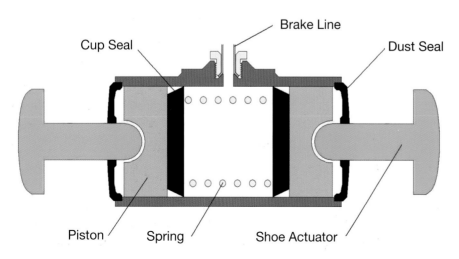

Cup Seal — Brake Line — Dust Seal

Piston — Spring — Shoe Actuator

Wheel cylinders are not complicated. When rebuilding one, the dust seal and cup seals are replaced. Most kits also include the spring. This spring keeps the pistons and the cups pushed against the brake shoes, preventing slack that can result in a low brake pedal or air entering the system.

Rear drum brake assembly. Note that the leading shoe has the shorter lining. Also, the axle flange makes rear brake reassembly more difficult.

Failure to rebuild the wheel cylinders will usually result in leaking later on, and this will either cause the brake pedal to sink or be low. Also, brake fluid on the shoes can cause grabby brakes.

Wheel cylinder refurbishing kits are inexpensive, but complete replacement wheel cylinder assemblies for most cars are inexpensive and save time as well. I simply replace wheel cylinders rather than refurbish them.

Begin the disassembly by cleaning the brake backing plate and wheel cylinder. Now remove the wheel cylinder and take it apart. For most cars, the two pistons, the two cup seals, and the spring simply press out. Clean the pistons and wheel cylinder with brake cleaner, lacquer thinner, or alcohol. Do not

Brake adjuster. There will be a right and a left side; the threads are reversed. If you mix these up, the adjuster will not work. Also, there is a washer between the star wheel and the shoe piece. Don't leave this out; it minimizes friction and therefore allows the star wheel to rotate freely when the adjuster attempts to move it.

use petroleum-based solvents. Immediately coat the pistons and wheel cylinder with brake fluid to prevent rust. Inspect the inside of the wheel cylinder for

Rear brakes with the axle removed. In this shot the adjuster can be clearly seen. The emergency brake actuator is behind the brake adjuster. Note that the shoe with the shorter lining is toward the front of the vehicle and also that the adjuster lever is resting on the adjuster star wheel.

signs of corrosion or pitting. If any pitting is found, replace the wheel cylinder. Also inspect the pistons for corrosion. Light corrosion or rust can be cleaned off with emery cloth. If the piston has heavy rust or pitting, replace the wheel cylinder.

Begin the reassembly by lubricating the wheel cylinder with brake fluid. Install the seal and piston on one side. Now hold the cylinder with the installed piston side down, keeping your thumb on the piston so it does not fall out. Drop the spring into the wheel cylinder. Install the other seal and piston. The two cup seals should be facing each other. Install the dust caps on each side and insert the brake pad actuators.

REASSEMBLING DRUM BRAKES

Install the wheel cylinder and connect the brake line. Hang the brake shoes. Make sure the leading shoe is installed on the correct side. For cars with two wheel cylinders per wheel, both shoes will be the same. For cars with a single wheel cylinder and fully floating shoes (no hard anchor opposite the master cylinder), the leading shoe is the shoe that the rotation of the drum will tend to help rotate away from the wheel cylinder. This is called self-actuation, and it results in significantly lower input force to make the brakes work. The leading shoe usually has a shorter lining than the trailing shoe. For most muscle cars, the leading shoe is the shoe that has its lining facing toward the front of the car. If the shoes are installed incorrectly, brake performance will suffer, and the shoes will wear unevenly.

Place a small amount of brake grease on the brake backing plate where the brake shoe touches against the backing plate. Next, turn the adjuster so that it is all the way in, or as short as it can be. The adjustor should turn freely; if it does not, replace it. Don't mix up the right and left side adjusters, as they rotate opposite directions. Install the adjustor between the brake shoes and then install the adjustor spring to hold the two shoes together. Install the rest of the brake hardware. Use a brake spring tool to install the return springs. These tools are inexpensive, and will save you considerable grief.

Once the brake system is reassembled, verify that the adjustor is working properly. The adjustor bracket should contact the adjustor wheel and prevent the wheel from turning. The linkage should also be tight enough that if the brake shoe moves up, the adjustor will move and cause the wheel to turn. Also watch how the spring that goes between the two shoes at the adjuster is installed. If it is installed incorrectly, it will interfere with the adjuster star wheel. For Chrysler vehicles, ensure that the adjuster cable is in good condition and properly routed. GM vehicles use a rod that attaches to the adjuster and the anchor pin.

For rear brakes, also verify that the parking brake works correctly. Verify that when the actuator lever is pulled, the shoes move out toward the drum. Also verify that the actuator moves freely. Check the emergency brake cable for wear, especially where it attaches to the actuator, and verify that the actuator is not damaged. Replace the cables if any signs of fraying are detected or if they don't move freely. Check the actuator for signs of damage or corrosion. Replace the actuator if damaged or corroded. The actuator usually has a cross-rod and an anti-rattle spring; check these components for damage. These parts are not included with the hardware kit. Replace

any components found to be damaged or defective.

Once the brakes are assembled, adjust them. Install the drum and rotate it by hand, checking for drag. If no drag is felt, remove the drum and turn the adjuster to spread the pads apart. Re-install the drum and check for drag. Once slight drag is detected, back the adjuster off slightly until no drag is detected. Do not drive the car unless the brakes are adjusted, as improperly adjusted brakes will result in low or no brake pedal pressure. Bleed the brakes and install the wheels.

When the rear brakes are rebuilt, the brake fluid needs to be changed. This can be accomplished by bleeding the front and rear brakes until the fluid comes out at each wheel clear and looking like new brake fluid. After bleeding, the brake pedal should be high and firm.

Most muscle cars did not have rear disc brakes, but if yours does, either OEM or aftermarket, use the procedure outlined next for troubleshooting the front disc brake calipers. And remember, if you upgraded either the front or rear or both to disc brakes, you must replace the master cylinder with one that provides sufficient volume and pressure to make the brakes work.

REBUILDING DISC BRAKES

Disc brakes are easier to service than drum brakes. Normally, front pads will last at least 30,000 miles. Therefore I recommend servicing the front brakes every 30,000 miles.

Start the job by removing the front wheels. Before removing the calipers, use a large screwdriver and pry the piston back in the caliper. Do this by inserting the screwdriver between the outer pad and the caliper housing. Pry until the inner caliper is fully seated. If the vehicle has multiple pistons, repeat the process by inserting the screwdriver between the inner pad and the caliper body.

Before pushing the pistons back, remove the lid from the master cylinder and check the fluid level. If the reservoir is full, remove some of the fluid so that it will not overflow when the piston is pushed back into the caliper. You can do this by taking it directly from the reservoir or by attaching one end of a hose to the bleeder valve on the caliper and placing the other end in a small container. Open the bleeder valve and slowly compress the piston with your screwdriver. The open bleeder valve will allow the excess fluid to drain into the container.

Once the piston(s) are retracted, remove the bolts that attach the caliper to the caliper bracket. If the caliper is going to be rebuilt, remove the brake hose from the caliper body before the caliper is removed from the bracket. To prevent the brake fluid from leaking out of the open hose, clamp a piece of rubber (such as a strip cut from an old inner tube) around the open banjo-bolt fitting. Note that sealing the caliper is more important than just preventing a mess. In some cars, the master cylinder is mounted in a position that makes bleeding air out of it impossible unless it is removed and bench bled. If brake fluid is allowed to drain from an open line, the master cylinder will have to be bled. If the caliper is not going to be rebuilt, remove it from the bracket and support it so it does not hang by the brake hose.

REBUILDING DISC BRAKE CALIPERS

Calipers should be rebuilt every other time the pads are replaced, or once every 60,000 miles. Calipers are easy to rebuild, and caliper rebuild kits are inexpensive.

Remove the caliper from the car and place a folded rag in the opening under the piston(s). Now apply compressed air to the brake hose fitting. Use a blow gun so you can control the air flow. Set the pressure to 10 to 15 PSI. You don't need any higher pressure. Now squeeze the trigger, and the piston(s) will pop out.

Clean the whole caliper, paying special attention to the cylinders, with brake cleaner, alcohol, or lacquer thinner. Do not use gasoline or any other petroleum-based solvents. Even soapy water is a better choice, as it will not leave any chemicals behind that will cause

problems later. Once the caliper is clean, immediately dry it and coat the cylinder walls with clean brake fluid. Clean the caliper piston(s) the same way. Also coat the piston(s) with brake fluid immediately after it is clean to prevent surface rust from forming.

Inspect the inside of the caliper cylinder walls for any signs of rust, corrosion, or pitting. If the corrosion is light, use a cylinder hone to clean up the cylinder bore. The cylinder walls must be smooth and clean. Do not go overboard; if the bore is too large, the piston may not slide smoothly. If the caliper is pitted, or if the corrosion is too severe, the caliper must be replaced.

Inspect the piston(s) as well. Light surface rust or corrosion can be cleaned up with 800-grit wet or dry sandpaper. Use brake fluid as the lubricant on the wet or dry paper. Just as with the caliper, do not go overboard; if the piston is sanded too much, it may cock in the bore and jam, or will not seal. If the piston is not salvageable, replace the caliper.

Install the new caliper seal in the caliper bore. Next, install the piston dust seal on the piston. The dust seal typically fits into a groove on the piston. Coat the piston with brake fluid. Align the piston with the bore, press the piston in, and work it into the bore. Once the piston is down, align the dust seal with the groove in the caliper and tap the seal into place.

REPLACING FRONT BRAKE HOSES

When you rebuild the calipers, the brake hoses should also be replaced. Since the hose has already been disconnected at the caliper, the job is only half as hard.

Before you remove the hose, spray the hose fitting with WD-40 or another penetrating lubricant. Make sure that the steel line is soaked where it threads into the fitting. These tend to seize to the fitting. If they do, the steel brake line will twist off when the fitting is turned. Carefully work the brake line loose from the hose. If the fitting feels tight, loosen and tighten the fitting several times to break the fitting loose from the line.

Once the hose is removed, clean and inspect the brake line. Wipe the WD-40 from the line and the fitting. Install the new brake hose, paying attention to how it is oriented. Also, make sure to properly install the hose-end restraining clamp; this is vital in order to prevent the brake line from moving and hardening.

REASSEMBLING DISC BRAKES

Before installing new pads, sand the rotors with 150-grit sandpaper by turning the rotor in the same direction it would turn when installed with the car moving forward. Clean the rotor to remove any traces of sand or grit. Measure the rotor thickness and verify that it is greater than the minimum thickness. This size is cast in the rotor, but if you cannot find this dimension, check the factory service manual. The rotor must be 1.25" or more. As a general rule, measure the thickness of each side, from the inside of the rotor vents to the pad surface.

Begin the reassembly by checking the caliper attaching hardware. Look for nicks, corrosion, and other types of damage. If the attachment hardware is damaged, your brakes may drag, resulting in short pad life. Also, damage to the attachment hardware can cause brake squealing. Clean up the hardware and lubricate with high-temperature silicone lubricant. Most brake calipers use O-ring seals in the caliper to trap the lubricant; these should be replaced at each brake job. Make sure that you get lubricant between the seals inside the caliper so that the attaching bolts will be properly lubricated.

Next, check the new pads. If the pads have a wear indicator, verify that it is properly positioned. The wear indicator is a thin, curved piece of steel designed to rub against the rotor and cause a squeal at low speeds when the pad is almost worn out. Verify that the edge of the wear indicator will contact the brake rotor when the pad has worn down to only 10 percent of the pad. If the pad is riveted, make sure that the wear indicator will touch the brake rotor before the rivets will. Also, make sure that the wear indicator is tight. If it is loose, tighten the rivet that attaches the indicator by placing it in a vice and crushing it tight.

This is a worn disc brake pad. Notice the cracks that come from heating the pad. Also, this is a semimetallic pad; the flecks you see are the metallic particles. This is a GM-style pad; the wear indicator is on the right side, and it is the curved piece of metal that is riveted to the pad. This one was bent and contacted the rotor too soon, indicating a worn-out pad while there was still 40 percent of the pad surface left.

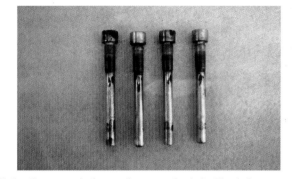

Notice the gouges in these caliper-mounting bolts. The dark areas are the deep gouges that the caliper has worn into the bolts as the miles rolled on. These will never properly support the calipers, and on this vehicle, brake squeal was the result. Simply replacing these bolts cured the brake squeal. The pads were not even replaced.

PREVENTING DISC BRAKE SQUEAL

Brake squealing is caused by the pads or some other component vibrating. If the components are not worn, the best way to prevent vibration is to ensure that all brake components are securely attached so they cannot move. For example, the disc brake pads should be securely fastened in the brake caliper. Check closely; the pads usually have ears or tabs that lock them in place. You'll usually find these tabs on the outboard (nonpiston) side of the caliper. If the part cannot move, it will not vibrate (and squeal).

Using channel locks, bend the tab on the brake pads so that it grips the caliper tightly. Make sure that the other jaw of the channel locks is on the brake pad and not the caliper. This prevents the pads from chattering when the brakes are not applied and also helps prevent brake squeal when the brakes are applied.

Another likely cause of squealing is rotors that are rough or warped. The rotor's finish must be smooth, with no ridges or other rough spots. Any variation in surface smoothness can result in brake howling, squeaks, or squeals.

Inspect the mounting hardware to ensure that the caliper is mounted properly. It must be able to slide in and out, but must not be loose or rattle. Also check that the caliper is held squarely in the brackets.

Check the mounting bolts for damage. They usually have a long smooth section that supports the caliper; make sure there are no nicks and that the bolt is not bent. Also check for corrosion or rust. These

bolts are inexpensive. If you are experiencing brake squeal, replace the bolts. Just be sure that they are properly greased and that the O-ring seals in the caliper body are also replaced, since these trap the silicone grease that is used to lubricate the points where the caliper slides on the bolts.

SERVICING FRONT WHEEL BEARINGS

When servicing the front brakes, the wheel bearings will need to be greased as well. As the miles roll on, the grease that lubricates the wheel bearings will pick up contaminants and the additives in the grease will break down. There is also a grease seal that will wear, and this can result in a loss of grease. Front wheel bearings should be cleaned and repacked every 60,000 miles. I do this when the calipers are rebuilt.

To service the bearings, the rotor must be removed. After the caliper and pads have been removed, pry off the wheel bearing dust cover and remove the cotter key that prevents the bearing retaining castle nut from turning. Now remove the castle nut and pull the rotor off. Only do one side at a time. If both sides are removed at the same time, do not mix the bearings. They wear with their respective race, and if you mix the bearings, they could fail.

Now remove the two bearings from the rotor; the smaller bearing is the outer wheel bearing, and the larger bearing is the inner wheel bearing. To remove the inner bearing, the grease seal must be removed. I remove the inner bearing and seal together by removing the outer bearing and washer. Now re-install the castle nut. Move the rotor so that the nut is behind the outer wheel bearing race, and lower the rotor so that it is almost resting on the nut. Give it a quick tug, pulling the rotor off. The inner bearing and grease seal will be sitting on the spindle.

Discard the grease seal, as a new one will need to be installed. Then clean each bearing in solvent. Do not spin the bearings once the grease has been cleaned from the bearings. Blow the bearings dry with compressed air, being careful to not allow the air to spin the bearings. Wipe all of the grease from inside the rotor, and also wipe all the grease from the spindle. The old grease must be removed, as it contains dirt and contaminants. Also, wheel bearing greases are not universally compatible, and the grease you use to pack the bearings might not be compatible with the old grease.

Carefully inspect the bearing rollers for signs of pitting or corrosion. Also check the bearing races in the rotor to make sure that the race is smooth and shiny. Do not mix up the bearings from the left and right side, as the bearings must be installed in their original races. Both the bearing rollers and races should be smooth and silver in color. Any discoloration indicates that the bearings have been overheated and must be replaced. Pitting, scoring, or scratching indicates a damaged bearing, and the bearing must be replaced. Don't forget to replace the race when the bearing is replaced. If a new bearing is purchased, it will come with a new race. When replacing wheel bearing races, use the proper tool to install the new race to prevent damaging it.

Pack each bearing with clean grease. The best way to pack wheel bearings is to place a large wad of grease in the palm of your hand and force the bearing through the grease until it is packed with grease. Do this to both of the bearings, and then install the inner bearing in the rotor. Force additional grease into the bearing, and install a new grease seal. Now stand the rotor up and fill the inside of the rotor with grease.

Install the rotor on the spindle. Force the grease back in around the spindle, verifying that there is sufficient grease so that as the wheel spins, grease will be present to lubricate the bearings. Now install the outer bearing and the keyed washer. Thread the castle nut back on the spindle. Snug the nut finger tight. Now spin the wheel while slowly tightening the castle nut. The nut should be just past finger tight. Install a new cotter key, and if the castle nut does not line up with the hole in the spindle, turn the castle nut tighter. Clean out the dust cap and install it.

Wipe the outside of the rotor around the dust cap with a rag soaked with solvent. You want to remove any trace of grease or oil from the area where the dust cap meets the rotor. Once clean, run a bead of silicone around the joint between the dust cap and rotor. This will prevent the grease from wicking out.

TROUBLESHOOTING YOUR BRAKES

Troubleshooting the braking system does not need to be time-consuming or expensive. One of the most common problems on an older car is low or no brake pedal pressure. This is not normal; the brake pedal on any vehicle should be high and firm. If it is not, don't drive the vehicle until it is fixed. Regardless of whether the brake system is stock or completely custom aftermarket, troubleshooting low brake pedal pressure is made much easier if you systematically test for problems. You need to isolate the subsystem within the brake system that has the problem.

Also remember that the brakes have most likely been serviced several times since the car was new. Unless you were the original owner and performed all of the brake repairs, there is a good chance that one or more replacement part is not correct. Also, try to determine if any modifications have been made. Don't forget that if the rear axle was swapped, the rear brakes most likely got swapped as well. Any modification to the brakes that was not properly thought out will most likely result in brakes that do not work as well as they should.

TROUBLESHOOTING LOW BRAKE PEDAL PRESSURE

Your brakes should begin to stop the car with no more than 20 percent of the brake pedal's travel. If the pedal will move farther than this without great resistance, the system has a problem that needs to be addressed. If the pedal travel is 50 percent or more before the brakes begin to function, do not drive the vehicle.

When diagnosing problems with your brake system, begin by adjusting the drum brakes. For vehicles with four-wheel drum brakes, all four wheels will need to be checked and adjusted. On cars equipped with front disc brakes, low pedal pressure can still be caused by rear brake drum that are out of adjustment. Although most vehicles have an adjuster hole that allow the brakes to be adjusted without removing the brake drum, I prefer to adjust drum brakes by removing the drum. This allows me to inspect the brakes completely. Either way, adjust the brakes so the brake pads just contact the drum, then back the adjuster off about 1/2 turn. Ultimately, you want the pad-to-drum clearance as small as possible without dragging.

After adjusting all the drum brakes, check your pedal pressure. If the pedal pressure is high, you

are done. Note that, once properly set up, drums brakes should adjust automatically and stay in adjustment (unless you own a really old vehicle). If you notice that the brakes don't stay adjusted, you may need to remove the drums and inspect the adjustment mechanism. Remember, drum brakes adjust when you back the car up. For GM vehicles, this will be each time you apply the brakes while the car is traveling in reverse, provided that you release the brakes completely and re-apply them while the car is still in motion. For Chrysler drum brakes, the car must move forward and be stopped; then when traveling in reverse, the first brake application will "release" the adjuster and perform a wheel adjustment. Subsequent reverse brake applications will not adjust the brakes until the vehicle has been driven forward and stopped, which reactivates the adjuster.

If the pedal pressure is low after you adjust the drum brakes, move to the master cylinder. Remove the brake fitting(s) and install pipe plug(s) into the output port(s). Check the pedal. If it is not high and extremely firm, with no play, bleed the master cylinder. On most GM muscle cars, the master cylinder must be removed and bled on the workbench, as the angle of mounting in the car will trap air in the master cylinder, making a proper bleed impossible. If this does not result in a firm high pedal when the pipe plugs are re-installed, the master cylinder is defective and must be rebuilt or replaced. Note: Never operate a vehicle with one or more brake sections disabled.

If the pedal is high and firm, with no signs of sinking, reconnect the brake line for the front wheels, leaving the rear brake port blocked. On cars with only a single section master, connect the brake line, and disconnect the brake line for the rear brakes at the junction block and install the pipe plug into the junction block.

If the brake pedal is not still high and firm, bleed the front brakes. If this does not correct the problem, proceed to "Checking the Front Brakes" on page 33. If the pedal is now high and firm, remove the pipe plug and reconnect the rear brakes. Now bleed the rear brakes, and if this does not result in a high firm pedal, proceed to "Checking the Rear Brakes" on page 34.

If you have an older vehicles or a street rod where the master cylinder is mounted low, check the residual pressure valve. This is particularly suspect if the brake pedal is high and firm immediately after bleeding the brakes, but becomes low and spongy after the vehicle has sat for several hours. The residual pressure valve is usually installed at the master cylinder outlet port or is part of the combination valve. To check it, pump the brakes several times and then release the brake pedal. Now open a bleeder valve at one of the wheels. If the residual pressure valve is good, there will be a spurt of fluid from the bleeder.

TROUBLESHOOTING PULLING WHILE BRAKING

If the vehicle pulls to one side under braking, especially at higher speeds, there are several items to check.

Begin with the brake pads and shoes. Inspect these for signs of foreign contamination, such as brake fluid, wheel bearing grease, or axle lubricant. These will drastically affect the friction coefficient of the brake material, resulting in a brake pull. Check the color of the linings; they should be the same general color for both sides of the vehicle. For example, check the rear shoes on the right and left side; the color should be the same. If not, this usually indicates that fluid has contaminated the lining at some point. If this is found, the pads on both sides must be changed.

Next, on drum brake vehicles, verify that the correct shoes are installed and that the leading and trailing shoes are in the correct position. Most brakes have equally sized shoes with different length pads. Normally, the longer lining is installed on the side of the brake backing plate located toward the rear of the vehicle. You might find that a previous installer reversed the leading and trailing shoe on one side of the vehicle; this will result in uneven braking force. Another common problem is that both leading shoes are installed on one side

and both trailing shoes are installed on the other, resulting in uneven braking action.

Finally, verify that the brake shoe linings are the same width. Some vehicles may have used a different width lining on the front drum brakes, and if the installer mixed up the shoes, anything is possible.

For disc brake vehicles, check for sticking calipers. This can happen due to corrosion or damage to the caliper or caliper bracket. The easy way to check for this is to remove the pads and re-install the calipers; they should slide back and forth with a smooth motion. Make sure that the sliding points are properly greased with brake caliper grease. Also check the caliper attaching hardware. These bolts should be smooth and not bent or scarred.

The caliper piston can also stick in its bore. This will also result in brake pull, or even brake drag. If brake drag is occurring, this will be obvious, as the wheel and brake will be extremely hot after a short drive. The vehicle may also exhibit a pull toward the side that is dragging. This is usually fixed by rebuilding the caliper, but be careful: a caliper usually sticks due to corrosion. If this is cleaned up, the bore or piston may now be the wrong size, and this can also lead to piston sticking if the piston cocks over in the caliper bore.

If the shoes and pads appear to be fine, next check for pinched or damaged brake lines. Begin by checking the brake lines on the side of the vehicle that is opposite of the direction of the pull. For example, if the vehicle pulls to the left, check the right side brake lines. Inspect them carefully for dings or creases. An easy way to check is to install a short piece of tubing onto each front brake bleeder, routing the other end of each tube to a cup directly under each wheel. Open each bleeder 1/2 turn and press the brakes slowly until the pedal stops. Have an assistant close the bleeder at each wheel, then release the brake pedal. Check the volume of fluid in each cup. If it is dramatically different, find out what is limiting the flow of fluid to the side with the lower volume.

CHECKING BRAKE PEDAL ADJUSTMENT

When was the last time you adjusted your brake pedal linkage? Most people do not give this any thought, but just like clutch linkage, if it is not adjusted properly, brake drag, long pedal travel, and/or power-brake groaning can result. The brake pedal linkage can be out of adjustment because of past work that was improperly done or because a master cylinder, brake booster, or other replacement part different from the original design was installed.

There can be one or two adjustment points, depending on your brake design and whether or not your vehicle has power brakes. To verify proper adjustment, first find out what is adjustable and where. If the vehicle has power brakes, you need to find out if the rod from the booster that actuates the master cylinder is adjustable.

Figure 12 shows how the piston in the master cylinder and the actuating rod from the booster are positioned with the master cylinder at rest. Note that there must be a gap here. If this is not the case, it can cause the pistons in the master cylinder to block the compensation ports, which will prevent complete brake release after repeated stops. This will result in dragging brakes. The booster may also emit groans

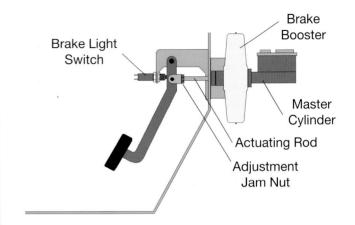

Typical brake linkage adjustment for a firewall-mounted master cylinder. Don't forget to adjust the brake light switch after the master cylinder has been properly adjusted. For Fords, the brake light switch is hydraulic and is not adjusted.

and other sounds if the brake pedal is released, but the actuating rod is not free to move without contacting the master cylinder piston.

If the actuating rod from the booster to the master cylinder is adjustable, adjustments are made by turning the rod. To make an adjustment, the master cylinder must first be removed. The easiest way is to first make sure that the brake pedal is adjusted so that it is not applying any pressure on the booster. Place a

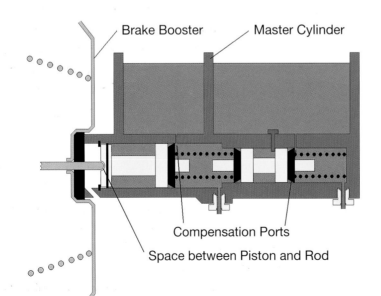

Key adjustment points for the master cylinder to the brake booster. Note that the pistons must be fully back against the stops in the master cylinder, exposing the compensation ports. Also, the actuating rod from the booster must have at least 1/8 inch of free play between the end of the rod and the piston in the master cylinder.

BRAKES

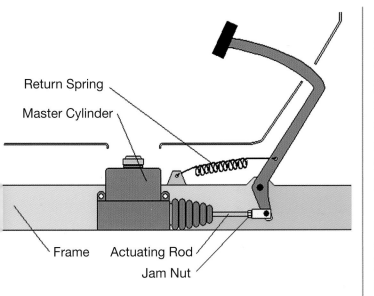

Return Spring

Master Cylinder

Frame   Actuating Rod

Jam Nut

Frame-mounted master cylinder. This type of arrangement was common on cars built before the 1960s. There is a boot that protects the master cylinder from water. Make sure that this boot is in good condition.
Also, this type of master cylinder will require a residual pressure valve because the master is at or below the wheel cylinders or calipers. There is also an inspection cover in the floor to allow the fluid to be checked.

small piece of clay in the piston indent. Now adjust the actuating rod between the booster so that when the master cylinder is temporarily re-installed, the clay is compressed to a thickness of 1/8 of an inch. Take off the master cylinder, clean off any traces of clay, and re-install the master cylinder. Some boosters are adjusted by placing shims between the master cylinder and the brake booster.

To adjust the brake pedal linkage, begin by checking for free play. There will be one of two styles of pedal. Most hanging pedals will not use a return spring on the pedal, but it will hang free, just contacting the actuating rod to the booster or master cylinder. For these, the pedal should be adjusted so that there is 1/8 of an inch of travel before the actuating rod that goes to the master cylinder begins to move. This translates to roughly a 1/2 inch of pedal travel. All brake systems have this adjustment; to achieve it you will need to find out where and how the actuating rod is adjusted.

For manual (not power-assisted) brake systems, it is important that the free play is set correctly; you want the rod to pull back from the master cylinder piston by 1/8 of an inch but no more. You don't want too much slack in the system so that the actuating rod can come out of position. If this happens, depending on how the vehicle is designed, the rod can move and interfere with the complete disengagement of the brakes, resulting in brake drag.

Don't forget the brake light switch. On cars that use a mechanical switch, it is usually mounted on the brake pedal linkage. After the pedal travel is properly adjusted, make sure that the switch is adjusted so that it is off while the pedal is at rest and comes on at the same time or just before the master cylinder piston begins to move. You don't want the brake lights on all the time or the brake lights not coming on when you stop.

For most Fords, this switch is hydraulic and is mounted on the distribution block. These types of switches are not adjustable. Verify that they work and also verify that minimal pressure activates the brake lights. If the switch is bad, it may not come on at all or it could require higher pressure levels to come on than may be reached during a light braking maneuver.

CHECKING FRONT BRAKES

Before checking the front brakes, check the front brake lines and hoses. On a car that is over 35 years old, the condition of these neglected items is most likely questionable. To check the front brake hoses, have someone press on the brake pedal while you inspect each hose. Check for swelling or signs of leaking along the length of the hose, as well as at each joint.

Also check the metal brake lines. Inspect along the entire length for signs of leaking brake fluid caused by mechanical damage, rust, or loose fittings. Replacement lines can be purchased for most cars from aftermarket sources. These will come prebent, with the proper fittings at each end. If you need to fabricate your own lines, they must be double flared.

Most auto parts stores also sell straight hard line, at various lengths, and these can usually be bent to fit.

For cars with front drum brakes, check for leaking wheel cylinders by carefully peeling back the dust cover on each side of the wheel cylinder and checking for moisture. If you detect any leaks, the wheel cylinder is bad. If the wheel cylinders check out OK, verify proper adjustment, as excessive clearance between the shoes and the drum will result in low pedal pressure. Also verify that the adjusters are working properly. The adjuster wheel should turn easily, and the adjusting arm should move freely, with no sign of binding. All springs and linkage should appear clean and not be rusted, broken, or distorted.

CHECKING FRONT DISC BRAKES

For cars with front disc brakes, check the calipers for signs of leaking at the pistons; any moisture indicates a bad piston. Check for proper adjuster operation; disc brakes adjust by having the piston seal move out in the caliper bore, thus holding the piston so that it is just in contact with the pad. Verify this by working the pedal, and then when the pedal is released, see if you can gently pry the pads away from the rotor. If you can, you have found your problem. Any clearance will result in low pedal pressure, as the pistons have to be moved back out to the rotors. This can be caused by loose caliper support hardware or bent or damaged support brackets.

CHECKING FRONT ROTORS

Check for warped rotors. If the rotors are warped, the brake pedal pressure can be low, as a warped rotor will work the pistons back into the cylinder bores when it rotates. Also, a warped rotor will usually cause the brake pedal to feel as if it is pulsating when the brakes are applied. In either case, it is easy to check the rotor. Place a straightedge so that it just contacts the rotor. Now rotate the rotor and verify that the straightedge remains in contact with the rotor and does not move. If the straightedge moves, or if you can see waves in the surface of the rotor, the rotor is warped and will need to be turned or replaced.

Remember, any clearance at all is a bad thing. Do the math: calculate the surface area of the pistons in your calipers and multiply this by the number of pistons. Now calculate the surface area of the piston in the master cylinder. The resulting ratio will show you how a little movement in the calipers is related to large movement of the piston in the master cylinder. This also multiplies the force applied to the disc brakes. Keep this in mind when upgrading to disc brakes or upgrading OEM disc brakes, as you may have to replace the master cylinder with one that has a larger bore in order to move sufficient fluid to make the brakes work.

CHECKING REAR BRAKES

Before checking the rear brakes themselves, check the rear brake lines and hoses. Rear lines and hoses suffer more abuse than front lines. To check the rear brake hose, have someone press on the brake pedal while you inspect each hose. This hose is usually located just off center from the rear axle differential, and should be securely clamped to the car and the rear axle. This hose is almost never inspected due to its location. Check for swelling or signs of leaking along the length of the hose, as well as at each joint. Finally, check the metal brake lines. Inspect along the entire length for signs of leaking brake fluid caused by mechanical damage, rust, or loose fittings. If this does not reveal the source of the problem, move to the rear brakes.

For cars with rear drum brakes, check for leaking wheel cylinders by carefully peeling back the dust cover on each side of the wheel cylinder and looking for moisture. If you detect any at all, the wheel cylinder is bad. If the wheel cylinders check out OK, verify proper adjustment, as excessive clearance between the shoes and the drum will result in low pedal pressure. Also verify that the adjusters are working properly. The adjuster wheel should turn easily and the adjusting arm should move freely with no sign of binding. All springs and linkage should look clean and should not be rusted, broken, or distorted.

BRAKE VALVES

Brakes require hydraulic control valves in order to function at their peak performance. Cars equipped with four-wheel drum brakes may have no valves, while cars with dual brake circuits might have nothing more than a simple brake-warning valve in the distribution block.

Cars use three types of control valves: the residual-pressure valve, the proportioning valve, and the hold-off valve. There is also the brake-warning switch, but this is not an actual control valve.

Correct control valving will make a substantial difference in braking performance. Muscle cars often have dismal 60-to-0 mph stopping distances—180 to 200 feet is not uncommon. Cars that have been converted to front disc brakes usually perform just as badly, if not worse, with the rears hopelessly locked and the front brakes not contributing much. Properly adjusting the control valves can allow a front disc–equipped muscle car to stop on par with most new cars. You want your 60-to-0 mph distances to be around 140 feet or less, and with proper valving this is easy to accomplish.

RESIDUAL-PRESSURE VALVE

Cars built in the 1950s or before commonly had the master cylinder mounted on the frame under the passenger compartment. On vehicles where the master cylinder is mounted at the same level as, or below, the wheel cylinders or brake calipers, the brake fluid can drain from the wheel cylinder back to the master. Since wheel cylinders only seal one way, when the fluid drains back, air can be introduced into the system. The residual-pressure valve prevents this by maintaining a low pressure, usually 2 to 10 psi, in the brake lines.

If the residual-pressure valve is bad or missing, the brake pedal will be high and firm right after bleeding the brakes, but sitting for some time or driving for a while without pressing the brakes will result in low brake pedal pressure. Also, if the vehicle is being converted to disc, a residual-pressure valve suitable for drum brakes may hold too much pressure for a disc brake car, resulting in brake pad drag. Keep this in mind when retrofitting or servicing the brakes on an early-model vehicle with a low-mounted master cylinder. Most drum brake applications will use a residual pressure valve with an operating pressure

This is an adjustable proportioning valve. This is installed in the line that feeds the rear brakes. This valve allows the knee point to be adjusted to find the optimum brake pressure and avoid rear wheel lockup.

of 10 psi while disc brakes will use a valve with an operating pressure of 2 to 3 psi.

PROPORTIONING VALVE

This valve is necessary for maximum stopping performance, particularly on cars with disc front and drum rear brakes. Most early factory disc brake–equipped cars did not have proportioning valves. For example, most GM disc brake cars built before 1971 did not have them, and the ones that did had separate valves for each function.

Disc brakes require higher pressure to work, and without a proportioning valve, the rear drum brakes will lock the rear wheels long before the front brakes have reached their maximum stopping power, resulting in longer stopping distances during panic stops. Whether on cars that were converted to front disc at some point in their past or on an early factory-equipped front disc–brake car, this is a common problem when there is no proportioning valve.

Proportioning valves work by limiting the pressure once the set point for the valve has been reached. For example, if the valve is set to limit at 550 psi, full brake pressure will be available to the rear brakes up until the 550 psi set point. From this point, any increase of brake pressure from the master cylinder will result in a much slower rise in pressure to the rear wheels. This pressure set point is also referred to as the knee setting.

The proportioning valve must be installed in line after the brake distribution block, as this is where the brake warning switch is installed. If you limit the pressure, the block may detect the pressure difference and trigger the warning light. Again, some brake line fabrication may be required to get the system plumbed properly. Do not add a second proportioning valve to a vehicle that already has one; replace the existing valve if you suspect it is bad.

Most factory disc brake cars built after 1971 had rear proportioning valves. Later models usually were equipped with a combination valve, which incorporates the proportioning valve in the distribution block.

Retrofitting a combination valve onto an earlier model car in place of its distribution block is an option. If you do this, use a new combination valve, as a used part might be defective or incorrectly configured. Also, a new rear proportioning valve will be calibrated for the vehicle the valve was originally intended for.

HOLD-OFF VALVE

Another valve required for front disc/rear drum cars is a hold-off valve. This valve is typically also a part of the combination valve on later-model cars built after 1971. This valve prevents the front brakes from receiving any pressure until 30 to 100 psi worth of pressure is available to the rear brakes. This allows the rear brakes to overcome their return spring pressure and begin application before the front brakes.

This has the benefit of preventing the front brakes from locking up before the rear brakes begin to work while stopping on ice or other slippery surfaces. When this valve is not working, the rear brakes might make noise but do little or no work under extremely light braking. If your rear brakes howl or make a grating noise under light braking, especially at slow speeds, suspect the hold-off valve.

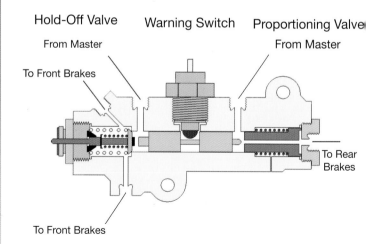

The combination valve combines the proportioning valve, hold-off valve, and the brake light warning switch in one assembly. It usually functions as the distribution block as well.

The hold-off valve also reduces wear on the front brake pads by using the rears more effectively under light braking. A defective hold-off valve will cause unusually short front pad life, especially if you spend time in stop-and-go traffic.

Finally, this valve helps promote vehicle stability by allowing the rear brakes to apply just before the front brakes.

Again, the first vehicles offered with front disc brakes may not have had this valve. Cars built in 1969 and 1970 may have had a hold-off valve but not a proportioning valve. Also, in 1970, your vehicle may have had separate hold-off and proportioning valves. Starting in 1971, most cars with factory disc brakes switched to a combination valve. Unless you are driving on ice or other extremely slippery surfaces, not having a hold-off valve will have no effect on stopping distance, but it can create noisy rear brakes if it is missing or defective. And if you do a lot of stop-and-go driving, this valve could increase the pad life of your front brakes.

For cars that are being converted to four-wheel disc brakes, this valve needs to be removed. If the car was originally a four-wheel drum brake car, then the output for the rear wheels just needs to go through a proportioning valve in order to get the proper brake balance so that the rear disc brakes don't lock up prematurely.

When bleeding the brakes on a car with a hold-off valve, the brakes will have to be pressure-bled or the valve will have to be defeated. For factory cars with a hold-off valve, there is usually a small stem that sticks out from the combination valve. By pressing this in, the hold-off valve can be deactivated for vacuum or gravity brake bleeding.

COMBINATION VALVE

The easiest way to convert a car to disc brakes or to upgrade an early factory disc brake car is to add a combination valve from a later model car. This gets you the proportioning valve, hold-off valve, and the brake-warning light switch all in one housing. See the diagram on page 36 showing what is inside a typical combination valve. The brake lines will have to be fabricated to fit the new valve, but you will have a neat all-in-one brake valve. This has a side benefit: if the front brake circuit fails and leaks, the combination valve will detect this and override the proportioning valve, allowing full pressure to be available to the rear brakes.

One final point: when you inspect a distribution block or combination valve, you will notice that the brake lines are usually made with differently sized fittings. This prevents the lines from being connected to the wrong ports. Especially on combination valves, the only ports that are the same size are for the two lines to the front wheels. If a vehicle is being upgraded to front disc, swapping in the appropriate combination valve is usually made more difficult by this, as the fitting sizes on the new valve will usually not match the size of the existing fittings on the car.

CHECKING THE COMBINATION VALVE

To check the distribution block or combination valve, disconnect one line at the master cylinder and plug the master cylinder port with a pipe plug. Now press hard on the brake pedal. The pedal should be high and firm, and must not sink. If it sinks or is low, check for brake fluid coming from the open line. Any sign of fluid or a sinking or low pedal is evidence that the combination valve is bad and must be replaced. If the valve does not leak and maintains a high firm pedal, the valve may still be defective. If you experience problems with excessive rear wheel lockup and the front and rear brakes have been checked out, the valve should be replaced. See page 38 for a drum brake distribution block diagram; note that the drum brake versions usually did not have a proportioning valve or a hold-off valve.

Remove the pipe plug and reconnect the brake line. Now remove the other brake line from the master cylinder and plug this port at the master cylinder and repeat the test.

These open line tests check for internal leakage. Internal leakage happens when the valve gets old and allows fluid to travel from one circuit inside the combination valve to the other. This defeats the purpose of having two separate brake circuits: safety in the event of a leak in one circuit. The internal leakage will allow the remaining good side to leak down as well, resulting in no brakes. On any vehicle that is 20 years old or older, it is a good idea to replace the distribution block or combination valve.

This internal leakage on a car with four-wheel drum brakes will usually not be noticed during braking, as the pressure is the same at all four wheels. For a car with front disc brakes, during hard braking the rear wheels may show an increased tendency to lock up. Provided that both the front and rear brake circuits are not leaking, this internal leakage in the combination valve will not cause the brake pedal pressure to be low. However, in the event of a break or leak in the front or rear circuit, a bad combination valve can result in no brakes.

This internal leakage can cause another problem: fluid creep. Many disc/drum cars had dual-bore master cylinders. The smaller-diameter piston is for the front disc brakes and develops higher pressure than the larger-diameter piston that is used for the rear drum brakes. If there is internal leakage, each time that the brakes are applied, some fluid will be forced into the rear brake system from the front brake circuit. When the brakes are released, not all of this fluid will make it back to the front brake circuit. This will result in an apparent leaky master cylinder, even though the fluid is really leaking from the front section of the system into the rear section, creating excess brake fluid in the reservoir that exits through the master cylinder cover.

On a GM vehicle, the drum brake piston is the rear part of the master cylinder. If the combination valve is faulty, the drum brake section of the master cylinder can overfill and then spill out, usually at the back of the fluid reservoir. The fluid will drain down the back of the master cylinder and drip from the rear of the unit, giving the appearance that the master is leaking from the rear of the bore. The clue

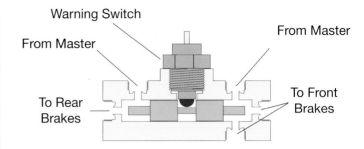

Distribution block with warning light switch. If the pressure between the two sides is not the same, the piston will move, activating the brake warning light. These types of blocks were used on most four-wheel drum brake vehicles that had dual-reservoir master cylinders. Note that there are no brake valves, just the warning switch.

that the combination valve is at fault is that the front of the master cylinder, not the rear, will be low on fluid with the rear totally full and overflowing. If the master was leaking, the rear would be low.

For Chrysler vehicles, the disc brake section is the rear of the master cylinder, so the leakage will be from around the front half of the master cylinder.

This same condition can also be caused by a pinched brake line. The high fluid pressure when the brakes are applied allows the fluid to travel to the rear drum brake, but because of the pinched brake line, when the brakes are released the fluid takes longer to return to the master cylinder. Since the cup only seals against positive pressure, as the piston moves back, the fluid stays in the other half of the dual master, resulting in an overfull rear section. If the front section is low and the rear section is overflowing, check for a pinched or restricted brake line on the end of the vehicle that is serviced by the rear of the master cylinder.

The combination valve is also responsible for turning on the brake warning light if one side of the brake system loses pressure. When performing the test outlined above, if the ignition switch is on, the brake warning light should come on when the pedal is pressed. If it does not, the valve could be bad. Test the wiring before replacing the valve. Ground the wire that was connected to the combination valve and verify that the brake warning light comes on. If the light comes on, the combination valve is bad and must be replaced. If the bulb does not come on, either the bulb is bad or the wiring has a problem. Refer to the electrical section for tips on troubleshooting electrical problems.

Note that for some Ford combination valves, once the light is on it would remain on. You have to reset the valve. To accomplish this, after the brakes are fully bled, open a bleeder screw on the circuit that is opposite of the last circuit bled. Now slowly

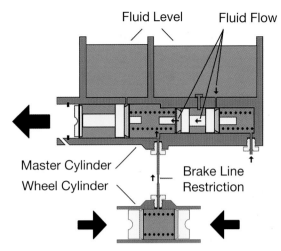

Master cylinder with pedal being released. The pinched line slows the return of brake fluid from the rear wheels. Once the front piston reaches its stop, brake fluid is able to pass by the cup that seals the rear cup pressure.

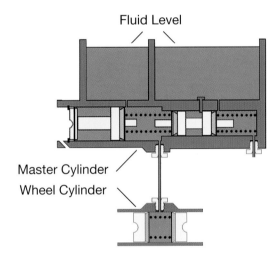

Master cylinder at rest.

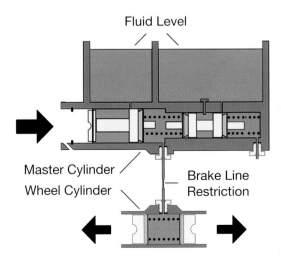

Master cylinder with brakes applied.

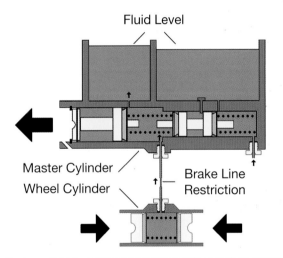

Master as fluid from rear wheel cylinders is finally able to return to the master cylinder. This results in the rear reservoir filling up and the front reservoir mysteriously dropping.

depress the brake pedal until the brake warning light goes out. Close the bleeder and release the brake pedal.

For vehicles with stepped-bore master cylinders, the combination valve was built to match the pressure difference. This is important. If the wrong combination valve is used with a stepped-bore

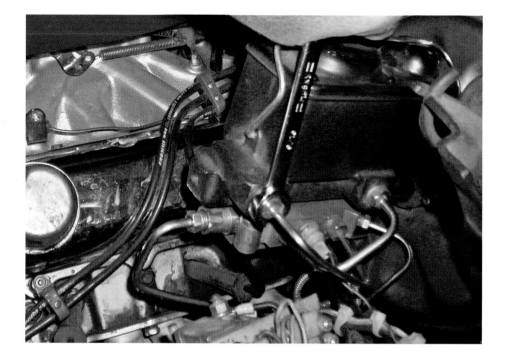

Always use a flare wrench when working with brake or other hydraulic fittings. The soft brass will round if a regular wrench is used.

master cylinder, it can result in the brake warning light coming on and in poor brake performance. The correct combination valve must be used with its corresponding master cylinder.

If the rear brakes lock up excessively, the combination valve should be suspect. Early distribution blocks do not have combination valves. If the vehicle was converted to disc brakes improperly, this feature will be lacking, resulting in early rear brake lockup. Also, even if the proper combination valve is being used, remember that the valve may have failed, resulting in early rear brake lockup.

Finally, if the brakes are working properly, but the rear brakes make excessive noise under extremely light braking, the hold-off valve may be defective. This can be checked by watching the protruding shaft from the combination valve; it should move slightly as the brake pedal is depressed. Also, as with the proportioning valve, drum brake cars do not have hold-off valves, and if the car was improperly converted, this feature will be missing. For four-wheel disc brakes, this valve is not required, and should not be present.

TROUBLESHOOTING POWER BRAKES

If your muscle car has power brakes and the pedal is hard to push, the brake booster needs to be checked. Check the vacuum check valve before assuming that the booster is defective. Start the car and remove the check valve from the booster. It should just pull out of the booster. Check for a strong engine vacuum at the open end of the valve. If the flow is low or not present, replace the check valve. If there is a strong vacuum present, the booster has a problem and must be replaced. Don't operate the vehicle with a failed brake booster. If the vacuum leak is in the seal between the master cylinder and the booster, the master cylinder may be damaged, resulting in a loss of brake fluid and brake system failure.

The last test you should do is to start the car and verify that the power-assist subsystem of the brakes are working properly. After starting the car, do not press the brake pedal, but let it idle for one minute, then shut off the car. Wait another minute and then press the brakes and verify that the power brakes still work. If not, either the check valve is leaking or the seal between the master cylinder and the power brake booster is leaking. The check valve is inexpensive and easily replaced. The seal between the master and the booster is usually not an available service part and a rebuilt power-brake booster is the only way to get one.

The seal between the master cylinder and the booster can be checked by finding the hole at the rear lower part of the master cylinder. This hole is present to allow any leaking vacuum from the booster to escape and prevent the rear seal of the master from being damaged by vacuum. By placing your finger over the hole with the engine running and checking for any sign of vacuum, the condition of the seal can be checked. There should not be any sign of vacuum. If there is, replace the booster. If this seal fails completely, the bleed hole in the master may not be sufficient to prevent eventual failure of the master cylinder rear seal and the loss of brake fluid from the rear master cylinder reservoir.

Also note that a rebuilt brake booster can usually be obtained with a new master cylinder for only a few dollars more than just the rebuilt booster. Check around; the cost of the rebuilt booster with the master cylinder is less than the cost for the rebuilt booster and master cylinder if purchased separately. As a general guide, I have found that the booster lasts about 15 years, and usually the seal between the master and the booster is what wears out. The first clue is that the booster will not store sufficient pressure for more than a minute after the engine is turned off.

I have also found that a properly maintained master cylinder lasts around 15 years, so I simply replace the booster and the master cylinder as a set. This prevents having to remove the master twice to service each component separately.

PEDAL EFFORT

If the brake pedal is high and firm but the pedal is hard to press and you are sure that the booster is not the problem, see if the vehicle was converted to disc brakes. It takes considerably more pressure to activate disc brakes, and this usually means a smaller diameter master cylinder. This sounds counterproductive, but a smaller diameter master cylinder acts as a pressure multiplier. It works like this:

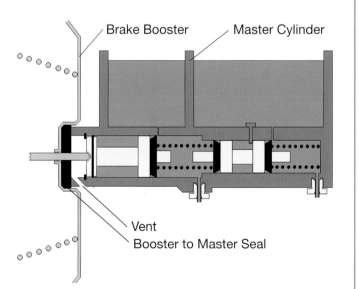

Master cylinder to power booster seal. The seal prevents the vacuum from reaching the rear seal on the master cylinder, and the vent bleeds any small vacuum leakage off.

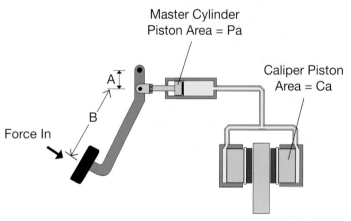

System multiplication factor is found by this formula:

Factor = ((A+B)/A) x Ca/Pa.

For multiple piston calipers, the force is multiplied by the number of piston pairs. From this, the pedal effort can be calculated. Divide the maximum required pressure by the multiplication factor.

Brake line pressure=Pedal force x pedal ratio x caliper area x $\left(\dfrac{\text{Brake line pressure}}{\text{Master cylinder area}}\right)$

You can see that making the diameter of the master cylinder piston smaller will increase the brake pressure for a given pedal pressure. There is a catch: the piston must be large enough in diameter to move sufficient fluid to make the brakes work. As the master cylinder piston gets smaller, the line pressure will go up with the same pedal effort, but so will the pedal movement. So like everything else, there's always a tradeoff; make the master cylinder piston too big and the pedal will be high but the required effort will also be high, so you may not be able to reach maximum braking power. Make the piston too small in diameter and your brake pedal will have more travel and be easier to push, but you may not have enough volume to reach maximum braking power before the pedal hits the floor!

The best advice: if the car was available with disc brakes, get the master cylinder that is for the disc brake version of the car. If the vehicle was never offered with a disc brake option, some research may be in order. If you are using an aftermarket disc brake conversion, get the manufacturer's recommendation for what type of master cylinder to use. This last bit of advice also applies if you are converting to rear disc, as most muscle cars were never offered with a rear disc brake option. Failure to get this right can result in a car that cannot be stopped safely in a short distance.

Another consideration for cars with front disc and rear drum brakes is a dual-bore master cylinder. These were used on several cars and they are just like a regular master cylinder except that the bore is stepped. For instance, a 1.125-inch bore is drilled at the back, with a 1.000-inch bore finishing the rest of the way. This type of master has the drum brakes at the rear of the master cylinder. The result of this is higher volume and lower pressure for the drum brakes. The 1.000-inch bore at the front provides higher pressure but lower volume for the front disc. This helps prevent a low pedal pressure feel while helping to overcome the pressure differences at which the two types of brakes operate. This is one reason

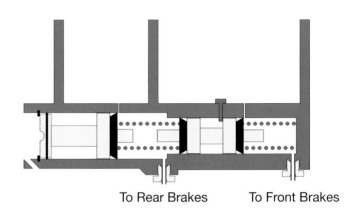

To Rear Brakes   To Front Brakes

The stepped bore master uses a smaller diameter for the front brakes, thereby increasing the brake pressure for the front disc.

that, when converting a car to front disc brakes, the master cylinder should be changed as well.

One more item to consider is the combination valve. The combination valve must match the master cylinder as well as the brake type. When diagnosing brake problems, verify that the master cylinder and the combination valve match and that they are the correct ones for the brakes that are on your vehicle.

BRAKE LINES AND FITTINGS

Muscle cars use 3/16-inch and 1/4-inch zinc-coated steel tubing for brake lines. After 30 to 40 years, especially if the vehicle is operated where salt is used on the roads, these lines will corrode and rust. Since brake-system pressure can reach 1,000 psi or higher, these lines should be replaced if they show any signs of corrosion. Look for roughness or a pitted exterior surface, especially around the fittings. If you see signs of this, replace the lines.

You can use the straight lines available at auto parts stores, but unfortunately these lines usually do not have the correct fittings to connect the master cylinder to the distribution block or combination valve. These lines will usually work when connecting the distribution block to the front brakes or when connecting the rear brakes to the rear distribution block. They also are rarely the correct length, resulting in a sloppy-looking job, as the excess tubing is bent to make the tube fit.

A better option is to purchase replacement lines. There are several companies that manufacture replacement brake lines for just about any vehicle imaginable. The advantage here is that the lines will have the correct fittings on each end, and they are the correct length with the proper bends. Furthermore, these lines will have spiral gravel shielding just like the original lines did. Also, most of these companies will give you a choice, original steel or stainless steel. The price is reasonable as well.

You can also fabricate your own lines. This may be the best option if you are performing a custom brake upgrade. Good sources for the tubing and fittings are the same companies that provide the brake line kits; they also sell lengths of tubing and the proper fittings. When routing the lines, a good tip is to use a length of solid copper wire. Bend and route it in place where the brake line will be routed. When finished, remove the copper wire and use this as your template to bend the brake line.

FLARING STEEL TUBING

The flaring at the ends is critical to a leak-free, long-lasting brake system. Use a good, high-quality double-flaring tool. Die-block flaring tools are what the professionals use, and they make really nice flares. They are also ten times the cost of the hand flaring tools that you can get at the local hardware store. You can still make a good flare with the hand tool. Only

flare new tubing. Never try to flare old tubing that has surface corrosion; the flare will leak.

Regardless of the tool used, begin by properly dressing the end of the cut tube. It must be perfectly straight, meaning perpendicular and flat. Next, clean out the inside and slightly ream the inside of the tube. The outside edge must be beveled back slightly at a 45 degree angle. This step is important; otherwise the tube will be difficult to flare. Now place the correct fitting on the tube, making sure it is oriented the correct way.

Clamp the tube in the flaring bar. Be absolutely sure that the correct length of tubing extends above the flaring bar. Also, make sure that both of the bars are exactly even. This is where most mistakes are made—either the tube is not at the correct height and or the bars are not even.

Next, clamp the flaring bar in a vice; it is difficult to get a good flare when you are wrestling the flaring tool around on the bench or floor. Place a drop of light oil in the flaring button so that the tube will slide easily while it is being flared. Now place the flaring button into the tube, stem side in, and then place the flaring tool in place. Tighten the tool to remove the slack. Now verify that the flaring tool is perfectly perpendicular to the tube and begin tightening the tool. Watch the flaring button to verify that it is going down straight. As soon as it bottoms out against the bar, stop. Do not tighten any further; this is what usually breaks the flaring buttons.

Remove the flaring tool and pull out the flaring button. Inspect the bell; it should be centered and even. There should also be no cracks or other deformations.

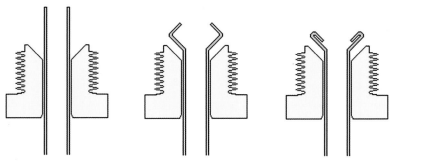

Brake tubing flare. Note that standard SAE flares are 45 degrees. Also, all brake lines should be double flared. This is where the tube is first bell flared, and then the tube is folded back over itself, resulting in a double flare. This prevents the flare from splitting or cracking at the outer edge of the flare. Never use a single flare for any brake line.

If all of this checks out OK, place the flaring tool over the tube and carefully line up the point of the flaring tools with the center of the tube and tighten the tool to remove the slack. Double check to verify that the tool is properly lined up and that the tool is perpendicular to the bar. Now tighten the tool with even pressure. As soon as the pressure begins to increase, stop. You are done. Do not overtighten, as this can damage or split the flare.

Remove the tool, loosen the bar, and remove the tubing. Carefully inspect the flare to verify that it is even and centered on the tube. Off-centered flares are usually the result of overtightening the flaring tool or allowing too much tubing to extend past the end of the flaring bar. Also, there should be no signs of cracking or distortion.

To check the flare, hand-tighten into a fitting. Then, using a wrench, lightly tighten. Now try to blow into the open end, checking for leaks. It should be sealed up tight with just light pressure from the wrench.

BRAKE SYSTEM UPGRADES

Most muscle cars came from the factory with drum brakes front and rear. From a braking performance standpoint, especially if you add a potent engine, this is marginal at best. Upgrading to front disc brakes is mandatory if you intend to drive the car on the street. The original four-wheel drum-brake system simply is not up to driving on a daily basis, especially in heavy traffic.

Consider this: a typical four-wheel drum brake–equipped car will take at least 220 feet to stop from 60 mph. This is for the first stop before the brakes are hot. The same vehicle will usually take over 1,000 feet to stop from 100 mph! This is totally unacceptable for daily driving compared to modern ABS-equipped vehicles; even a new delivery van will out-stop your vintage four-wheel drum brake–equipped muscle car. You need to be in the 130- to 150-foot range for your 60-to-zero braking distances, and with a proper front disc upgrade combined with the correct valving, this is easy to achieve.

Most muscle cars had disc brakes as a factory-installed option, or other models from the same manufacturer had disc brake options, and these can be easily installed. You can also install disc brake upgrade kits that can be purchased from aftermarket vendors. These have the advantage of all-new or refurbished components and typically include all the required hardware.

If you choose the OEM approach, remember that the parts you are looking for have probably been out of production for quite a while. The GM A-body direct bolt-on disc brake system was produced from 1969 until 1972, with the spindles being the key part. These spindles have not been produced since 1972, so good luck finding a used set. Also, the vast majority of the 1968–72 A-bodies were drum brake cars. Ford and Chrysler were similar. Federal safety standards mandated front disc brakes starting with 1973 models, so if your platform crossed from 1972 to 1973, you should be able to find the brake parts you need.

You will need all the parts beyond the ball joints: spindles, dust shields, rotors, caliper brackets, calipers, hardware, and the brake hoses. You might even need to get the front brake lines, and their frame mounting brackets. The calipers will most likely need to be rebuilt, or replaced, but these are typically affordable pieces. Also, replace the brake hoses and wheel bearings. If the brake rotors are worn or damaged, replace them as well.

The master cylinder will need to be replaced with the disc brake version that was available for your car. If none was offered, some research will be in order for later versions or other model versions that will fit. For cars that came with a single-reservoir master cylinder, get a 1968 or later version, as it will be a dual-reservoir model.

The next thing to check is the valving. Most drum brake cars used a simple distribution block, and unless the master was mounted below the wheels, no control valves were used to limit or control brake pressure. When converting to front disc, this will have to be changed if you expect to achieve maximum braking performance. This is important. Many cars have been converted to disc brakes at some point, and the conversion may not have included the proper valves. This will result in a brake system that never works properly.

For starters, you will need a proportioning valve. Under maximum braking, the rear brakes will need less pressure than the front. For front disc and rear drum, the rear pressure will be lower than the rear pressure for a vehicle with rear disc. But even a four-wheel disc car requires less rear brake pressure than front.

Just remember, even an adjustable proportioning valve is not an ABS system. It will only provide maximum braking potential under the conditions it was designed or adjusted for. For example, if the system was designed (or adjusted, for an adjustable model) for best braking performance on level, flat concrete, it will allow rear brake lockup on a wet road. It will also allow rear wheel lockup on a downhill slope, due to increased weight transfer to the front.

AFTERMARKET DISC BRAKE CONSIDERATIONS

If you are adding aftermarket disc brakes, consider that the larger the rotor, the more leverage the brakes can apply to stop the car due to the increased surface area's improved heat removal. Remember, brakes work by converting motion to heat. Since energy cannot

Aftermarket combination valve under a disc drum master cylinder. This is installed on a vehicle that was converted to front disc. With this combination valve and master cylinder, the brake performance is on par with modern cars. This vehicle no longer exhibits premature rear brake lock.

be created or destroyed, all of the kinetic energy of motion must be converted to heat. The ability of the brakes to dissipate this heat will determine how effectively the brake system can resist fading.

The caliper piston bore determines how much brake pressure is required to achieve the clamping force. If the bore is large, then the clamping force will be higher compared to a caliper with a smaller piston area at the same line pressure. There is a tradeoff: the larger-piston caliper will require a lower pedal effort when compared to a smaller-piston caliper, but the volume of fluid that needs to be moved will be greater, resulting in more pedal movement. If this is taken to extreme, the master cylinder may not have sufficient piston travel to safely stop the car!

If rear disc brakes are being installed, you must pay attention to the ratio between the front and rear caliper piston bore diameters. Since weight transfers forward while braking, the rear piston area needs to be less than the front caliper piston area. Even with a good proportioning valve, it is possible to have the minimum pressure still be enough to lock the rear wheels if the rear caliper piston area is too big. As a rule of thumb, the rear piston area should be no more than 70 percent of the front caliper piston area. This will allow the proportioning valve to be set to prevent rear wheel lockup under panic braking.

The best way to install the correct system is to talk with the aftermarket brake component supplier and get their complete kit for the front wheels, rear wheels, master cylinder, and valving. Make sure that the components are for your car, and that the supplier can tell you how and why they were sized the way they were.

Vehicles with front disc and rear drums should have a hold-off valve for the front brakes. These are usually incorporated in the combination valve, and they are harder to find as standalone parts. These are not absolutely necessary, but it will make the vehicle easier to drive on ice. Also, this valve can increase the life of your front pads if you do a lot of driving in stop-and-go traffic.

If you add a combination valve, make sure that you modify the wiring that connects the brake warning light. The combination valve will replace the distribution block. If the vehicle is older and originally had a single-piston master cylinder, there will be no sensor in the original distribution block. If you want to add this feature, run an 18-gauge wire from the emergency brake pin switch and connect this to the electrical connector that is on the combination valve. To test the indicator, open a front or rear bleeder and press the brakes. With the ignition on, the brake warning light should come on.

CHAPTER 4
SUSPENSION

In order for your car to perform at its best, you must have a suspension system that works properly. The starting point is to test the system.

Begin the suspension check by raising the vehicle and supporting the vehicle with jack stands under the frame. You usually do not have to remove the wheels. Do not grease the suspension before checking the components, as fresh grease may restrict the movement and mask a faulty component.

CHECKING BALL JOINTS

For cars with springs on the lower control arm (or torsion bars) place a jack under the lower arm, at the spring pocket, and raise the jack enough to take the load off the ball joints. When the suspension is hanging free, the rebound is limited by the upper control arm bumper. If your car has the spring on the upper control arm, you are ready to begin as soon as the vehicle is jacked up and supported on jack stands.

With the ball joints unloaded, slide a pry bar under the tire and try to rock the tire up and down as well as in or out. Be careful; do not confuse movement caused by a loose wheel bearing for ball joint movement. Check both the upper and lower ball joints for movement, either in and out or up and down. You may have to place your hand around the ball joint and the spindle to feel for movement. If the ball joint has play, it is defective and must be replaced.

CHECKING CONTROL ARM BUSHINGS

To check your control arm bushings, visually inspect the bushing for signs of torn or missing rubber. Any damage to the rubber in the bushing signals a bad

Rubber (OEM) or Other Active Material

Inner Sleeve

Outer Shell

This is a cross-section of a control arm bushing. It is really quite simple. The design prevents any metal-to-metal contact between the moving surfaces in the suspension.

bushing. Also check for proper centering in the bushing. If the rubber is damaged, the bushing will not hold the bushing centered on the bolt. This may also allow the arm to rub against the frame. If there is any evidence of problems, the bushings must be replaced. The rubber cap that is on each bushing is also important; this rubber is responsible for keeping the control arm from moving from side to side.

SUSPENSION MAINTENANCE

While no car should be operated unless the suspension system is in good working order, it is especially vital for a daily driver. When performing suspension maintenance, do one side at a time. This way you have the other side to use as a reference for how things go together. Do not attempt to unload or remove a coil spring without a spring compressor. Remove all of the components and clean them thoroughly. Inspect all components for signs of impact damage or fatigue. Replace any component that shows any sign of fatigue, bending, cracking, or previous impact (collision) damage. Pay particular attention to the load-carrying A-arm, checking for signs of fatigue around the ball joint and the spring pocket. Replace it if any problems are found.

Begin the suspension rebuild by jacking up the front of the vehicle and firmly supporting it with heavy-duty jack stands placed under the frame. I prefer to place large wood timbers (I use 4 x 16) under the frame, as the vehicle cannot slip or fall from these. Rotate the front wheels and look for any signs of bending or other damage. Next, remove the front wheels. Inspect the wheels for signs of cracking around the bolt holes, and also inspect the wheel where the center is attached to the rim. Look for corrosion or cracked welds. Keep in mind that if these are the original wheels, they are at least 30 years old!

Remove the front brakes. Inspect the mounting hardware for signs of corrosion or cracking. See the section on brakes for how to inspect and rebuild the brakes. At this point you should be staring at the spindle. The spindle is a machined cast part. Wipe away the wheel bearing grease, and carefully check the spindle for damaged threads. Also inspect the spindle for any signs of fatigue or previous collision damage. If the spindle shows evidence of collision damage, do not attempt to straighten it. Replace it.

Unbolt and remove the shock absorber. The next step is to remove the sway bar end links. Also, if the car has brake-reaction or strut rods, these need to be removed as well. Now the suspension system should have everything detached other than the control arms and the spring. Before proceeding, a spring compressor will need to be applied to the spring to hold the spring in place. Do not attempt to service a coil spring without using a spring compressor. The spring may fly out under considerable force and cause serious injury or death.

Remove the outer tie rod end from the spindle. Remove the cotter key and the retaining nut. Now use a pickle fork or a tie rod puller and separate the tie rod from the spindle. Since the steering is also being rebuilt, remove the cotter key and the nut that holds the center link to the pitman arm. Using a pickle fork, separate the center link from the pitman arm. Now remove the bolts that hold the idler arm to the frame. Remove the entire center link, idler arm, and tie rod assembly as a unit. This will save considerable time.

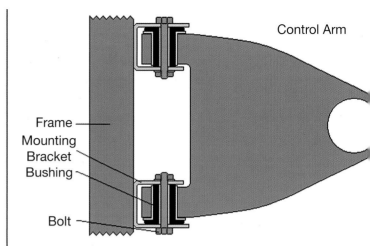

Here is how the bushings install in a control arm. Note that the bushings install with the pad sides facing away from each other. This prevents the control arm from moving forward or backward.

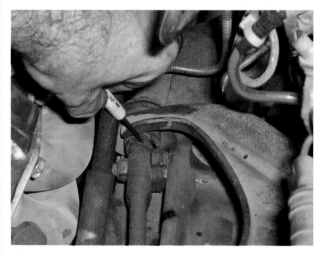

Even polyurethane bushings go bad. These have over 100,000 miles on them and are 10 years old. Note the space between the bushing and the cross shaft. This results in unacceptable movement in the suspension.

DISASSEMBLY OF UPPER A-ARM (COIL SPRING SUSPENSION)

Depending on your car, the coil spring will either be pressing on the upper control arm, or it will be pressing on the lower arm. For upper control arm springs, such as the Ford Mustang, compress the spring with the spring compressor and remove it from the car. Now the ball joints can be separated from the spindle. Remove the cotter keys and the nuts. Next, use a pickle fork to separate the spindle from the A-arms. Do not pound or hammer on the spindle or ball-joint studs. Most cars that have the spring on the upper A-arm also use a brake-reaction or strut rod that connects the lower A-arm to the front of the frame. This also needs to be removed and the bushings need to be replaced. Now continue with the final suspension disassembly.

DISASSEMBLY OF LOWER A-ARM (COIL SPRING SUSPENSION)

If the car has the coil spring pressing on the lower control arm, place a jack under the lower control arm and raise the jack until the spring begins to compress. Now remove the cotter keys and loosen—but do not remove—the ball joint nuts. Next, insert a 1/4-inch diameter or larger steel rod into the shock absorber hole, through the spring, and down through the shock hole in the lower control arm. Lower the jack until it is 1/2-inch below the lower ball joint. Use the pickle fork to pop each ball joint stud free from

Separating the upper ball joint with a pickle fork. Position the fork between the ball joint and the spindle. Now drive the fork in using a hammer. This will destroy the grease boot on the ball joint, but it will separate the ball joint from the spindle. Note that the brake caliper is wired up to prevent it from hanging by the hose.

Modern front suspension. This is a late-model SUV front suspension. Notice that it is an unequal length A-arm front end, just like most vintage muscle cars. The big differences include the rack-and-pinion steering, coil over shock spring, forged A-arms (most muscle cars used heavy stamped sheet steel A-arms), and the ABS sensor.

the spindle. The spring tension will help. Once loose, remove the steel rod and install the spring compressor and compress the spring.

Remove the spindle and clean it. Inspect the spindle for any signs of damage. Check around the ball joint stud holes for cracking. If you find any damage, the spindle must be replaced. The bad news is that new spindles are not available for most cars, and good used spindles are getting hard to find.

The last step is to remove the A-arms. Remove the bolts that hold the A-arms to the car. Once removed, clean the A-arms. Next, remove the ball joint. For a pressed-in ball joint, remove it with an air-powered chisel. If the ball joint is riveted in, use a drill to remove the rivets. Be careful not to damage the control arm. Use a chisel to remove the bushings. When removing parts with a chisel, be careful to not nick or damage the A-arm. For bushings, the best way is to deform the bushing, then force it out.

Once the bushings and the ball joint are removed, inspect the A-arm for signs of damage. Check carefully around the bushings and ball joint holes for cracks. Also check the spring pocket on the load-carrying arm for cracks. Check for signs of previous collision damage. If any cracks or deformation is found, the A-arm must be replaced. Do not attempt to straighten a bent A-arm. Just like the spindles, A-arms may be hard to find, as not all cars have replacement arms available. If the A-arm passes inspection, paint it.

SUSPENSION REASSEMBLY

The reassembly process begins with the A-arms. First install the bushings. The best way is to use a press. Do not pound the bushings in with a hammer, as the bushing and the A-arm will most likely be damaged. Before installing a new bushing, coat the outside of the bushing with door-hinge wax lubricant. If you do not have a press, take the parts to an auto parts store or a mechanic to be pressed into place.

Install the ball joints by using a ball joint press. Do not hammer ball joints into the control arm, as the joint and the A-arm will be damaged. To make the installation easier, coat the outside of the ball joint body with door-hinge wax lubricant. For non-load-bearing ball joints, such as those on GM A-body upper control arms, the ball joint is installed with four bolts.

Install the A-arms. With the new bushings, the arm may be difficult to install. The tight fit

Using an air chisel makes removing old bushings a snap. Just don't contact the control arm with the chisel blade.

is mandatory to prevent the suspension from moving during braking or cornering. To ease installation, apply wax or silicone to the bushing before working the arm into the brackets. Use a large pry bar, not a hammer, to force the arm into position.

Use a hydraulic press or a ball joint press to install the new bushings. Do not hammer the bushings into the A-arm. Also, for arms that are open-channel design, such as this GM A-body arm, a suitable-sized spacer must be used to pass the force through and prevent distorting the arm. Here I found some sockets that are the correct length.

Here is a ball joint being installed using a ball joint press. These make the job simple, and this type of tool can be used with the A-arm on the vehicle.

Once the A-arms are installed, the spring can be installed. Compress the coil spring and install it. Do not loosen or remove the spring compressor. Install the spindle and tighten the ball joint stud nuts. Torque the ball joint nuts to the factory torque specifications. Tap on the spindle, on the sides by each ball joint stud, and recheck the tightness. Line up the cotter key holes and install new cotter keys. Remove the spring compressor.

Assemble the inner and outer tie rod ends and match their length with the old assemblies. This will result in alignment that is close. Install the new idler arm. Next, attach the new center link to the idler arm and pitman arm. Ensure that the castle nuts are torqued

Snug, but don't tighten, the mounting bolts until the car is back together with the wheels installed and sitting on the ground. If the vehicle has rubber bushings, the outer edge of the bushing needs to be tightened down while the suspension is at the correct ride height. Once back on the ground, tighten the mounting bolts to the factory torque specifications.

properly and that the cotter keys are installed. Install the new tie rod assemblies, making sure that the castle nuts are properly torqued. Install the cotter keys.

When installing castle nuts, torque the nut to the recommended torque specifications, and then tap on the side of the part that the stud is inserted through. Then re-check the torque to make sure that the stud was properly seated. Check the cotter key hole. If it lines up, install the cotter key and you are done. If not, tighten the castle nut a little more, until the cotter key hole in the stud lines up.

Install the shock absorbers and the sway bar end links. If the car used brake-reaction or strut rods, install the new bushings and the bars. Double check that everything is correctly assembled. Get out the grease gun and lubricate the ball joints, tie rod ends, center link, and the idler arm. Re-install the brakes. Now it is time to align the front suspension.

ALIGNMENT

Proper alignment is critical for proper vehicle handling characteristics and maximum tire life. If the alignment

Uneven tire wear caused by excessive negative camber. Excessive toe-out will result in a similar wear pattern, except the tread ribs will have an angled wear pattern on each rib, with the high edge toward the outside and the low edge toward the inside.

is wrong, expect poor handling, wandering, pulling, and short tire life. Optimum alignment will also help fuel economy.

A proper alignment can be performed by a competent tire shop or mechanic. You can also perform an alignment at home, and you will know your settings exactly and that the job was done properly. You can find the proper settings in the factory service manual.

The tools that you need include the proper wrenches to loosen the adjustment bolts or the bolts that hold the shim packs. You will also need some alignment tools. A camber gauge can be purchased for about the cost of a single good alignment. Any precision angle gauge can be used; for example, I use a 5-0-5-degree bubble level.

Note that the vehicle must be parked on a flat, level surface to do the alignment. This is critical because you are checking angles where 1/4 degree can make a difference. It is also a good idea to simulate the driver's weight in the front seat. Suspension loading changes the angles. After performing your first alignment, you might want to take the vehicle to a competent alignment shop and have the alignment checked to verify your settings.

By reading the tires that were on the front of the vehicle, most alignment problems can be identified by the wear pattern. Be careful; if the outer edge of the tire is worn, this could be from excessive positive camber or because the vehicle is being driven hard and the wear is from cornering forces. It could also be improper toe setting. Excessive toe-in will result in the outer tire edge wearing and excessive toe-out will cause the inside edge to wear.

When using a tool for setting camber and caster, there are two basic types. The first mounts to the hub and the second mounts to the wheel rim. When using the hub type, it is imperative that the wheel center cap is perfectly mounted to the wheel. Any error here could result in an improper alignment.

Begin the alignment by checking the camber and caster. Now evaluate what needs to be changed.

Center worn

This type of wear indicates that the tire was operated while overinflated. This bulges the center of the tire out. This type of wear can also be observed if the tie is too wide for the wheel.

Feathering

This type of wear is caused by incorrect toe. Each tread rib will be worn at an angle. This can be felt by running your hand across the tread. The side of each rib with the greatest wear will tell you how toe is set incorrectly. If the outer edge of each rib is the most worn, then there is too much toe-in. You can detect this type of wear before it is visible by rubbing your hands from side to side.

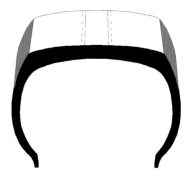

Both sides worn

If the tires are worn down at the edges and the wear is similar for the inside and outside edge, then the tire was most likely operated constantly underinflated. This allows the center of the tire to bulge up while the sides bulge out where the tire contacts the pavement. This can result in the tire overheating while traveling down the road.

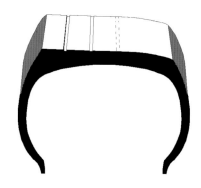

One side worn

This type of wear is caused by camber being set incorrectly. The wear will be on the inside edge if the camber is too negative; if the outside edge is worn, the camber is too positive. Don't confuse this for toe, as usually there will also be the feathering effect across the tread if the toe is incorrect. Also, for outside tread wear, this can be the result of continuous hard cornering, especially with older suspensions that exhibit a positive camber increase while under load.

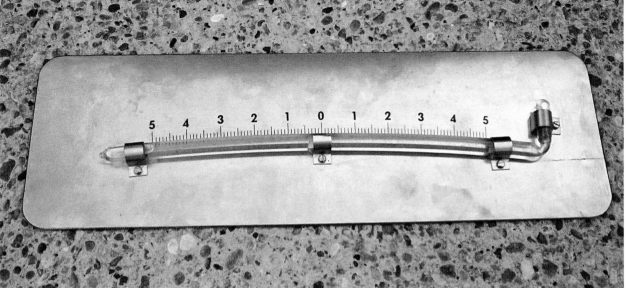

Bubble level used for front end alignment.

For example, on GM front ends, shims are used to set camber and caster angles. If the camber is wrong, add or subtract the same number of shims from the front and back. If caster is wrong, you need to change the relationship between the front and back shim stacks. If only caster is incorrect on a GM vehicle, remove one shim from the front and install it in the rear to make the caster angle more positive. For Ford, camber is set by adjusting the offset bolt that mounts the lower control arm to the frame. Caster is adjusted by the brake strut rod.

Not all vehicles provide adjustment provisions for all settings other than toe. For example, Ford trucks from the 1970s and 1980s with the twin I-beam suspension do not have provisions for adjusting camber. If camber is off, the truck needs to be taken to a frame shop so that the beam can be tweaked.

After camber and caster are adjusted, the toe can be set. For toe, you will need some additional tools. For starters, you will need two 3- to 5-foot straightedges (levels work well). Also, four supports for the levels are needed. I use gallon paint cans. Set the cans so that the levels rest against the tire sidewalls and extend forward. Now make one mark on the level, two feet back from the end. When checking toe, measure at the end of the level and at the 2-foot mark. Subtract the two, and the difference is the toe. Since most vehicles run with toe-in, the measurement at the end should be less than the measurement that is 2 feet back.

OPTIMUM SUSPENSION SETTINGS

After checking the recommended settings from a factory service manual, you might feel that there are better settings for your front end. You are probably correct. Some trial and error is needed to find the optimum settings. You should always begin with the factory settings as a baseline. But don't go to extremes. Proper handling requires that the tire's contact patch remain as flat as possible. Also, excessive angles or settings will result in shortened tire life.

First, most vehicles will respond well to additional negative camber. So for your first setting, use the most negative of the factory-recommended settings for camber. If the service manual shows a camber setting of +3/4 to +1/4 for camber, use +1/4, as this is the smallest (i.e., most negative) setting. Also, the wider the tires, the closer to zero you need

This is a typical muscle car upper control arm. By adding or removing shims, the caster and camber can be changed. Adding shims pulls the upper ball joint in. Adding or subtracting the same number of shims from the front and rear points will make camber move more negative or positive. By moving a shim from the front to rear, caster will move more positive while camber will not change. Always adjust caster and camber before adjusting the toe. Caster and camber changes move the suspension mounting points, and this will change the toe settings.

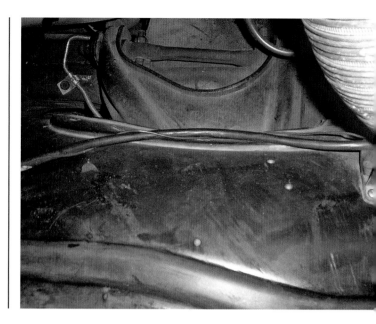

Checking camber, the bubble shows 0 degrees. For this type of gauge, the center cap must be perfectly mounted to the wheel.

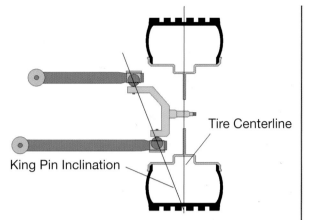

Kingbolt inclination angle. This is the angle of a line that is drawn between the ball joints. The closer that this line intersects the pavement under the center of the tire tread, the easier the steering will be. The vehicle stability will be increased as well. Most muscle cars will not achieve this, but will be within a couple inches. This angle is created by the design of the suspension and is not usually adjustable.

to run. When testing, if the vehicle understeers, you can move more negative, in 1/4-degree increments. Make changes and evaluate how the handling changes. Don't forget to see how the car feels when being driven straight at slow and high speeds as well as judging the turning performance.

Next, caster should be adjusted. Caster affects how stable the car feels, especially at higher speeds. Caster is the angle at which the spindle lays back. The farther it is from straight up and down, the more positive the caster is, and the greater the vehicle's high speed stability and resistance to crosswinds. If caster isn't positive enough, the vehicle will feel loose and it will wander. You will be constantly working the steering wheel to keep the car centered in its lane. Also, if caster is different from side to side, the vehicle will pull, usually toward the side that is the most positive.

Setup for checking toe. Make sure that the raised letters do not interfere with the level. Duplicate this setup on the other side and you are ready to measure toe.

When adjusting toe, the adjuster sleeve can be rotated with channel-lock pliers. After loosening the pinch clamps on each end of the sleeve, the best method is to grab the sleeve so that the direction that you want to rotate will have the jaws of the pliers hook the slot in the sleeve and be attempting to open or spread the sleeve as you rotate. Also, before you begin, spray a good penetrating lubricant in the sleeve.

After adjusting toe, check to be sure that both tie rod ends still have full rotational movement before tightening the pinch clamps. Do this by rotating both tie rod ends in the same direction and then backing them both up so that they are at the halfway point of their rotation. Next, hold the adjuster sleeve, and using a large screwdriver, rotate the pinch clamps so that they are pointing straight down. This ensures that the steering does not hang up due to the clamps interfering with anything on the vehicle. Now tighten the pinch clamps.

Begin with the most positive caster setting that the service manual recommends. For example, if the service manual shows +1 to +2.5 degrees of caster, start with +2.5 degrees. Usually, 2 to 3 degrees of positive caster is sufficient. If caster is correct, the vehicle will feel stable when traveling down the highway and will be easy to keep on track, with little steering input.

Caster works with kingpin inclination for straight-line stability. Kingpin inclination causes the vehicle to be lifted any time that the wheels are turned from straight ahead. This naturally promotes the return of the wheels to the straight-ahead position. Even though vehicles have not used kingpins since the 1950s, the name refers to the angle that would be created between an intersection of an imaginary line drawn through the upper and lower ball joints and another imaginary line that is perpendicular with the ground. The first line can also be referred to as the steering pivot point. This is not an angle that can be adjusted.

Be careful if wheels that use a different offset from stock are installed on the front. They will change where the center of the imaginary line, or steering pivot point, intersects the tire tread. As this moves away from the center of the tire, the wheel will swing, not pivot. This can dramatically affect how the vehicle handles.

Toe also affects straight-line stability. Most vehicles will run a slight toe-in. Usually 1/16 to 1/8 is the range that should be run. This means that the front of the tires are closer together than the rears. Just like camber, the wider the front tires, the less toe that should be run. If toe is incorrect, the car will not handle well and the tires will wear prematurely. If toe is 3/16 inch or more in or out, tire wear will be excessive, with the most wear on the outer edge of the tires for excessive toe-in and on the inside edge for excessive toe-out.

Bump steer is how much the tires will turn in or out as the suspension travels up and down. Most modern vehicles are designed to prevent bump steer. This is accomplished by placing the tie rod pivot points so that they intersect the pivot points that correspond with each end of the suspension components. This allows the tie rod to move in parallel with the suspension and prevents the wheel from turning because of suspension movement. Be careful when considering any suspension modifications; this is one angle that will be affected if any mounting points are changed or control arm lengths are modified.

There are times where toe-out can be used. It makes the vehicle feel more responsive and quicker to respond to steering input. The downside is that the vehicle will feel twitchy and have a tendency to wander.

A proper toe setting will also increase fuel economy.

SUSPENSION SYSTEM UPGRADES

Modern aftermarket parts can tremendously improve the handling of old muscle cars. For starters, a good set of modern radial tires will make a world of difference. For now, we will focus on the suspension.

Suspension systems work best when all of the components are selected to complement each other. Just adding large swaybars, stiff springs, and firm shocks may not result in a better handling car. While these changes may make the car handle better, chances are that you will end up with a marginally better handling car that rides like a buckboard. You could also end up with a poor riding car that actually handles worse.

You must understand what makes a car handle, and this can be summed up in a suspension system that maintains the largest contact patch possible, given the driving conditions, at each of the four tires, and also keeps the vehicle's weight evenly distributed on all four tires. So to make your car handle better, you need to correct the areas where your car falls short.

REMOVE THE SLOP

Before making radical suspension modifications, incorporate basic improvements in order to eliminate slop and improve handling. Your stock suspension uses rubber bushings to mount the control arms to the suspension mounting points. Rubber bushings are used because they last a long time and are compliant. They allow some flexibility in movement, which can prevent suspension binding. They also provide ride

This is a spherical rod end. Note that this type of joint is free to move not just in a plane that is perpendicular to the mounting point. This allows some freedom and twisting to be accommodated while positively locating the endpoint.

isolation, meaning they keep road noise from being transmitted from the tires through the suspension and into the passenger compartment.

Under normal driving conditions, rubber bushings will perform reasonably well. But they also allow excessive movement when placed under heavy loads, like aggressive cornering. This contributes to lower handling performance and a loose feel, both of which can be minimized by switching to stiffer bushings. A good choice is polyurethane, as this material is much stiffer and resists deflection.

However, polyurethane can also cause problems, since rubber bushings work by stretching. The outside of the rubber is attached to the bushing shell and rotates with the control arm while the inside of the rubber is attached to the hollow shaft that is pinched between the suspension mounting points, so the rubber stretches as the control arm moves up and down. This actually provides some damping action to suspension movement. It is also why the attaching bolts for a stock rubber-bushing suspension system must not be tightened until the suspension is compressed down to the vehicle's normal ride height.

Polyurethane or other hard bushings do not stretch. Instead, they are lubricated and move by rotating, with the bushing sliding between the hollow shaft and the bushing shell. This results in the polyurethane slowly wearing away. Also, if silicone grease is not present, the bushings can squeak. Finally, do not get conventional brake fluid on them, as it will deteriorate the polyurethane.

There is one other important point to remember. You can only use hard bushings, like polyurethane, in suspension components that only move in one plane. Think about this for a minute. For a double

A-arm front suspension that uses two mounting points per A-arm, the arms only move in a single plane. But for vehicles that use a brake reaction rod, like the Ford Mustang, the lower A-arm moves slightly forward and back as it moves up and down. This is because the brake reaction rod swings in an arc. So for this type of suspension, the upper A-arm can use hard bushings, but between the lower arm and the brake reaction rod, one or the other needs to retain the softer rubber bushings in order to allow for this slight forward and back motion.

Another example of hard bushings and potential problems is on the GM A-body rear suspension. This is a four-link-style rear suspension, with the upper arms angled to provide the side-to-side stability of the axle. The problem with solid bushings here is that, when one tire travels over a lower or higher point than the other side, the axle twists. This twisting is accommodated by the rubber bushings. A hard bushing, like polyurethane, by design tries to resist this twisting motion. This forces the control arm to flex and it also can cause the bushing to bind.

If the vehicle is cornering at a high rate of speed, normal body roll also requires the bushings to flex, and if the bushing binds, it will not exhibit smooth suspension travel. Rather, it will bind up and then suddenly let go, which can result in a sudden change in the handling behavior, usually resulting in what is called snap oversteer. So for suspension points where the bushings must also accommodate some off-axis movement, you must use a compliant bushing or a custom suspension part that uses a spherical rod end.

HANDLING PROBLEMS

So what exactly happens when a car goes around a corner? If you don't understand this, you will not be able to diagnose problems or achieve the results you are after. When you are turning, the vehicle's weight will be transferred from the inside tires to the outside tires. If the car is balanced, with the same amount

This is a 1.125-inch diameter sway bar with polyurethane bushings that can be greased. This replaced the factory 7/8-inch bar and helps minimize cornering roll.

of weight on the front and rear tires, and speed is constant, then the shift from side to side will be the same for each end of the vehicle. The more the car rolls, the greater the weight transfer. Eventually, this results in the car overloading the outside tires and slipping. The first goal of tuning suspension to achieve maximum cornering performance is to limit weight transfer.

Bear in mind that changes that improve handling should not increase the total load on any one part of the suspension or tires. In fact, usually the worse a vehicle handles, the more load is placed on its outside front tire. The goal is to spread cornering forces more evenly across all four tires.

The perfect suspension prevents any vehicle roll-induced weight transfer while allowing each wheel to freely travel over irregularities in the road while maintaining optimum tire patch contact with the road. In such a perfect scenario, each tire will carry exactly 1/4 of the vehicle's weight under all turning and braking conditions. Of course it is impossible, but a properly set up suspension works toward achieving this.

Simply installing stiff springs or stiff sway bars will not achieve this goal. A balance needs to be maintained between these components, and they have to be sized for the weight of the vehicle. Be careful, as these items tend to work against each other. For example, to limit body roll, you can tighten up the springs or use huge sway bars. Go too far with this, though, and you will reduce the body roll, but the suspension will not be free to move. As the vehicle tries to roll, weight on the inside tires will be reduced and simply transferred to the outside tires.

"Understeer" and "oversteer" define which end is slipping. When the car does not turn as much as the steering input dictates, this is called understeer. An example is when you enter a corner too fast and the front wheels are turned but the car still wants to go straight. A car that exhibits this kind of handling is said to be tight. This is how most factory suspensions are set up. Rear-wheel-drive cars will usually understeer if too much braking force is applied while in a corner.

Oversteer is when the car turns more than the steering input dictates. For instance, you enter a corner too fast, and as you turn the steering wheel the rear of the car swings around. A car that oversteers is said to be loose. Oversteer can easily result in a spin. Rear-wheel-drive cars can oversteer if too much throttle is applied while turning a corner.

As you tune your suspension, you will find that the vehicle dynamics change, and as the handling speed increases, the vehicle may shift from understeer to oversteer. On a neutral handling car, applying the brakes will shift the car to understeer. On a neutral car that is rear-wheel drive, applying the throttle will shift the car to oversteer. If the car is front-wheel drive, applying the throttle will result in understeer. This is why the top-performing road race cars are rear-wheel drive. A properly set up rear-drive car can be made to understeer by braking, and oversteer by applying the throttle, but a front driver is not capable of throttle-on oversteer.

Normally, you will want your car to understeer slightly. This is the safer of the two conditions, as a car that tends to oversteer is much more likely to spin. Just as with engine tuning, make changes one at a time, and evaluate the results. Remember, if a change results in quicker handling characteristics, evaluate the handling at the limit, and determine what change will enhance the characteristics of the car. Your goal should be a smooth transition from neutral to slight understeer at the limit. When set up properly and driving at the cornering limit, brake application should result in a smooth transition to understeer and applying throttle should cause a smooth transition to oversteer.

The weight transfer that reduces cornering performance can be minimized by lowering the vehicle, increasing the spring rates and adding stiffer sway bars. Changes such as this will result in less weight transfer and greater cornering speed. Also, body roll can be minimized by lowering the vehicle, but more than a couple of inches is usually hard to accomplish. Lowering the engine and transmission will also improve handling, but changes such as this are not usually practical.

There are two schools of thought on improving handling—stiff bars or stiff springs. Both of these will work to minimize body roll and weight transfer. Each also has its own advantages and disadvantages.

A vehicle with stiff springs will limit weight transfer, but the vehicle will ride rougher. Stiffer springs limit body roll and weight transfer by restricting suspension movement. One advantage is that for a street-driven vehicle, cornering on rough roads will be better than a vehicle with stiff sway bars, as the tires will not be disturbed by the movement of the tire on the other side of the vehicle.

A vehicle with stiff sway bars can be set up to ride smoother than a vehicle with stiff springs. The sway bar will limit body roll by restricting the independent movement of the suspension, especially the opposite movements that occur during cornering. The problem is that when cornering on rough surfaces, the movements of one wheel will be transferred to the other side of the vehicle, possibly disturbing the other wheel.

But there are limits. As the sway bar is made stiffer, the inside tire is unloaded more on turns and this will actually increase the outside tires' tendency to slide. For example, if the rear bar is made too stiff, the vehicle will want to oversteer. If the front bar is too stiff, the vehicle will want to understeer. This is due to the fact that the bar limits body roll. The body is attempting to roll out of the turn, and to counteract this, the bar pulls up on the inside tire and presses down on the outside tire. This transfers weight from the inside wheel to the outside wheel. Take this too far and the outside wheel is overloaded while the inside wheel is unloaded and the vehicle begins to slip.

So the correct sway bar rate will be directly related to how stiff the springs are, and the proper bar will limit body roll to maximize cornering potential without excessive unloading of the inside tire and overloading the outside tire. Looking at the front, if the front bar is too soft, the body roll will be excessive, resulting in understeer as the body roll transfers too much weight to the outside tire. If the bar is too stiff, the body roll will be minimal, but the bar will exert too much force and unload the inside tire while transferring too much weight to the outside tire, resulting in understeer. So just like everything else, the bar has to be just right or the vehicle will not handle properly.

SUSPENSION SYSTEM GEOMETRY

The reason stiff springs improve handling is because most muscle cars exhibit excessive body roll and also have suspension systems that tuck the front tires in when loaded. For these reasons, stiff springs help handling, but they also sacrifice ride quality. Stiff springs mask but don't fix the fundamental suspension problems. Stiff springs also cause another problem: they result in substandard handling on rough roads. The higher spring rates limit the effective suspension travel, so the suspension system is unable to maintain good tire contact with the road surface.

Instead of overly stiff springs, first investigate how your vehicle reacts when the suspension system is loaded. If your car reacts like most muscle cars, the wheels will tuck in at the bottom (gain positive camber) when loaded. This results in the tire riding around the corner on the outside edge. To test for this, place an angle gauge on the hub, then jack the vehicle up under the front crossmember. You don't need to raise the vehicle off the ground, but lift the suspension about three inches. Now check the camber angle again, and if it has moved more negative (the top of the wheel is leaning in more at the top than before), then you have the classic muscle car suspension. This movement is exactly the opposite of what you need, as you want the tire to lean out at the bottom as the car compresses the suspension (remember, this test decompresses the suspension).

This problem can be corrected by either lowering the upper control arms or making the front spindles longer. This is not as radical as it sounds. The Ford Shelby Mustangs used relocated upper control arms, and the templates are still available from Ford Mustang parts houses; it is a simple matter to redrill the mounting holes lower. Other cars have readily available solutions, such as the GM intermediate tall spindle conversion. This uses the taller spindles from later model full-size GM cars. The conversion is straightforward: use the spindles and upper and lower ball joints from a late '70s Camaro or Caprice (the Camaro used the same spindles as the full-size Caprice). The lower ball joints will have to be turned down to fit in the A-body lower control arm. The outer tie-rod end for the tall spindle will also be required. There are various suppliers that offer complete kits, even including brakes, that make this conversion easy. These kits can be ordered with new control arms as well.

The geometry change will reverse the camber change under load, and the tire will move out under suspension compression. This will reduce the spring rate required. You will still need springs stiffer than the factory rate, but you no longer have to use the brute force method. You can now choose a combination of springs and sway bars that minimizes body roll in corners, yet still absorbs the inevitable bumps in the road.

Remember that tightening up the suspension can be detrimental to acceleration traction. Weak springs allow more suspension travel, and this is what is needed for acceleration traction. Stiff springs limit suspension travel, thus minimizing weight transfer to the rear under acceleration. This is where the front geometry corrections can pay off, since the spring rates can remain lower than they would otherwise have to be to minimize body roll in corners. The geometry correction will not impact straight-line acceleration traction. Also, rear sway bars usually help stabilize the rear suspension, and help reduce tendency of the right rear tire to lift during acceleration.

Combining a heavier front bar with reasonable spring rates and revised front suspension geometry will usually result in a good-handling car that also accelerates well. But what spring rates to use? This is a tough one. Spring rates depend on the car's weight, weight distribution, and desired usage. It is best to find a chassis expert to help with spring rate recommendations. Also, there are several good books on suspension and chassis tuning that will help. For a start, I have found that 600 lb/inch front springs work well on GM A-bodies running big-block engines. This rate results in a reasonable ride that is not overly rough.

CHAPTER 5
STEERING SYSTEM

The steering system consists of the steering wheel, steering shaft, steering box, tie rods, center link, and the idler arm. The spindles are part of the suspension. Just like it is with the suspension system, it is vital to maintain the steering system. Lubricate the tie rod ends and the idler arm at each oil change. If your vehicle has manual steering, check the steering box gear oil at each oil change. For power steering cars, check the power steering fluid at each oil change.

Begin checking the steering components by jacking up the front of the vehicle. All of the following tests

Checking tie rod ends is simple. Grasp the end so that you palm is attempting to squeeze the joint together. Any sign of up or down movement indicates that the joint is loose and needs to be replaced.

This is a recirculating-ball power steering box, the type used on most muscle cars.

should be performed with the wheels off the ground. Properly support the vehicle on jack stands before crawling under the vehicle. The jack stands should be placed under the frame behind the front tires.

To check the tie rod ends, grab each tie rod behind the ball joint at the end of the tie rod. Now attempt to push each tie rod end toward the part that it is mounted to. For example, the outer tie rod end should be pushed toward the spindle. Inner tie rod ends should be pushed toward the center link. If the rod can be moved, the tie rod end is defective and should be replaced. Also check the rubber seal that covers each tie rod end ball joint. If the seal is torn or missing, replace the tie rod end. This seal keeps

the grease in the joint and also keeps dust and water out. When the cap is missing, dirt gets in and quickly wears out the joint.

To check the idler arm, grab the center link at the point where it connects to the idler arm. Push up and pull down on the center link. If the idler arm moves, it is worn and must be replaced. Also check the rubber grease seals at the top and bottom of the idler arm. As with tie rod ends, if the seals are torn or missing the idler arm must be replaced.

Checking the center link is similar to checking the idler arm. Grab the center link next to the point that it connects to the idler arm. Push up and pull down on the center link and watch for evidence that the ball joint is compressing or expanding. Repeat this test, but grab the center link right next to the pitman arm. Any compression or expansion of the center link ball joints are signs that the part is worn and must be replaced. The center link also has rubber grease seals at each end ball joint. Check these for signs of damage, and if they are torn or missing, the center link must be replaced.

Finally, check the steering box. Begin by verifying that the pitman arm is not loose. This can be checked when checking the center link. Then check for smooth operation of the steering box by turning the wheel from lock to lock. On power steering cars, this test should be performed with the engine off. If any tight spots are detected, disconnect the center link from the steering box and check for smooth operation again. If the steering is now smooth, the steering components must be checked for signs of damage. If the steering box still shows signs of binding, the box must be replaced or rebuilt.

Also check the steering box for signs of fluid leaking from the gear box. Check at the base where the pitman arm connects to the box. Also check around the steering shaft input. On power steering cars, check the hose connections for signs of leaking. Finally, most steering boxes have a large cup plug at the end opposite from the steering shaft input. Check around this plug for signs of fluid leakage. If any leakage is detected, the steering box should be rebuilt or replaced.

REPLACING THE STEERING BOX

The steering box is replaced by mounting the new box to the frame. Check the bolts carefully; any signs of damage or corrosion means the bolts should be replaced. If nuts are used, they should be the type of nuts that do not loosen. New hardware should be used. If an aircraft or vibration-resistant nut is removed, only a new nut should be used during assembly. Tighten all of the bolts just snug. Once all of the bolts are in place and snug, torque the bolts to the recommended torque.

Aftermarket steering boxes can improve steering feel and performance. Quick-ratio boxes really wake up a slow-responding car. Several of these look like OEM boxes, so this is a change you can make and still retain your car's stock appearance.

CENTERING THE STEERING BOX

If you disconnect the steering shaft or pitman arm from the steering box, the box must be centered. Centering the box is also necessary if previous maintenance of the steering system is deemed questionable or if the vehicle seems to turn further one direction than another. The instructions below assume that the input shaft and pitman arm are removed, but the check can be performed with these connected.

Begin by rotating the input shaft all the way to one direction and placing a mark on the input shaft and the housing. Now count the number of turns to get to the other lock. Pay careful attention to the last turn, as it is never a full turn. Count the number of splines past the mark on the gear box housing. Make a new mark on the input shaft that lines up with the original mark made on the housing and turn the shaft back one half the number of full turns plus

Here is the steering box coupler. This is a flexible joint that allows some flex between the steering shaft and the steering box. Check this joint if play is detected in the steering system.

This power steering cap is shot. It is hard to see from this picture, but there is an obvious groove where the pump filler neck contacts the rubber seal. Even though this cap still fits, it no longer seals the reservoir, resulting in a slow and mysterious fluid loss.

one half the number of splines counted from the last step. Doing this will center the steering box.

Install the steering shaft. It usually goes through a steering coupler, another component that should be replaced, as they tend to rot. New ones are inexpensive, and a loose coupler will add considerable play to the steering wheel. Use only new nuts of the correct type (most vehicles use vibration-resistant nuts) and grade 8 bolts when replacing the steering coupler.

Install the pitman arm. Make sure that the steering box and wheels are centered. Press the pitman arm back on the shaft. Install the retaining washer and retaining nut. Tighten the nut to the recommended torque. If a cotter key is used, install a new cotter key.

If the vehicle does not drive straight with the steering wheel centered after centering the steering box, check the alignment. Also, check that the pitman arm and idler arm are straight ahead with the steering wheel centered. If not, check that the steering wheel is installed properly. Not all cars use a keyed shaft where the steering wheel mounts. Some used splined shafts, and if the wheel is mounted even one spline off, it will result in the steering wheel being noticeably off center when the vehicle is going straight. Do not correct an uncentered steering wheel by aligning the front wheels until you have verified that the steering wheel and pitman arm are properly installed on a centered steering box.

For a manual steering box, fill the box with the correct lubricant. Use synthetic lubricant of the weight recommended by the manufacturer. If the steering box was rebuilt, use a lubricant that the rebuilder recommends.

For power steering boxes, install new pressure and return hoses. Always replace the hoses, as the hoses wear from the inside out. Ensure that the new hoses are routed properly before tightening down the fittings or clamps. If your vehicle uses a return hose that is held on by hose clamps, use only automatic transmission cooler hose. If fuel or vacuum hose is used, it will fail in a short time. Fill the pump with the recommended power steering fluid. Never use automatic transmission fluid. Follow the bleeding instructions in Flushing and Bleeding the Power Steering System on the next page.

CHECKING THE
POWER STEERING PUMP

Power steering pumps are usually long lived. It is not unusual for a power steering pump to go 200,000 miles or more without any problems. What usually does them in is running low on fluid. If the fluid level is properly maintained, the typical problem will be fluid leakage as the seals age. If your pump is leaking, find the source of the leak before replacing the pump. Check the hoses first. Also, check the cap and pump housing.

If your steering is hard at slow speeds, the pump is most likely defective. Also, if the pump is locked up or making excessive noise it is obviously bad. When replacing a failed pump, the steering box must be flushed.

If you have a power steering fluid leak and cannot find the source of the leak, check the cap. There is a spring that pulls the cap against a rubber seal in the top of the cap. After years have gone by, the rubber gets hard and the spring is no longer able to seal the pump reservoir. This will result in a leak that occurs as the vehicle travels down the road and the fluid is sloshed around in the reservoir.

REMOVING THE
POWER STEERING PUMP

Loosen the pump-adjusting bolts and remove the fan belts. Place a drain pan under the pump and remove the hoses and discard them. When replacing the power steering pump, always replace the hoses. Let the fluid drain from the pump. Remove the pump from the vehicle. Usually the brackets must be removed with the pump, as the pump shaft passes through one of the brackets.

To remove the pulley, use the appropriate puller. Do not use a two- or three-finger gear puller, as the pulley will be destroyed. Instead, a power steering pulley puller must be used. If your pulley is retained by a nut, remove the nut and the pulley will come off. For pulleys that are retained with a nut, save the cotter key, as it will be required for reassembly. Better yet, use a new one.

Once the pulley is removed, the brackets can be removed from the pump body. Make note of what fasteners are used, and what holes they go into. Clean the brackets and check them for cracking and other signs of damage. Any defective brackets must be replaced.

REBUILDING THE
POWER STEERING PUMP

You can either rebuild or replace your pump. Replacements are not very expensive, and rebuilding the pump is easy. The choice is yours. Either way, the pump usually must be removed from the housing. Be careful to not damage the housing when removing the pump. Also check the housing for any signs of damage or distortion, which will cause the pump to leak. When installing the pump in the housing, ensure that the seals are all in place and lightly lubricated with power steering fluid.

Install the brackets to the pump. If your pump has a bolt-on pulley, install the key, line up the pulley, and slip it into place. Tighten the nut to the recommended torque. If your pulley is a press-on type, use a power steering pulley installer. Do not use a hydraulic press or hammer, as either of these will destroy the pump.

This is a power steering pump, the portion that fits in the housing. Notice the groove where the large, square-cut O-ring seals the pump to the housing. The housing must be perfect, or there will be a constant, slow leak at this point.

INSTALLING THE POWER STEERING PUMP

Position the pump and install the bolts that secure the brackets to the engine. Do not tighten the bolts until all of them have been installed. Once all of the bolts are in place, torque them to the recommended torque specifications. Check the pulley for proper alignment with the water pump and crankshaft pulleys. Use a straightedge in the pulley grooves. The straightedge and the pulleys should all be in the same plane. Do not install the belts yet.

Install new hoses; never reuse the old hoses, as power steering hoses deteriorate from the inside out. Before tightening the fittings or clamps, ensure that the hoses are routed properly, and that they will not rub against anything. If they do, the hose will fail. For return hoses that are retained by clamps, use only transmission cooling line; do not use fuel or vacuum hose, as it will not last very long.

FLUSHING AND BLEEDING THE POWER STEERING SYSTEM

Fill the reservoir to the normal full mark. Begin bleeding by rotating the pulley by hand in the direction that the engine rotates. If you are standing in front of the vehicle facing the engine, turn the pulley clockwise. Watch inside the housing for bubbles rising from the return hose port. Keep the fluid level full and continue turning the pump until no more bubbles are seen. If the steering box was replaced as well, you will add over a quart of fluid to get the pump and the steering box full. Don't skip this step by installing the belts and simply starting the engine; you will immediately drain the reservoir and destroy your new pump.

Get in the vehicle and turn the steering wheel in a normal manner 10 times from lock to lock. Add fluid when needed to keep the reservoir at the full line. The fan belts can now be re-installed. Tighten the belts. Be careful; the housing on most power steering pumps is thin sheet metal. Do not pry on the case, or the housing could be damaged. Check the fluid level and make sure the pump is full but not overfull. Start the vehicle and check for leaks from the hose fittings. Turn the wheel lock to lock several times, listening for excessive noise or whining. Shut the engine off and check the fluid level. Also check for any leaks. Lower the vehicle and test-drive it to verify proper power steering operation.

CHAPTER 6
ENGINE

The engine is the heart of the muscle car. Part of what makes a muscle car a fun daily driver is the big block with all of that torque. The majority of muscle cars did not have special engines; most used an engine that was standard equipment for the manufacturer's full-size models, albeit with a slightly larger camshaft, and perhaps a larger carburetor. What you do to your engine will obviously have the largest impact on your muscle car's performance and reliability.

Remember that the major manufacturers were in the business of selling cars. Muscle cars had to be reliable to prevent an uproar of warranty claims from the dealerships. All of the manufacturers had edicts during the 1960s requiring that all cars had to start and run with no issues, and idle smoothly. This forced the

The big block is the heart of a muscle car.

engineers to select cams and carburetors that met these drivability requirements.

To keep reliability high, carefully consider each change you want to make. Consider the effect it will have on the entire package, and what special requirements it will dictate. Also, be careful to select components that are intended for endurance racing or other high-reliability applications. Be extremely careful in selecting components that are designed for all-out performance, but not intended for long life or endurance racing. One example is aluminum connecting rods; while light and strong and ideal for a drag race engine, these are not going to make 150,000 or 200,000 miles, and should not even be considered if you are attempting to build a reliable street-driven car.

Finally, consider this: if you are not having a problem with a particular part or system, think potential changes through carefully. The last thing you want to do is increase the likelihood of a failure. For example, if you have driven the car for thousands of trouble-free miles, and are considering an oil system modification, think it through. If you are not having a problem with the stock setup, be careful if you are going to make a change. If, on the other hand, you are increasing horsepower and rpm, the oiling system that gave you those thousands of trouble-free miles may fall short.

STOCK OR MODIFIED?

The first thing is to decide on how much power you want and how much temperament you are willing to put up with. A 600-horsepower naturally aspirated engine may sound great—until you try to drive the thing every day. Set a realistic goal on performance, and also decide if you need air conditioning, power brakes, or an automatic transmission. Remember that a really radical engine will require a steep rear axle ratio to take full advantage of the engine, and this will have a dramatic impact on drivability and gas mileage. And the high-rise cams used in highly tuned engines typically create a rough idle that will rattle your fillings at every stoplight.

First, develop a plan. Most components function best when matched. For example, camshaft selection depends on head-flow characteristics, and both dictate the intake and exhaust system components. An engine will perform best only if all of the key components are matched. A realistic goal is 1.1 horsepower per cubic inch. This is easily achievable without sacrificing drivability. Just as important, a goal of 1.2 lb/ft of torque per cubic inch should also be your goal. For a big block, this results in impressive power that must be felt to be appreciated.

Engines that develop a broad torque curve are much stronger than engines that have a high but narrow power peak. It should also be your goal to have 80 percent of your torque peak from 2,500 to 6,000 rpm. For example, if your engine develops 500 lb/ft at the torque peak, your goal should be to select components that will flow and fill the cylinders to ensure that you have 440 lb/ft of torque from 2,500 to 6,000 rpm. Realistic goals for a street-driven 450-cubic-inch engine with no power adders (nitrous or blower) are 480 to 500 horsepower with peak torque of 550 lb/ft. These are relatively easy numbers to achieve without sacrificing drivability.

BASIC UPGRADES

Unless you are performing a 100 percent restoration, there are probably a few items that you will want to upgrade on your engine. Even if your goal is to keep the engine basically stock, there are still several areas where technology has advanced, and taking advantage of what has been learned over the last 30 to 40 years will really pay off.

Regardless of how mild or wild you want your engine to be, one of the first modifications is to upgrade your timing chain and gears. Especially if the engine is original, and has not been rebuilt, or you don't know when it was rebuilt, this is one area that most likely needs attention. The factory chain and gears, especially on GM muscle cars with the nylon upper gear teeth, are not very reliable. You don't want a failure, as it will definitely leave you stranded.

Use a name-brand American-made timing set. Do not use bargain gear sets; the machining tolerances are not very good, and the timing can be off by as much as 6 degrees. I only use a true roller double chain set. You will have to change the upper and lower gears, but these are included in the timing set. This is also the time to check the harmonic balancer and replace the front seal. Replacing the timing set will ensure that your engine will not strand you due to a timing set failure, and a good true roller timing chain will last 150,000 miles or more.

Another area that needs attention is gaskets. Even if the engine is not being rebuilt, it is a good idea to tear the covers, such as valve covers, oil pan, timing cover, and intake manifold, off the engine and replace the gaskets. This will eliminate several leak points and keep your engine from leaving deposits on the garage floor. Also, the engine itself will be much easier to keep clean if it is not leaking oil. Finally, this is the time to clean and paint items such as valve covers, front covers, and intake manifolds.

FASTENERS

One final recommendation for basic upgrades is to replace the fasteners. If the engine is being rebuilt, replace all critical fasteners, such as rod bolts, main cap bolts, and head bolts, with quality performance fasteners. Don't forget the flywheel or flexplate bolts;

these high-stress bolts should be replaced if they are removed. Also, don't overlook the clutch-pressure-plate-to-flywheel bolts, or for automatics, the torque-converter-to-flexplate bolts (except Fords, which use studs on the torque converter).

For head bolts, if the engine needs to look stock, use high-quality replacement head bolts. If the look is not important, studs are the only way to go. When replacing head bolts, always ensure that the block and head surfaces are clean, smooth, and straight. Use high-quality gaskets, and use the sealer(s) that are recommended by the gasket manufacturer.

The torque sequence is the same for bolts and studs; for example, if the torque specification is 90 lb/ft, first snug all fasteners finger tight, then torque all of the fasteners to 30 lb/ft. Next, follow the torque sequence and tighten the fasteners to 60 lb/ft. Follow the torque sequence and tighten the fasteners to 80 lb/ft. Finally, follow the torque sequence and tighten each of the fasteners to 90 lb/ft. Notice the second to last torque step—it takes the fastener to 85 to 90 percent of the final torque. Even better, for rod bolts, use a rod bolt stretch gauge and follow the rod bolt manufacturer's recommendation for fastener yield. All bolts stretch when tightened, and a fastener develops maximum clamping force when stretched to the design yield point. All good fastener manufacturers can furnish the yield specifications for their fasteners.

This is important. If the bolt is not fully tightened, the fastener will not provide the maximum

A three-angle valve job refers to how the seat is cut. Instead of a single angle, where the valve face contacts the seat, there are two additional cuts, one in the chamber that blends the seat into the chamber and one in the throat that blends the seat cut with the port throat.

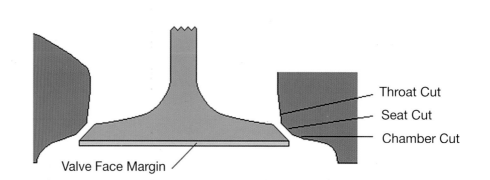

Throat Cut
Seat Cut
Chamber Cut
Valve Face Margin

clamping force and may allow the parts to separate when placed under stress. For a connecting rod, this would be when the piston is moving toward TDC and the crank is attempting to slow the rod down, or when the crank is moving the piston down on the intake stroke while operating at high rpm, especially with the throttles closed. The force being applied on the rod cap will attempt to separate the rod from the rod cap. If the connecting rod bolt stretches, the rod cap will separate from the rod and it may be enough to allow the bearing to move. Or worse, the bolt may fail or loosen, resulting in a catastrophic engine failure.

REBUILDING HEADS

If you are going to keep the engine relatively stock, the original cylinder heads will work just fine if properly reconditioned. First, if the heads were manufactured before 1975, the valve seats may not be hardened. If not, they will need to be replaced with hardened seats. This is necessary to prevent the exhaust valves from slowly receding into the head. Earlier heads relied on tetraethyl lead in the gasoline to lubricate the valve and valve seat to prevent this problem. With the removal of lead from gasoline, the valve seats must be replaced with hardened valve seats to prevent this problem.

When rebuilding a cylinder head, the first step is to clean the head and inspect it for cracks. Pay particular attention to the area between the valves. If a cast iron head is cracked, it is most likely junk, especially if the crack is in the chamber area. There are a few welding shops that can spray weld cast iron, but unless the crack is located outside the chamber, and not under a valve spring seat, it is just not worth the cost. Of course, if the head is rare, such as a set of Boss 429 heads, then cost is less of an issue. If the heads are aluminum, a good welder can repair the crack.

Once the heads are clean and verified to be free of cracks, inspect the valve seats to determine if hardened seats are present. You will probably have to consult either the factory service information or a reputable source to determine this. Most factory iron heads did not use a separate valve seat. Instead, the valve seat was induction hardened. If the head was manufactured before 1973, it probably does not have hardened valve seats and will need to have hardened valve seats installed.

After the valve seats have been replaced (or verified to be hardened), the guides can be machined. Most cast-iron factory heads do not have separate guides; the cylinder head is simply machined for the valve stem. As the miles roll by, the steel valve stem rubs against the iron head and the guide wears. Check the guides for wear, and if the clearances are found to be excessive, the head must be machined for a replacement guide. There are two main types of guides: replacement hard guides and bronze wall threaded inserts.

The hard guide is basically a cast-iron tube that is installed by machining the original guide to allow the tube to be pressed into place. This is also a good time to have a reputable machine shop verify the position of the valve, and the hole can be machined to properly locate the valve. In extreme cases such as when oversize valves are going to be installed, the valves can be relocated slightly farther apart to create additional room.

The bronze wall guide is installed by machining the original guide to the appropriate size, then tapping the guide, and finally screwing in the bronze wall insert in place. After installation, the insert is reamed to create the final size. This type of guide holds oil in between the coils to help lubricate the valve stem. It is not possible to correct any valve positioning errors with this style of insert, as the machining does not remove enough metal to allow repositioning.

With the seats checked (or replaced) and the guides taken care of, the valve seats can be ground. Always have a three-angle valve job performed. The valves will be replaced or ground at this time as well.

Make sure that a competent machinist performs the seat work. As the valve face is cut and the valve seat is ground, this will result in the valve sitting lower in the head, and the valve stem protruding higher on the top of the head. A good majority of muscle cars did not have adjustable valvetrains and this additional height will result in the lifter plunger being farther down in the lifter. Even for an adjustable valvetrain, the increased height can result in the geometry being off, especially if the heads are milled as well. This can be rectified by changing the pushrod lengths.

Also, after the valve face is cut, verify that the margin is still wide enough. For intake valves, this is typically no less than 0.070 inch. For exhaust valves, the margin is typically not less than 0.085 inch. The margin provides the valve with tolerance to expand as it heats up, and if the margin is too thin, the valve will fail.

Now the head deck surface can be machined. This is done to ensure that the head-to-block surface is perfectly flat and straight. Do not remove excessive material, or you may have serious problems with head gaskets. A thin deck surface will not be able to properly seal the combustion pressure. Remove the absolute minimum amount to achieve a straight head deck. If you really want higher compression, change the pistons.

Finally, check all intake and exhaust manifold bolt holes. If any are stripped, they can be fixed by installing a Heli-Coil or other type of thread-repair insert. These are installed by drilling out the stripped hole, tapping the hole, and threading in the insert. Also check the valve cover bolt holes and the accessory mounting holes. And don't forget to replace the freeze plugs in the heads.

ALUMINUM HEADS

One area that technology has really advanced in is cylinder head design. Modern cylinder heads will do more for the power of your muscle car than anything else. Technology has really advanced, especially in combustion chamber design. Modern heads use small chambers that promote smooth, even flame front travel and efficient cylinder filling. Also, most

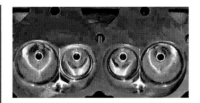

Most modern cylinder heads use small heart-shaped chambers.

now have a heart-shaped combustion chamber that promotes swirl and turbulence. This helps prevent detonation. Even the best muscle car–era cylinder heads pale in comparison to modern performance cylinder heads.

Better yet, out-of-the-box aftermarket aluminum cylinder heads will outflow just about any stock muscle car cylinder head. Even if the original head is ported, it will usually at best just equal a set of modern out-of-the-box aftermarket heads. So the cost of rebuilding the heads plus the porting work will usually end up costing more than just buying a set of modern performance heads. So consider the aftermarket cylinder heads; you can spend less and get a better head that is brand-new.

The good news is that modern performance cylinder heads can be had for almost any make of muscle car engine. The cost is really not bad, and when you factor in the true cost of reconditioning a set of used heads, the cost difference is really not that much.

The best possible design will match a flat-top piston with a small chamber. The current trend is a small, heart-shaped chamber matched with a flat top piston. Several engine builders also prefer the spark plug to be angled toward the exhaust valve. Small chambers limit the amount of metal available to absorb heat from the combustion process. You want the lowest possible total surface area exposed to the flame front. By contrast, a large open chamber head with a dome-top piston will result in a large total surface area that will absorb excessive amounts of heat from the combustion process and slow the flame front's travel, thus lowering efficiency. Also, fuel next to the metal is less likely to ignite, so a larger surface area will result in slightly more unburned fuel, and a corresponding decrease in horsepower along with an increase in HC emissions.

HORSEPOWER AND AIRFLOW

There is no magic here; engine performance is directly related to airflow and cylinder filling. Volumetric efficiency is how an engine's pumping capacity is defined. Peak torque occurs at the rpm that has the highest volumetric efficiency. This is the rpm at which the engine's induction system best fills the cylinders with air-fuel mixture. On a naturally aspirated racing engine, the volumetric efficiency will exceed 100 percent. For most high-performance street engines, volumetric efficiency can approach 100 percent or more at the torque peak. Most older factory stock engines will be around 80 to 85 percent at the torque peak and 70 to 80 percent at the horsepower peak. Several things influence the volumetric efficiency, and as you have probably guessed, they are all dependent on each other.

Horsepower is directly related to how efficiently the engine pumps air. You can't make horsepower without airflow. A rough estimate for the required airflow is given by the formula CFM = HP x 1.338. This is an approximation assuming a fuel consumption of 0.49 lbs/hr per horsepower. This formula does not account for items that increase the efficiency of the engine such as thermal barriers or friction reducers. Nevertheless, it will give you a rough idea of the amount of air required to support a particular horsepower level. Notice that engine size is not a part of the calculation. Horsepower is related to the amount of air and fuel burned, not to the size of the engine. A larger engine will usually have a higher horsepower potential simply because it is capable of pumping more air.

A true high-performance engine will have the cylinder heads, camshaft, intake, exhaust, and compression ratio all matched. You will be extremely disappointed if these components are not properly matched with one another. As you select a more aggressive camshaft and larger cylinder port heads, the rpm where volumetric efficiency (VE) and torque peak occurs will be higher. Larger cylinder heads are required to properly fill the cylinders at the higher rpm at which the larger cam will be operating.

Another point to remember is the relationship between density and temperature of the intake air. Engines draw in airflow by volume, so if the air is denser (packs more oxygen molecules in a given volume), the engine will develop more horsepower. As a rule of thumb, for every 10 degrees that the intake air is cooled, the engine will develop 1 percent more horsepower. This should be kept in mind, as it is usually extremely easy to feed the engine cool air. Even on a hot day, feeding the engine 100-degree air is better than 150-degree air from under the hood.

PORTING CYLINDER HEADS

Regardless of what type of cylinder heads you are running, porting them can add substantial amounts of power. But don't just assume that by making the ports larger the airflow will automatically improve. This is not always true, and in fact, airflow may actually decrease.

No matter what components are used, an engine cannot produce more power than its intake ports can flow. As a rule of thumb, for normally aspirated engines, the formula HP = 0.25714 x CFM x CYL derives a good approximation of an engine's horsepower potential. Let HP be the maximum horsepower; CFM is the intake port flow, in cubic feet per minute at a pressure difference of 28 inches of mercury. CYL is the number of cylinders. If the engine has two intake ports per cylinder, then the CFM is the total flow for both intake ports. The bottom line, the maximum airflow determines the horsepower. If a power adder such as a supercharger or nitrous oxide injection is used, the horsepower will be greater due to the fact that more oxygen (and fuel) will be packed into the cylinder. The flow ratio between the intake and exhaust port should be 70 to 75 percent. So if the intake flows 300 cfm, the exhaust should flow a minimum of 210 cfm.

On most cylinder heads, it is a safe bet that cleaning up the bowl area will result in a flow gain. Unless you have access to a flow bench, you should limit your work to simple cleanup of the bowl area and transition from the bowl to the short side. Do not alter the shape of the port mouth, but do match the intake port opening to the intake gasket by grinding the cylinder head and the intake manifold so their port openings match the gasket opening. Also, a clean transition from the valve seat to the bowl area will also enhance airflow. This work should be performed after the valve seat has been cut. A three-angle valve seat cut results in maximum flow around the valve head.

Another important point: the area just below the valve seat is called the throat. This should be 80 percent as big as the valve size. So if the engine has a 2.07-inch intake valve, the throat should be 1.65 inches. Making the throat larger can hurt airflow and performance. The transition from the valve seat through to the throat should be smooth, with no sudden changes or steps.

As with the intake port, limit most of the exhaust port work to the bowl area. The port can be worked smooth, but do not worry about making the exhaust port mirror smooth. The extra work will not benefit the flow. Again, just like the intake, the throat area is most important. Make sure it presents a smooth transition from the valve seat to the port. Most modern high-performance heads have a D-shaped exhaust port. The curve is on the roof. When you look at the exhaust port, it looks like a D lying on its back.

Also, if the headers are matched to the exhaust gasket by grinding the cylinder head and the exhaust manifold or header flange so that the port opening matches the gasket opening, leaving the exhaust port smaller will create a port that flows gas out easily while limiting reversion. This can increase mid-range horsepower, broadening the torque curve.

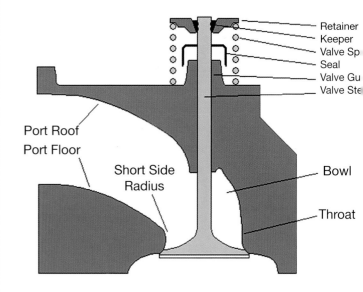

This is a cross-section through a typical intake port showing the valve components as well as the common port names.

Unless you are experienced and have access to a flow bench, leave the serious port work to one of the experts in this field. Porting heads takes time. Why waste a good set of heads, as well as your time, only to be disappointed by a porting job that results in little or no power gains, or worse, a power loss? There are experts who can work magic with a set of heads.

If you are working with a head porting shop, they will suggest pistons and camshaft specs that will work well with your newly ported head. Matching the engine's components to cylinder head modifications requires careful coordination. If the machinist who will be porting your heads cannot give you specific recommendations for piston and camshaft selection, you should probably find another shop. They should also ask what your power expectations are, as well as your anticipated rpm range.

CAMSHAFT SELECTION

Another area in which technology has really advanced is camshafts. The lobe profiles on modern performance camshafts can really wake up your big-block engine, and significant performance gains can be had without sacrificing drivability. The old muscle car grinds can't hold a candle to modern lobe profiles, so unless you are performing a 100 percent original restoration, I recommend that the camshaft be replaced.

Don't go overboard when selecting a camshaft. On most engines, the maximum power will most likely be limited by the intake port, with maximum rpm being limited by the valve springs (valve float) as well as the bottom end (catastrophic failure). The good news? Big-block engines can swallow a relatively large cam with ease.

For a modest build-up with stock or mild heads, a cam with .050-inch duration numbers between 224 to 230 degrees with a lift around .510 inch will provide a good idle and slightly more power than stock. A cam in this range will also be easy on the valvetrain parts. Also, a modest 9.5:1 to 10.0:1 compression ratio will work just fine, and the rear end gears do not need to be steep. For an automatic, the stock torque converter will work just fine. Power brakes, power steering, and air conditioning will also work with a camshaft in this range. For big blocks, 400 to 450 horsepower can be achieved with an engine such as this.

For a strong street engine with modified or aftermarket heads, a cam with .050-inch duration and between 230 to 240 degrees with a lift around .550-inch will provide a rougher idle and significantly more power than stock. This is the 500-horsepower realm, and depending on your heads, your 450-cubic-inch engine can reach 500 horsepower with a camshaft in this range. Most cams in this range won't be overly rough on the valvetrain parts. Also, 10.0:1 to 11.0:1 compression should be used, and the rear end gears should be no lower than 3.30:1. For an automatic, the torque converter should stall to 2,400 rpm. It may take some work, but power brakes, power steering, and air conditioning can be made to work with a camshaft in this range.

For an all-out street engine with highly modified heads, a cam with .050-inch duration and between 240 to 250 degrees with a lift above .600-inch will provide a rough idle and significantly more power

than stock. Your 450-cubic-inch engine can reach 550 horsepower with a camshaft in this range. Do not even consider a camshaft in this range unless you are running modified heads.

Most cams in this range will be rough on the valvetrain. Also, 11.0:1 to 12.0:1 compression should be used, and the rear end gears should be no lower than 3.70:1. For an automatic, the torque converter should stall to at least 3,000 rpm. Power brakes will only work with an auxiliary vacuum pump, and power steering will work as long as you keep the engine rpm up while turning at slow speeds; otherwise low-speed parking maneuvers can stall the engine. Air conditioning will only work if the compressor is shut off when at idle, or if a solenoid is used that increases idle speed when the air conditioner is engaged. A cam this size can be tamed somewhat with fuel injection.

The above are simplifications meant to help with your selections. There are numerous other aspects to camshaft selection, such as lifter type.

Camshafts can be had that are designed to work with hydraulic lifters, solid lifters, roller hydraulic lifters, roller solid lifters and mushroom lifters. Each type has advantages and limitations. Talk to your engine builder or shop about selecting the proper cam for your application.

OIL AND YOUR CAMSHAFT

Oil has changed significantly since your muscle car was built, and one change is the reduction of zinc. Zinc helps minimize wear under high-pressure load conditions, such as the camshaft-to-lifer contact area. Modern cars use roller lifters, and therefore the amount of zinc required in the oil is significantly reduced. Furthermore, zinc in the oil can contaminate the oxygen sensor and catalytic converter. There is always a small amount of oil that gets past the rings into the combustion chamber, and when this oil is burned, the zinc additives end up as ash that slowly coats the oxygen sensor(s) and catalytic converter, reducing their efficiency. For these reasons, the oil manufacturers have reduced the amount of zinc in the oil.

ENGINE

When you purchase a new camshaft, follow the manufacturer's recommendations to the letter. Use the prelubrication coatings they recommend and use the viscosity of motor oil they recommend. They may even recommend a certain brand or type of oil as well. If the engine has just been rebuilt, prelube the engine before starting it the first time.

You may also want to call the camshaft manufacturer's tech support line and ask if you need to use an oil supplement during the camshaft break-in process, specifically one that is high in zinc. Another consideration is to use diesel or four-cycle motorcycle oil for the first 1,000 to 3,000 miles after the camshaft was installed, as these usually have higher zinc content. Also, most true racing oils have higher zinc content.

During the break-in process, keep the engine rpm at or above 2,500 rpm for at least 20 minutes, or longer if recommended by your camshaft grinder. Never let the engine idle during the break-in process. These procedures are even more critical now that the zinc level in the oil has been reduced.

The reduced zinc content in modern oils helps protect the high-pressure contact area between the lifter and the camshaft, and the emphasis on improved oil control results in less oil ending up on

Adjusting hydraulic lifters is easy. With the cam on the back of the lobe, loosen the adjuster two to three full turns and let the lifter rise up for a couple of minutes. Now twist the pushrod while slowly tightening the adjuster. As soon as resistance is felt, tighten the adjuster a half turn and you are done. Lock your adjuster in place. Be careful; the internal spring in the lifter is not very strong, and the change will be subtle.

Adjusting valve lash on a solid lifter engine is straightforward. First, the lash specifications must be known. Then, with the lifter on the backside of the lobe, slowly tighten the adjuster until the feeler gauge fits snugly between the rocker arm and the valve stem. Now tighten the lock while holding the adjuster.

the cam lobes. Put these together and the importance of proper lubrication and break-in are even more important if a flat-tappet camshaft is used.

HYDRAULIC LIFTERS

Hydraulic lifters can be had in solid or roller configurations. Hydraulic lifters offer the advantage of low maintenance, as the lifter automatically adjusts the valvetrain. Once set up, a hydraulic lifter usually requires no adjustment or maintenance. The downside is the lower peak rpm range; hydraulic lifters can "pump up" at high rpm and this results in premature valve float.

Lifter pump-up occurs when the valve is being opened at a high rate of speed. Due to inertia, as the lifter reaches the top of the lobe, the valve keeps opening, resulting in slack in the valvetrain. The lifter adjusts and becomes too tall. This will delay or prevent the valve from closing, resulting in a loss of power. For this reason, camshafts ground for use with hydraulic lifters have a carefully designed lobe that slows down the rate of opening as the valve approaches maximum lift. This will result in a small overall power loss, as the valve does not reach maximum lift quite as fast as a solid lifter cam profile.

For a mild to hot street engine, hydraulic lifters work quite well. They are reliable, maintenance-free, and quiet. Also, for most big blocks, a high-rpm lifter pump is usually not an issue, as the rev range of most big blocks is below 6,000 rpm. For a high-winding small block, however, hydraulic lifters can limit performance. As an interesting side note, lifter pump was used by most of the OEMs as a crude rpm limiter.

SOLID LIFTERS

Solid lifters are the only way to go for an all-out performance engine. Just like hydraulics, solid lifters can be had in flat tappet and roller-lifter designs. Unlike hydraulics, solid lifters do not pump up at high rpms. Solid lifters also weigh less than hydraulic lifters, further increasing the engine's top rpm range. Since lifter pump is not a concern, the lobe profile can be more aggressive. They also allow slight camshaft tuning, as the valve lift can be lowered by opening up the valve lash.

Solid lifters have their drawbacks. They require periodic adjustment, which is time-consuming. They also clatter; some may find this annoying. For these reasons, the factories only installed solid lifters in their high-end, low-volume performance machines. If you are building an all-out performance engine, solid lifters are the only way to go, as they will yield the highest RPM capabilities with proper valve spring selection. Just be sure you are willing to adjust the valves regularly.

FLAT TAPPET LIFTERS

Solid and hydraulic lifters are either of flat tappet or roller design. Flat tappet lifters have a smooth hardened surface that rides directly on the cast-iron cam lobe. The lobe does not wear perceptibly due to the smooth hardened steel of the lifter riding on the dissimilar cast-iron cam lobe. The lifter base may appear to be flat, but it has a slight crown that forces the lifter to rotate as the lifter follows the cam lobe.

Flat tappet lifters and cam lobes develop a wear pattern, and a flat tappet lifter must never be reused on any other cam lobe. If a used flat tappet lifter is installed on a different camshaft lobe, both will be destroyed in just a few miles. It is OK to install new flat tappet lifters on a used camshaft, but used flat tappet lifters should never be installed on a new or used camshaft.

Also, the pressure created between the flat tappet lifter and the camshaft lobe is extreme, higher than any other point in the engine. For this reason, when installing a new camshaft or lifters, there is a specific break-in procedure that must be followed or the camshaft and lifters will fail.

ROLLER LIFTERS

Roller lifters, regardless of whether they are solid or hydraulic, reduce engine friction, as the lifter does not slide across the camshaft lobe. The lifter is constructed with a needle-bearing-supported roller wheel that rolls over the camshaft lobe. This results in a significant reduction in engine friction. The camshaft profile can be more aggressive, as there is no danger of the edge of the lifter "digging" into the side of the cam lobe. Even if it has the same valve lift and duration as a flat tappet design, a roller camshaft will usually produce more power.

The downside of roller lifters is that they must be held so that the roller is perfectly aligned with the cam lobe. If the lifter rotates or the roller is not properly aligned with the cam lobe, both the lifter and the cam will be destroyed. All roller lifters use some form of alignment feature. Roller lifter conversion systems

Here is a pair of solid roller lifters. These are for retrofitting a roller camshaft to an engine that did not have one. The link bar prevents the lifters from rotating.

ENGINE

usually use a link bar that ties two lifters together so that they can move up and down independently, but cannot rotate. Most factory roller lifter engines use a collar system, and the lifters have a flat edge that holds the lifter in alignment when the collar is installed. The engine block is set up to hold the collar in place, either directly or with some sort of retainer.

If you are converting an engine from flat tappet to roller lifters, shorter pushrods will be required because roller lifters are taller. Ensure that the lifter retaining system is properly installed and that each lifter roller is precisely aligned with the camshaft lobe. Roller lifters are also heavier, and stiffer valve springs will usually be required. But because internal engine friction is so much lower with roller valves, stiffer springs are usually not a problem.

Roller lifters do not develop a wear pattern, and can be reused. In fact, you can replace a roller camshaft and use the old lifters with the new camshaft. As long as the lifters are not damaged, they can be reused. Most factory engines have used roller lifters since the mid-1980s.

One caution: roller camshafts are steel, and therefore cannot be used with the stock distributor gear. Most muscle car distributors are intended by the factories to be driven by a cast-iron camshaft. When replacing a stock cast-iron camshaft with a steel camshaft, a bronze or fiber distributor gear must be used to prevent the steel camshaft from being damaged. This bronze gear will need to be replaced at regular intervals, usually every 12,000 miles.

Some roller camshafts have pressed-on iron gears for the distributor drive. These eliminate the need for a bronze or special distributor gear. Always talk with the cam grinder about the gear types available and what options you will have.

Finally, roller camshafts will also require a thrust plate or cam bumper to prevent the camshaft from "walking" in the block. Flat tappet lifters force the camshaft toward the rear of the block as the engine rotates. Roller lifters do not do this, so the cam is free to float forward and back in the engine. This is

called walking. To prevent it, modern engines use a camshaft retaining plate. Older engines use a thrust button added to the front of the camshaft to keep the camshaft from moving. Flat tappet cams are held in place by the force of the lifters. Roller cams need to be retained, or the ignition timing will be erratic—since the distributor and camshaft drive gears are cut at an angle, the forward and backward movement of the camshaft will cause the timing to change.

VALVE SPRINGS

Unless you are performing a 100 percent original rebuild, use the valve springs recommended by the camshaft manufacturer. When choosing springs, you need to consider three things: the installed seat pressure, the pressure at maximum valve lift, and the maximum lift before coil bind.

The valve spring must be strong enough to keep the lifter in contact with the camshaft lobe at all times. When the cam is opening the valve at high engine speeds, the inertia of the valve, rocker arm, pushrod, and lifter will try to keep moving up, even as the lifter passes over the top of the lobe. The valve spring must have enough pressure to stop the valvetrain and keep the lifter on the cam.

Another problem is valve spring oscillation. Valve springs have a resonant frequency, and each valve spring has a particular opening and closing rate (which occurs at a certain engine rpm rate) at which the valve spring resonates, or oscillates. When this happens, the valve spring is ineffective at controlling the valvetrain.

To combat this problem, most performance valve springs will either use multiple springs or a damper. Multiple-spring solutions usually consist of two springs, with the inner and outer spring having different pressures, and the inner and outer spring wound with different gauge wire. The inner and outer springs are also wound in different directions. None of these differences eliminate spring oscillation, but the inner and outer springs will oscillate at different rpms, resulting in a valvetrain that remains under spring control over a wider operating range. The damper solution uses a single spring with a flat wire damper that is wound in the opposite direction inside the spring. This damper is in contact with the spring and helps stop or damp out the spring oscillations. Most factory muscle car valve springs were of the damper type.

Modern engines and performance valve springs are moving toward a different solution to the valve spring oscillation problem. By progressively reducing the diameter of the spring's coil wind, the valve spring no longer has a resonant frequency, and therefore is not prone to oscillation. These types of springs are called "beehive" springs because the spring resembles a beehive. They work well, but require unique spring retainers.

One final note: the lighter the valvetrain, the more effective the springs will be, and the higher the engine's potential rpm. Titanium retainers will reduce valvetrain weight, but in reality, most big blocks will not experience valvetrain rpm limits as long as a good camshaft and the proper springs are used. You have to be operating the engine above 7,000 rpm before really exotic valvetrain components are required.

INSTALLING VALVE SPRINGS

When installing new springs, check the installed height as well as the coil-bind height. Next, compute maximum lift by multiplying the gross lift of the cam lobe by the rocker arm ratio, then adding .050. The resulting number must be less than the installed spring height minus the coil bind height. If the number is equal or greater, then the spring will bind, immediately destroying the cam and lifter and possibly damaging other valvetrain components as well.

Also, spring retainers and retainer locks, or keepers, must match. The valve stem will be a certain diameter, and there will also be grooves cut near the end of the valve stem for the keeper or valve lock. The keepers must match the valve stem diameter and have the proper ridge to match the groove, or grooves, in the valve stem. Finally, the keeper is machined at an

angle, and this angle must match the spring retainer. The factories used a number of different angles. Using the wrong lock can cause a retainer to fail, dropping a valve into the engine. The valve keeper must fit the valve stem properly as well. So when replacing valves, make sure that they fit your keepers and retainers.

Finally, valve seals are important for preventing excessive oil consumption. There are two main types of valve seals: umbrella and positive. I prefer umbrella seals that are long enough to shroud the valve stem even when using high-lift cams. Positive seals may work too well for a street car, preventing the valve stem from obtaining sufficient lubrication. If umbrella seals are used, use only high-quality seals that will hold up. Most factory engines came with umbrella seals.

ROCKER ARMS

The rocker arm has a simple task to perform: it changes the direction of the pushrod movement in order to open the valve properly. It also performs a ratio multiplication. Because of its simple functionality, unless you are experiencing problems with your valvetrain, the rocker arms will receive little or no attention.

TYPES OF ROCKERS

There are three basic styles of rocker arms in American V-8 engines. The original is the shaft-mounted rocker. The most common is the stud-mounted rocker. Finally, the pedestal or bridge rocker was used on some production engines. Original muscle car rockers, regardless of style, were direct contact and did not use a roller tip for the valve-to-rocker contact point. They also did not use roller bearings for the pivot joint.

Shaft-mounted rocker arms place all of the rocker arms on a single shaft, and this shaft is bolted to the cylinder head. The Chrysler Hemi used two shafts per head, one for the exhaust rockers and one for the intake rockers. Each rocker arm is free to pivot on the shaft and the shaft does not move. Pressurized oil is fed into the shaft, and there is a small oil feed for each rocker arm. The rocker arms are located in a precise

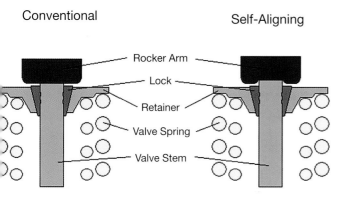

Conventional   Self-Aligning

— Rocker Arm —

— Lock —

— Retainer —

— Valve Spring —

— Valve Stem —

Conventional and self-aligning stud rocker arms. Note that the self-aligning rocker arm has "rails" that extend down on each side of the valve stem. This keeps the rocker arm properly aligned over the valve stem. This also requires that the valve stem extend higher above the spring retainer.

position on the shaft, thus solving the rocker-arm-to-valve-stem location problem.

Shaft-mounted rocker systems can be made very strong, since the rockers are on a single shaft. The shaft is usually bolted to the head at five points, spreading the load across multiple mounting points and reducing the change of a failure. Flex and movement can occur when a single mounting point is used. Also, the valve-stem-to-rocker-tip alignment is easy to maintain on a shaft-mounted rocker arm setup.

Cost is the big disadvantage of a shaft-mounted rocker arm setup, which is why most manufacturers did not use them. The number of components is high—there is a rocker shaft, support pedestals, springs and spacers to keep the rocker shaft in place, and finally, the rocker shafts themselves. The design complexity is also higher—all OEM shaft-mounted rocker setups require that pressurized oil was fed to the cylinder head to provide the oil for the rocker arms. Finally, to make the valvetrain adjustable requires an adjustment screw and locknut where the pushrod meets the rocker arm.

Stud-mounted rocker arms were the most popular. These have the advantage of low design

and manufacturing costs. There are only three components: the rocker arm, the trunion ball, and the stud. Also, most engines used the same parts for the intake and exhaust rockers. The rocker arm was usually stamped steel, further reducing cost. The pivot point, or trunion, is formed by stamping the rocker with a smooth circular contact area and then installing a semi-circular support or "ball" that is held in place by a retention nut on the stud. By design, these are easy to make adjustable.

Disadvantages of stud-mounted rockers are that some sort of alignment must be provided to keep the rocker arm tip in proper alignment with the valve stem. This requires either a guide plate that the pushrods pass through or specially designed rocker arms that have guides or rails that straddle the valve stem. Also, stud-mounted rocker arms transmit all of the valve actuation force to the single stud, and this can actually cause the stud to flex at high RPMs. For high-performance applications, an aftermarket stud girdle may be required.

One item to watch with stud-mounted rocker arms is how they are aligned. There are two styles. The traditional style has no self-aligning feature, and these must be used with a pushrod guide plate. The newer style that both Ford and Chevrolet introduced in the 1980s is the self-aligning or rail-style rocker arm. This rocker has guides on each side of the valve stem contact point that keep the rocker arm centered over the valve stem. These rail rocker arms must not be used with guide plates, and they also require valve stems that are slightly longer so the tip of the stem extends higher above the spring retainer. The two styles of stud-mounted rocker arms are not interchangeable unless the valves are also replaced.

Pedestal or bridge-style rocker arms have the same low-cost advantages as stud-mounted rocker arms, and they also solve the rocker alignment problem without requiring a guide plate. This is accomplished by stamping the rocker arm with a cylindrical trunion and replacing the trunion ball with a bridge that has a cylindrical support. Since the rocker and the bridge are cylindrical, not spherical, the rocker is free to pivot in only one direction. The cylindrical support is held in alignment because the bridge bolts to the head in two places. This bridge supports the exhaust and intake rocker for one cylinder.

The disadvantage of pedestal rocker systems is the lack of valve-lash adjustment. Because of the way the pedestal works, it must be firmly clamped to the cylinder head. Since the rocker arm is stamped steel, there is no provision for adding an adjuster at the pushrod cup. This is not a problem for a lower-RPM hydraulic lifter setup, as the lifter can accommodate some degree of manufacturing variance. It can become a big issue after a valve job that leaves the valves further up in the head, resulting in valve stems that are now too tall, thus disturbing valve train geometry.

HIGH-PERFORMANCE ROCKERS

Because of the way rocker arms work, there is considerable sliding friction, both at the trunion and at the rocker tip. To reduce this friction, high-performance rocker arms will use roller bearings at these high friction points. The first step up is to add a roller bearing where the rocker tip contacts the valve stem. This style is called a roller-tip rocker. Besides reducing friction, it also has the advantage of reducing the side load on the valve stem, reducing valve guide and valve stem wear.

The next improvement is to add a roller bearing at the rocker arm fulcrum, or trunion. This style of rocker arm almost always has a roller tip as well, and since this is a full roller rocker, it is referred to as a roller rocker arm. These are available for stud and shaft rocker systems. Vehicles that use bridge- or pedestal-style rockers must convert their cylinder heads to stud rocker arms, usually by adding a custom guide plate and machining the head for rocker mounting studs.

High-performance full roller rocker arms also reduce lubrication requirements, due to the substantial reduction in friction. This allows the oil system to be modified to keep more of the oil in the lower part of the engine, usually by using oil-restricted pushrods for stud-mounted rockers or block oil restrictors for shaft roller rocker systems.

ROCKER ARM ANGLE

Valvetrain geometry is critical to long engine life. This is something that is relatively easy to check. What you are attempting to avoid are excessive angles that produce sideways pressure on the valve stem. If not set properly, the excessive side loads will result in rapid valve guide wear. Changing the operating geometry usually requires a different pushrod length. Also, the valvetrain must be adjustable; many factory engines came with hydraulic lifters and nonadjustable valvetrains.

If your engine is stock, the stock pushrod lengths will be fine. If the engine has been converted to roller lifters it will definitely require shorter pushrods. Changes such as milled cylinder heads, a decked cylinder block, or roller rockers may also require custom-length pushrods.

Since the rocker end moves in an arc, the tip of the rocker arm will move across the top of the valve stem. What you want is the rocker arm to contact the top of

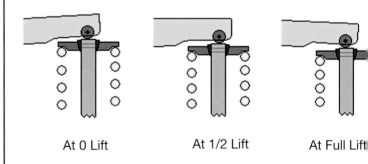

At 0 Lift   At 1/2 Lift   At Full Lift

Proper rocker arm geometry is critical for long engine life. The end of the rocker moves in an arc, so if the geometry is correct, the rocker arm contact point will move the same distance to and from the center of the valve stem. Also, with the valve at half lift, an imaginary line from the rocker pivot point to the rocker to valve stem contact point should be perpendicular to the valve stem.

ENGINE

the valve stem as close to its centerline as possible. Also, when the valve is at full rest (fully closed) and at full lift (fully open), the rocker arm saddle's contact point should be the same distance from the centerline of the valve stem top. This will make the rocker arm contact point move across the centerline of the valve stem top as the valve opens and closes. As the lift is increased, proper geometry becomes even more critical, since the rocker contact point (or roller if a roller rocker is used) can walk right off the edge of the valve stem if the geometry is not correct.

With the valve at exactly half lift, an imaginary line drawn from the center of the rocker arm pivot through the rocker arm to valve stem contact point should be exactly perpendicular to the valve stem. If the angle is less than 90 degrees, a longer pushrod is needed. If the angle is over 90 degrees, a shorter pushrod is needed. Also, while the valve is at exactly half lift, the rocker arm contact point should be on the side of the valve stem top that is farthest from the pushrod. When the valve is fully open or fully closed, the rocker arm contact point should be at the same point on the valve stem top, and on the side of the valve stem top that is closest to the pushrod.

BOTTOM END

The longevity of the engine depends on the bottom end. Spending money on premium components here will not result in performance gains, but will definitely result in increased reliability, especially if the power level has been increased. This is one area where shortcuts should not be made, as a failure here will usually result in catastrophic (costly) engine failure.

Begin with the crankshaft. You don't have to have a forged-steel crank to have a reliable engine. For power levels up to 500 horsepower, a cast-iron crankshaft that is properly prepared will work just fine. A nodular-iron crankshaft will handle 550 to 600 horsepower. A forged-steel crank will handle outrageous power levels of the most radical engines.

Regardless of which type of crankshaft is used, it must be properly inspected and prepared in order for

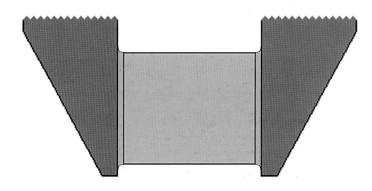

Radiused crankshaft journal. This is much stronger than a journal that is relieved. The caveat is that the bearing must have a corresponding radius at the edge to clear the radius at the edge of the journal.

it to last. Begin by inspecting the journals thoroughly. Check for any signs of cracking or hot spots. If the journals are scratched or scored, the crank must be turned. Also check the crank for a proper radius where the journal meets the counterweights. Some cranks are undercut at the ends of the journals, and this will result in a crankshaft that can fail under heavy loads.

A proper radius at this location is critical for a strong crankshaft. If the crank is undercut, consider locating a replacement crank if the engine's output is going to be increased. Also, when using a radiused journal crank, it is imperative to ensure that the bearings are relieved to clear the radius. If the bearings do not have the proper clearance, your machine shop can trim them, or you can do it yourself. Be sure the bearing clears the radius by at least .0015 inch when the bearing shell is pushed all the way to the edge of the journal.

Watch the bearing clearance! Don't get the clearance too large. Look at the specifications for your engine and set the clearance on the tight side. For example, if the specifications list .0015 to .0035 as the allowable main clearance, shoot for .0018 to .0025 as the clearance in your motor. Don't go below the minimum, but get close to it. The tighter clearance will help the oil do its job and also keep the oil pressure up.

Another consideration for the bottom end is the main cap support. Big-block engines have heavy crankshafts with long strokes. Keeping the crankshaft stable in the engine is important. Several engines have aftermarket solutions for adding additional support for the main caps. Solutions such as main cap girdles that tie all of the caps together to minimize "walking" are one example; straps that fit across the top of the caps are another. Aftermarket studs that are much stronger and do a better job of retaining the cap than the factory bolts are available for most engines. Again, find a good book on your particular engine and see what is recommended to help keep your bottom end alive.

One of the keys to building a strong engine is balancing the rotating parts. Big-block engines have a heavy reciprocating assembly, and proper balancing is vital to reducing vibration and stress, especially at higher rpms. Make sure the machine shop that is going to balance your reciprocating assembly is familiar with your engine. When selecting a harmonic damper, replace the factory rubber ring with a high-quality SFI-rated harmonic dampener. Make sure that it is provided to the machine shop before the engine is balanced.

PISTONS

For a stock rebuild, cast pistons will work just fine. High-performance engines that use nitrous oxide or are built to make 500 or more horsepower require the reliability offered by forged pistons. For higher rpm engines, forged pistons are a must. Do not even consider cast pistons, as they will fail in these types of engines. For a stock rebuild, cast pistons will work just fine.

If cast pistons are used with a high-horsepower engine, expect ring land failures. Detonation will also cause this type of damage. The continuous pounding caused by high horsepower or detonation fractures the ring land under the top compression ring. This allows the ring to move down, and because rings are not flexible, the ring breaks. The engine will have a noticeable miss and it will be down on power. A compression check will show a cranking pressure of 10 psi or less. Fortunately, this failure typically does little damage to the cylinder wall.

Running nitrous with cast pistons may result in broken ring lands or even a broken piston top. Nitrous-injected engines generate powerful pressure spikes that can destroy a cast piston. Cast pistons cannot tolerate preignition or detonation; forged pistons can tolerate more detonation than a cast piston.

Forged pistons do have drawbacks. They require greater cylinder wall clearances. Your machinist must be aware of the type of piston you will use, as this will affect how much clearance will be required. This extra clearance can cause piston slap when the engine is cold, which will last until the piston warms up and expands. This also requires that the engine be driven slowly until the pistons have warmed up and expanded.

Finally, forged pistons are no excuse to tolerate detonation in the engine; the pressure spikes caused by detonation will destroy an engine.

PISTON RINGS

Use only chrome or chromemolybdenum (moly) rings. Uncoated cast-iron rings will not last more than 50,000 miles. Moly rings are porous and will hold oil better than chrome. In order to use them, the cylinder bores must be finished properly; moly rings require a fine finish. Talk this over with your machinist. Also check to see what finish is recommended by the ring manufacturer. In addition to the grit of the finishing stones, there may also be crosshatch-angle recommendations.

With modern oils, cylinder and ring wear should be minimal, allowing for up to 200,000 miles between rebuilds. In order to achieve the upper end of this estimate the carburetor will need to be properly calibrated to prevent an overly rich mixture from continually washing the cylinders. Keep this in mind when rebuilding the engine. Select parts for the long haul. Build the engine using parts that are recommended for endurance racing.

When you install the piston rings, fit them to the cylinder bores. Use a squaring tool, or an inverted piston to push the ring one inch down in the cylinder bore. Check the end gap and set it on the tight side of the specifications. If the gap is set too small, the ring gap may close completely as the ring warms up, which can gall the cylinder wall, break the piston, or seize the engine.

TABLE 3: TOP RING GAP GUIDE

Engine type	Top ring gap
Normally aspirated engine	Bore x .0045
Moderate turbo boost or nitrous	Bore x .005
High turbo boost or nitrous (over 200 or more additional horsepower)	Bore x .007

Use the table above to get the ring end gap as tight as possible for the type of engine that you are building. Notice that for turbocharged and nitrous-injected engines the gap gets wider. This allows for the extra expansion that will come from the additional heat that these types of engines will experience. You want the tightest gap that is safe to run, as this improves engine sealing. The better the seal, the more efficient the engine will be, increasing horsepower and torque. Fuel consumption per horsepower will also go down as the ring seal improves.

OILING SYSTEM REQUIREMENTS

The oiling system modifications you need to make will vary depending on how heavily you modify your engine as well as how the car will be used. For a basically stock engine, a higher-capacity oil pan is all that is required, especially if the vehicle is not going to see much performance driving.

For sustained high-speed operation such as endurance racing, the stock oiling system will not cut it. The oil will rapidly overheat, and the bearings will be starved for cool, fresh oil. The only way an engine can be expected to survive sustained high-speed operation is with a modified oiling system. Driving your engine hard will almost certainly require an oil cooler as well as high-performance parts that maintain adequate oil pressure under extreme conditions.

A high-volume oil pump can be found for virtually any muscle car engine. But don't use one unless the engine really needs it, and then only if the engine is properly set up to handle the increased oil flow. The problem is that the high-volume pump will move more oil in less time. Unless oil capacity is increased, and the drain back from the block is improved, you can end up with all of your oil up in the engine's heads and cam valley. Once this happens, your oil pressure will go to zero, and your main and rod bearings are in serious trouble.

To properly handle a high-volume pump, your engine will need a larger oil pan. You should look for a six- or seven-quart pan (not counting the filter) as a minimum. Don't even consider using the factory four-quart pan with a high-volume oil pump, as your first high-rpm blast will suck it dry. If you are going to run a factory four- or five-quart pan, stick with the stock pump. Your main and rod bearings will be much happier.

With a high-volume pump, oil-restricted pushrods should also be used. This will help limit the amount of oil sent to the top of the engine. If you are running restricted pushrods, roller rockers are a recommended modification as they can handle the reduced amount of oil the restricted pushrods will deliver to the top of the engine, especially at low rpms. The stock stamped rockers will not survive the reduced oil flow. And finally, don't forget the oil pump driveshaft. If you are using a nonstock pump, you must use an oil pump driveshaft that can handle the extra load.

Now how much oil pump do you really need? This really depends on what you will be doing with the car. If you plan on making spirited runs down a drag strip, you should explore oiling system modification, especially if you are going to be increasing the rpm and horsepower. If the engine is stock or mildly modified, perhaps with headers, then a properly setup and blueprinted stock oiling system equipped with a high-capacity oil pan should be more than adequate.

If you need a higher-capacity oiling system, use a high-volume pump, higher-capacity oil pan, and the required oil restrictors. Check the numerous engine building books for guidance in this area, like *Big-Block Mopar Performance* by Chuck Senatore, *Ford Performance* by Pat Ganahal, and *Chevy 454 Through 512 Hi-Po* by R. M. Clarke. There are several available for almost every muscle car engine, so you should be able to find one to use as a guide.

Before adding a high-volume pump, check the rest of the oiling system. Just like the induction system, where a large carburetor does no good if the intake ports are restrictive, if the rest of the oil system cannot pass the increased volume of oil, you can install a high-volume pump and not see any increase in oil pressure. A high-volume pump will move more oil, but if the oil cannot pass through the oil system, it will simply be relieved out the oil pressure relief valve and may actually result in increased aeration of the oil and a subsequent decrease in pressure.

Oil pressure is the indicator of how much oil is really available to lubricate the engine. While high oil pressure may look impressive, excessive pressure does nothing more than rob horsepower, and can cause other problems as well. For starters, since heat and pressure are directly related, increased pressure will add heat to the oil. More oil will be thrown from the crank onto the cylinder walls for the rings to remove. You can also have problems with oil pump driveshaft or distributor gear failures, as the extra power required to create the greater oil pressure has to be delivered through the pump. Finally, if oil pressure is too high, a ruptured oil filter may be the result.

So how much oil pressure is enough? The old rule of thumb is rpm x .01. So if your engine has a 6,000 rpm redline, you need 60 psi of oil pressure at 6,000 rpm. This is to ensure that there is sufficient pressure at the main bearing to force oil into the rotating crankshaft. This pressure is the hot oil pressure. Remember: as the crank spins, centrifugal force is attempting to push the oil back out the main bearing oil intake hole. It requires pressure to overcome this force. Also, the faster the bearing is rotating, the more oil is required to keep the oil wedge in place and to replace the hot oil with fresh, cool oil.

Oil pressure is not the same at every point in your oiling system. The oiling system is a complex maze of passages, with openings delivering oil to each lifter and bearing. When the system is operating, pressure is regulated at the input to the system by the oil pressure relief spring at the oil pump. Then, as oil flows through the system, its pressure steadily decreases. As the oil flows through the oil galleys, each opening siphons off some of the available oil, resulting in a pressure drop. By the end of the oil galley, the pressure is significantly lower. This is compounded by the fact that the oil galley passages are not always large enough for the task at hand. Remember, pressure is the result of volume in minus flow out.

Engines with the oil pressure sender located at the end of the oil galley are indicative of this. For example, Oldsmobile big blocks have the oil pressure sending unit located at the front of the engine, at the end of the oil galley (the oil enters the galleys at the back of the block). This results in the gauge showing oil pressure at close to the lowest pressure point in the oiling system. Small- and big-block Chevy engines usually have the oil sender mounted at the side of the block, close to the oil galley input from the filter. This results in the oil pressure gauge showing a pressure much closer to oil pump output, but it doesn't show the lowest oil pressure in the system.

This is a typical aftermarket Chevrolet big-block oil pump. This one uses a bolt-on pickup assembly. Most factory pumps use a press-on pickup.

This is an Oldsmobile oil filter adapter. Note the cast in passages that the oil must flow through. These are a restriction, and when you consider the path that the oil must travel in and out of this and the filter, it is no wonder that this adds a 10 psi pressure drop. This one has a tap to route oil to a turbocharger, and that is the fitting that is exiting at the top.

Neither of these situations are a problem, but something to be considered when modifying an oiling system. Be aware that oil pressure indication is a relative thing, and a good pressure reading for one engine family is not necessarily the ideal pressure for another.

TROUBLESHOOTING LOW OIL PRESSURE

Low oil pressure can be frustrating, particularly when you discover it on a freshly installed engine. Who wants to take the engine back out? You need to determine if the problem is a bad pump, incorrect engine part clearance, or a faulty gauge. This can be accomplished without having to remove the engine from the car.

First change the oil and filter to see if this solves your problem. Do not use a 0W30 or 5W30 oil, as these will usually be too thin for the large journal sizes used in most big-block engines. The oil volume

required to maintain decent pressure will be too high. Instead, use a 10W40, or for hot climates, a 15W50 or 20W50 synthetic oil.

CHECKING THE GAUGE

The first component to test is the gauge. You don't want to spend considerable time or money on other parts just to find that the gauge is defective. For electric gauges, check for signs of oil around the sending unit. On high-quality gauge sets, the sending unit will normally only leak a little if the sending unit fails, thus preventing engine failure. However, the gauge reading will be wrong. The easiest way to check for a broken electric sending unit is to loosen the electrical connection and then loosen the jam nut at the base of the terminal. Start the engine and check for any oil coming out around the electrical connection. If you see any sign of oil leaking out, the sending unit is bad.

If there are no obvious signs of problems, check the gauge by disconnecting either the sending unit (for an electric gauge) or the oil pressure feed line (for a mechanical gauge) from the engine and connecting it to a steel or brass tee fitting that fits the gauge's sending unit threads, which are usually 1/8 NPT. The other two ends of the tee fitting should be connected to a 0-to-100 psi gauge and an air tool quick-connect fitting. If the oil pressure gauge is electric, run a wire from the body of the tee fitting to the battery's negative terminal. Now connect an air hose to the quick-connect fitting and start your air compressor. Adjust the air pressure regulator at the compressor and compare the reading on the tee block gauge with the reading on the gauge in the car. Check the pressure from 15 psi up to 80 psi (or the maximum reading on your vehicle's oil pressure gauge). Make a note of where the gauge is wrong. If the gauge is off by more than 5 psi at any point, it should be replaced.

GETTING STARTED

If the oil pressure is always low, regardless of rpm or temperature, the oil pump is the likely culprit. Even if the engine is a little loose, oil pressure should be higher at a given rpm when the engine is cold than it is when the engine is warm. Also watch for improper clearance between the oil pickup and the bottom of the pan. There should be a minimum of 3/4 of an inch from the bottom of the pickup and the oil pan.

The next possibility is that the oil pressure relief valve is stuck or the spring is weak or broken. For MoPar or Buick engines, the spring can be accessed without having to remove the pan. For the rest of us, the only way to gain access to the relief valve is to remove the oil pan. If the spring is broken or weak, or if the relief valve is stuck open, oil pressure will be low when the engine is cold, and even lower when the engine warms up.

Another pump problem is debris blocking the oil pickup. All factory pumps use a screen in the oil pickup. Excessive debris will restrict the flow of oil, thereby leading to low oil pressure. Don't discount this too quickly; several factory engines, especially GM, used a nylon upper timing gear. When it failed, the teeth were usually ground off. These nylon gear teeth end up in the pan, and then in the oil pickup. Also, past work on the engine could have resulted in gasket material or blobs of silicone sealer being left in the engine. Again, this stuff will make it to the pan, and then into the pickup. The end result is the junk clogs up the system and causes insufficient oil flow, and therefore low oil pressure, especially when the engine warms up.

If you eliminate all of these problems, the next step is to check the engine. Start by checking for oil passage restrictions or missing galley plugs. These types of problems usually result in no oil pressure. Most engines have several points where the factory had to drill an oil galley through and a plug is required. Some of these ports are located outside the block, so a missing plug will be immediately evident. But for the ones located inside the engine, a missing plug will not be obvious, although the resulting near zero oil pressure will be.

If the internal clearances are a little loose, the engine's oil pressure will be close to or normal when

Here is a dual remote oil filter adapter with -12 AN fittings. Also note the oil temperature sensor that is installed into the other side. If a cooler is used, always flow the oil through the filters first, then the cooler. Hot oil is thinner and will flow through the filters better. Remember, oil enters the filters on the outside edge. Also, if remote oil filters are being used, place them so that they get as much airflow as possible; this will help in removing heat from the oil.

it is cold. As the engine warms up, oil pressure will drop. The loose clearances will require higher oil volume, and the pump and oil passages may not be able to meet these higher volume requirements. Note that the rod bearing clearance will not have as much of an effect on oil pressure as the main bearing clearance will.

The excess clearance can be in the main or rod bearings, cam bearings, or at the lifters. Lifter clearance can be problematic. Several engine families share similar engine lifter bores, but the oil grooves are at different heights. Using the wrong lifters will result in excessive oil bleed-off. One example is Oldsmobile and Chevrolet. Both are .842 inch in diameter, but if you use a Chevrolet lifter in an Oldsmobile, your oil pressure will be extremely low due to the Chevrolet lifter oil groove location being too high for the Oldsmobile lifter bore. This results in the lifter oil groove being lifted up above the lifter bore, thus opening the main oil galley to the inside of the block. Also consider this when installing a high-lift camshaft, or a roller cam conversion.

If the lifter bore is worn and excessive clearance is detected, don't fret. The block can be machined and liners can be installed. This is also a good time to verify that the lifter bores were properly machined at the factory. If not, the machining process when installing the liners can correct this.

Another cause of low oil pressure is aeration or foaming of the oil, which is caused by the oil being whipped by the rotating crankshaft. This problem can be recognized by a decline in oil pressure as rpm increases, usually starting around 3,000 rpm. It can take several minutes for the foaming to subside. Proper oil control will minimize this problem. Quite simply, the oil must be kept away from the rotating assembly. A good windage tray will help.

Also, if the engine oil temperature is excessive, oil pressure will drop due to the loss of viscosity.

ADDING AN ENGINE OIL COOLER

If operation causes oil temperature to exceed 235 degrees Fahrenheit, the oil temperature is too high. This may only occur during higher speed operation, such as freeway cruising speeds. There is only one solution for this problem: an oil cooler. If sustained high speed operation is being considered, such as competing in the Silver State Classic, an oil cooler is an absolute must. Drag racing will not require an oil cooler—the race does not last long enough. If the engine is basically stock and you do not plan on operating the engine at more than 3,500 rpm for more than 5 to 10 minutes, you do not need an oil cooler.

Before installing an oil cooler, keep the following points in mind, because the last thing you want to do is increase the chance for a breakdown due to an oil cooler failure or leak. The tubing sizes used must be at least 3/4 of an inch in diameter, or -12AN. If smaller diameter tubing is used, oil pressure will be low due to flow restriction. Also, the oil cooler itself must not be a flow restriction. Most oil coolers available over the counter or in a catalog are set up for 1/2-inch diameter oil hose, and the cooler element itself is a flow restriction. These coolers are fine for a four- or six-cylinder engine, as well as for stock small-block V-8 engines, but they will not flow sufficient volume for a big block.

This means you must find a high-volume oil cooler, such as the stacked plate type, with 3/4-inch NPT fittings. Also, the hose or pipe lengths must be kept as short as possible. If using hose, it is strongly recommended that braided-steel hose and aircraft-quality fittings be used. As stated before, for a big-block engine, -12AN is the size that should be used. Also, these hoses should be changed every three years or 50,000 miles. Even braided-steel aircraft hoses do not last forever, and a hose failure at the oil cooler has the potential to destroy your engine bearings, especially at highway speeds.

To install an oil cooler, begin by removing the oil filter. Find a suitable adapter with large fitting sizes. For engines with removable oil filter adapters, you can usually find an adapter that is drilled and tapped for oil filter hoses. The resulting system will also have

Here are some -12 AN fittings. Note that the 1/2-inch to 37 degree -12 AN fitting on the right is steel. The steel versions are available in all popular sizes. I prefer the steel fitting, as it will last forever. Also, when the aluminum AN hose adapter is tightened, the aluminum will form to the steel fitting, resulting in a leak-free connection.

Here is the remote oil adapter for Oldsmobile engines. This takes the place of the oil filter adapter and is set up to accept 1/2-inch NPT fittings. Better yet, these are drilled directly to line up with the passages in the block.

to have a remote oil filter. Ensure that the filter is plumbed the correct way, as oil filters have an anti-drainback valve that will prevent flow in the reverse direction. Keep in mind that the oil enters the filter at the outside ring of holes and exits through the center hole. Run the oil to the filter first, then to the cooler, as the hot oil travels through the filter more easily. Finally, route the oil back to the engine block.

When routing the hoses, ensure that they cannot come in contact with the exhaust system. Also make sure they are routed so they are not subject to excessive flexing or pulling. Where hoses pass near the exhaust system, install a heat shield or use metal pipe. Fabricate a bracket to support the hose and prevent excessive flexing or pulling at the hose fittings. If you are installing a remote filter, make sure that the filter bracket is a high-flow model without excessive restrictions. The filter housing is also a good place to install a temperature sensor, as most have inlet and outlet fittings on both sides. Just make sure that the temperature sensor can handle the pressure.

Only use AN-style hose fittings and high-quality steel-braided hose. But one suggestion: since the hose fittings are aluminum, most manufacturers also sell aluminum pipe fittings. However, the steel pipe fittings can be purchased as well. I prefer to use the steel pipe fittings. They last forever, and the aluminum hose fittings will seal up just fine against the steel pipe fitting. Also, there is less chance of distorting steel pipe fittings when installing them in oil filters, block adapters, or oil coolers.

One final point: run fine-grit sandpaper on a roll attached to a drill through all metal pipe and pipe fittings to remove any flash. If a lower-cost remote oil filter is used, run the sanding roller through the passages to remove all traces of chrome and any casting flash from the inside. The chrome must be removed to prevent the chrome from flaking off and circulating inside your engine. After all of the sanding is finished, scrub out the internal passages with a bottle brush and soapy water. After it is all clean, blow it dry with compressed air.

PREVENTING OIL LEAKS

Oil and other fluid leaks are preventable problems that often plague most older vehicles. While it is true that modern cars have been designed with greater attention to gasket surfaces in order to help minimize or prevent leaks, your older muscle car can also be leak-free if careful attention to detail is used when replacing a part that uses a gasket.

To begin with, use only premium gaskets! This may sound like a cop-out, but using no-name or house-brand gaskets will almost certainly result is a leak. It really is that simple, and all of the preparation and gasket sealers cannot compensate for a low-quality gasket. Use the famous name brand, and only use their premium offerings. Also pay attention to options, or application notes. For example: some factory muscle cars were equipped with aluminum intake manifolds. If you are replacing an intake manifold, pay attention to the options or application notes that the gasket

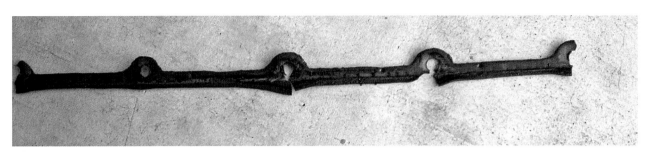

This is an old gasket. Notice that besides cracking and breaking, the gasket also crushes and hardens in the shape that it was compressed.

manufacturer points out. They may have a different gasket for aluminum intakes.

For aluminum intake manifolds, periodically check the torque of the bolts. Due to the increased rate of expansion and contraction caused by warming and cooling the manifold compared to the rate of expansion and contraction of the cast-iron block, the bolts may loosen. This should be performed every 3,000 miles. I check mine when I change the oil. These bolts should be checked and re-tightened only when the engine is cold, so if you perform this during the oil change, wait until the engine has cooled.

Another key point to consider is that gaskets have improved. For most engines, you can now find gaskets that have O-rings around the ports. These gaskets are intended to survive greater surface movement, such as what you will be experiencing with aluminum cylinder heads and manifolds. If you are using the original cast-iron heads and manifold, premium-quality OEM gaskets will work fine. Aluminum intake manifolds and heads require modern gasket sets to avoid having to change intake gaskets every two to four years.

Cleanliness is critical! All old gasket material, sealer, and other junk must be removed. The two mating surfaces must be oil- and grease-free. Think of it this way: if paint won't stick, neither will the gasket! Clean the two surfaces as if you are going to paint them. As a final step, I prefer to wipe the surfaces with lacquer thinner to ensure that there is no residual oil or grease.

Gaskets and sealer will not fix warped or misaligned mating surfaces. After the mating surfaces are clean,

check them with a straightedge. If they are not straight, the gaskets will not seal. This is most often the problem with leaky oil pans or valve covers. The sheet metal is bent or distorted at the bolt holes. For sheet metal parts, they can be worked back into place, but be sure that they are perfectly straight or you will have no chance of maintaining a leak-free seal.

If you are installing chrome parts, all of the chrome must be sanded off where the gasket seals. If you don't believe this, try painting chrome and see how well the paint sticks! Be careful not to scratch the finish where the chrome is visible. Any other type of shiny finish must also be sanded. I use 100-grit paper on steel and 150-grit paper on aluminum, as a slightly rough surface will clamp the gasket better.

Before using a chrome-plated engine accessory, remove all of the chrome from the side that is exposed to the inside of the engine. This is to prevent chrome from flaking off and getting inside the engine. Chrome is extremely hard and, if improperly applied, it can flake off inside the engine and scar or gouge bearing surfaces and cylinder walls. Remove all traces of chrome from the inside of any part unless you are sure that it is properly applied and will not flake off. No matter how it was applied, chrome must be removed from gasket-sealing areas or the gasket will not properly seal.

Before replacing a gasket to fix a leak (or rebuild a component), verify the cause of the leak. Begin by washing the suspect component or area. Run the engine for 15 to 20 minutes (or drive the car if the leak is from a transmission or rear axle), then check

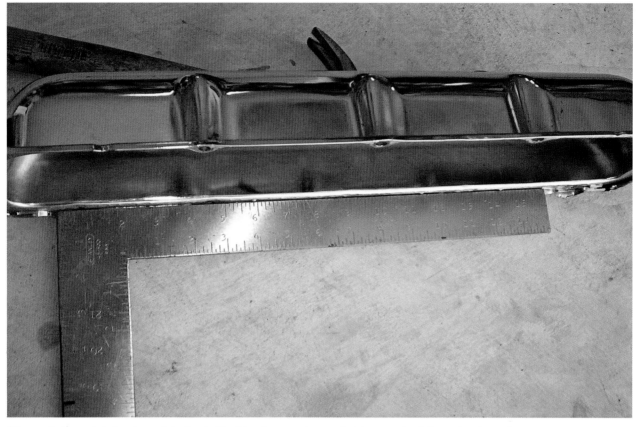

When replacing gaskets for stamped steel parts, like this valve cover, be sure that the mounting holes and gasket surfaces are straight or you will never be able to prevent leaks.

for the source of the leak. The last thing you want is to spend time and money and still have a leak!

A good way to detect the source of leaks is to wash the engine and transmission thoroughly. Drive the car a short distance, like 5 to 10 miles, and park it over a large piece of cardboard. Let it sit overnight and check for spots. The spot will be directly under where the oil dripped from the leaking part. Work back up and find the source.

Intake manifold end seals are just as problematic as valve covers, and most engine oil leaks are usually due to one or the other. If your engine has a manifold that seals the front and rear of the block, throw away the gasket or rubber seal! Use an RTV silicone gasket maker like Permatex Ultra Black instead. But just like any other gasket surface, the two mating surfaces must be clean and oil-free. Sand the mating surfaces on the intake manifold end seal area with 100-grit

sandpaper, parallel to the sealing surface (always sand perpendicular to the path the fluid would take if it were to leak). Clean the block's mating surface with lacquer thinner. After the gaskets are in place on the block, with the proper gasket cement on them, run a thick, uniform bead of RTV along the front and rear block mating surface. Be sure and force the RTV into the joint where the heads meet the block.

Now lower the manifold straight down; do not slide it forward or back, as the RTV could be moved off from the block and cause a leak. Ensure that the RTV is in contact with the underside of the manifold. Do not let the RTV cure enough to form a skin before setting the manifold in place; you want the RTV to seal to the manifold. Once cured, the RTV will flex enough to maintain a seal as the manifold expands and contracts.

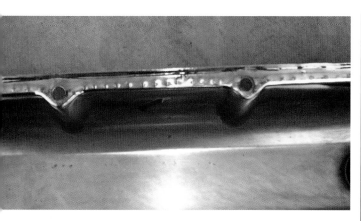

Dimpling the valve cover gasket surface will help prevent the gasket from moving or creeping; this can be a problem with stamped steel engine covers.

For rotating seals, such as the crankshaft rear oil seal, ensure that the seal is properly installed. Since most muscle car engines used a two-piece seal, use a small dab of gasket cement on the ends to seal the two halves together. You can prevent leaks by rotating the two seal halves slightly so their parting line is not aligned with the rear main bearing cap parting line. Apply a thin coating of wheel-bearing grease to the seal surface in order to protect the seal on initial start-up.

Most older engines used a rope seal for the rear crankshaft seal. This type of seal is essentially a wax-coated rope. The engine has a groove cut into the block and the rear main cap. The rope must be fitted into the block and rear main cap or the seal will leak.

Rope seals come as two strips, one for the block and one for the rear main cap. Begin by working one strip into the groove in the block. Now install the crank (note that all bearings must be installed and pre-lubed). Work the crank down in order to force the rope into the block. Using a sharp razor knife, cut the ends of the rope so they are even with the surface of the block. Do not nick or scratch the crank. Next, remove the crankshaft and carefully remove the trimmed rope section. Install this section into the main cap. Now install the second rope segment into the block, re-install the crankshaft, work the crank down to seat the second section, and carefully trim

the ends. Once complete, remove the crank, place a light coating of prelube on the rope seal (block and main cap segments), re-install the crankshaft, and finally install the rear main cap. One warning: if a rubber seal is used in place of a rope seal, make sure to remove the retaining pin from the main cap. This pin is located in the receiving groove for the rope seal to prevent the rope seal from moving. If this pin is not removed, you will not be able to install the rubber seal properly. It will be damaged and cause an oil leak.

For press-in seals, such as those at the front of the engine, the key is to apply gasket cement to the outside of the seal before pressing the seal into position. Use a seal installer to drive the seal into place. If the seal is hammered in without the proper tool, the seal can be damaged. Also, the seal will leak if the shaft that is being sealed is not smooth. If an existing seal is being replaced, check the shaft carefully. A groove may be worn into the shaft where it contacted the old seal. On most engines, the harmonic balancer contacts the seal. If this groove is present on engines on which the harmonic balancer contacts the seal, the balancer must be replaced to ensure that the new seal will hold. Use a thin coating of wheel-bearing grease on the surface of the seal.

Finally, don't forget to check the bolts. Unless the bolt is in a blind (not drilled through) hole, or is located so that the gasket and sealer completely seal the threads from the oil, oil will wick up around the bolt threads and seep out from under the head of the bolt even if the gasket is properly installed. To prevent this, a small dab of RTV can be used on the bolt. Apply it around the bolt, just under the head. This way, when the bolt is tightened, the RTV will seal the threads. For studs, the same trick will work; just apply a small dab of RTV around the base of the stud before installing the washer and nut.

ALUMINUM INTAKE MANIFOLD CONSIDERATIONS

Sealing aluminum intake manifolds can present special challenges. Aluminum expands at a higher rate than cast iron, and therefore will move around more as engine temperature changes. This movement affects the gaskets and eventually results in leaks. Careful installation techniques are required to achieve a long-lasting seal. But even a proper job will still usually have to be redone every five years. Also, check the bolts and make sure that they are tight. Check them at every oil change or every three months, whichever comes first.

In order to install a new gasket on an aluminum intake manifold, remove the manifold and clean the mating surfaces thoroughly. Before cleaning, place a towel or rag in the valley area to prevent old gasket material and other trash from entering the engine. Also place a rag in each intake port prior to any cleaning. Carefully scrape all traces of old gasket and sealant from the heads and the intake manifold. Be careful to not scratch or gouge the mating surface. Use lacquer thinner as the final step to remove any trace of oil and grease. Don't forget to clean the end rails, as this is where most engines leak oil.

Now evenly brush on a high-quality gasket sealer, such as Edelbrock Gasgacinch, around each intake port and all areas except around the water ports. Do not use RTV on the intake port area of the gasket. Around the water ports, run a smooth, even bead of RTV. Place the gasket on the block. Repeat for the other side and then run a nice, thick, even bead of RTV along the end rails.

Immediately place the intake in position, being careful to not slide the manifold. You must drop it straight down into position. Make sure that the gaskets do not move but remain properly positioned.

Start the bolts in all of the mounting holes. Beginning with the center bolts and following the recommended sequence, torque all of the bolts to 10 lb/ft. Allow the manifold to sit for 30 minutes and then torque the manifold again. Torque it to about 10 lb/ft below the final value, and then go back and tighten it fully to the recommended value, which is usually 25 lb/ft. Allow the engine to sit for 24 hours and then recheck the torque value of each fastener before filling the engine with coolant and starting the engine.

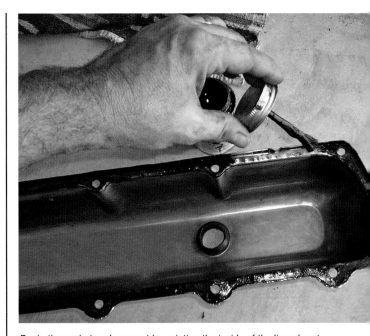

Begin the gasket replacement by painting the inside of the lipped part with a high-quality gasket sealer. Next, install the gasket to the part. Then paint the gasket with the sealer. Now install the component on the engine. If the part has a lip that retains the gasket, do not install the gasket on the engine and then install the part; there is a chance that this will result in the gasket pushing in, causing a leak.

Pressure check the cooling system before filling the radiator. Pump the cooling system up to 10 psi with a cooling system pressure tester and be sure that the pressure holds. After this test, fill the cooling system with the recommended antifreeze and coolant. Start the engine and set the ignition timing. Note that for most engine types the distributor has to be removed in order to remove the intake manifold, and you will have to set the ignition timing. Run the engine until warm, checking for leaks. Shut the engine off.

Allow the engine to completely cool and recheck the manifold bolts to be sure they are all still tight. Check the manifold bolts every three months, only when the engine is cold. Use anti-seize compound rather than thread-locking compound on the bolts for aluminum heads. The proper torque value will help keep the bolts from loosening.

Before removing the manifold, clean around the mating surface thoroughly. Scrape all debris loose and then remove. I use a shop vacuum to remove the dirt and debris. This prevents all of this from falling into the engine when the manifold is removed.

Cover the valley and place wadded-up paper towels in the intake ports before scraping off the old gaskets. The goal here is to prevent the debris from entering the engine.

CRANKCASE VENTILATION

Proper crankcase ventilation is a must for long engine life. This is because the rings do not seal 100 percent; some air and fuel escapes the combustion process and finds its way into the crankcase. And once the air fuel mixture is ignited, the pressure forces some combustion by-products past the rings. This results in unburned fuel, water vapor, and other compounds finding their way into the crankcase. If not released, these gases can build up to levels that are harmful to the engine.

The easiest way to minimize the buildup of harmful compounds in the crankcase is to force air to circulate through it. All factory engines built after 1966 came with a crankcase ventilation system. Do not discard or de-activate this system! It has no effect on full-throttle performance or part-throttle drivability, and if properly set up it can more than double the life of the engine.

For older engines, I strongly recommend that a crankcase ventilation system be added. Remember that roughly one-third of all vehicle hydrocarbon emissions come from crankcase emissions. Routing these gases back into the intake manifold eliminates them as a pollution source. This is one emissions control system that has no negative impact on vehicle drivability, horsepower, or fuel economy, and it increases the life of the engine.

In order to maintain a crankcase ventilation system, check that the fresh air intake of the crankcase ventilation system is in the air cleaner, either going through a separate filter, or drawing air from the filtered side of the air cleaner. This ensures that only clean air is allowed into the crankcase. Never allow the crankcase to breathe air without a filter. I recommend that the fresh air intake be in the air cleaner housing; this will prevent engine blow-by gases from escaping into the air during low-vacuum engine operation.

The PCV valve must be the correct one for your engine. They are not all the same, as the valve regulates airflow based on vacuum. The wrong PCV valve may flow too much or too little air, resulting in a lean- or rich-running engine. Make sure that your valve cover has an oil baffle so the PCV valve is not directly exposed to the inside of the engine. This could cause the PCV valve to draw in oil that is being thrown from the rocker arms, increasing oil consumption.

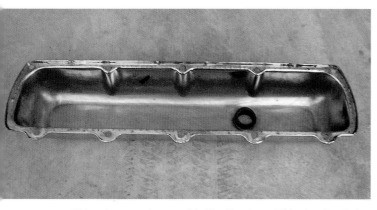

This valve cover has no oil baffle. Running a PCV valve directly in this valve cover will result in excessive oil consumption, as the PCV valve will pick up the oil mist.

Oil being drawn in is a common problem in engines that cruise at higher rpms. At higher rpms, the rocker arms are moving faster and create more of an oil cloud under the valve covers. When the PCV valve allows air to flow into the intake manifold from the valve cover, some of this oil is drawn as well. So if your engine works fine at lower rpm, but mysteriously loses oil when operated at higher rpm for any length

This is an oil separator. Inside are a baffle plate and a wire mesh that separate the oil from the airflow.

After the mating surface is clean, remove the paper towels from the ports. I use a shop vacuum to catch and remove any debris that may have fallen in the ports as the paper towel is removed from the port. This prevents the debris from falling out when the paper towel is removed. After the paper towels are removed, I then vacuum out each port and the valley.

of time, this could be your problem. This type of oil loss is especially common in boats.

To check for this, remove the PCV valve from the hose and check for signs of oil in the hose. If any is found, this is most likely your problem. There are a couple of solutions. You can install taller valve covers that have oil baffles. These will help and can be made more effective if they are packed with coarse stainless steel wool. The steel wool helps separate the oil droplets from the air. Only use stainless steel wool, as it will not rust.

The second method is to use an oil separator. Oil separators function by having a larger internal volume that allows the air to slow down, which gives the oil droplets time to settle out. Just like the valve cover breather trick, loosely packing the breather with stainless steel wool will help to separate the oil droplets from the air.

CHAPTER 7
COOLING SYSTEM

A reliable cooling system is a must for a daily driver. There is nothing more frustrating than being stuck in traffic and helplessly watching the temperature gauge rise past the boiling point. There are several things that can be done to ensure your muscle car does not overheat.

The cooling system has a single job: to remove engine heat and transfer it to the atmosphere. There are only four main components, the radiator, fan, thermostat, and water pump, and each has a specific function. Maintaining and troubleshooting a cooling system will involve focusing on these components.

RADIATOR

The radiator is the primary component, and the performance of the cooling system is ultimately defined by the radiator. The size and construction of the radiator defines the amount of heat that can be transferred from the coolant to the atmosphere. Surface area defines the efficiency and heat removal of the radiator. Surface area involves both the overall footprint of the radiator itself in the air stream, and the surface area of the core element tubing in which the coolant flows. For this reason, muscle cars came with large radiators that used multiple rows of core elements.

FAN

To cool the engine when the vehicle is not moving, the radiator has a fan. The only function of the fan is to move air through the radiator when the vehicle speed is low. Above 35 mph, the fan is not needed. Heavy-duty cooling systems usually added a fan clutch. The job of the fan clutch is to disengage the fan when the air temperature exiting the radiator is not hot. When the car is moving

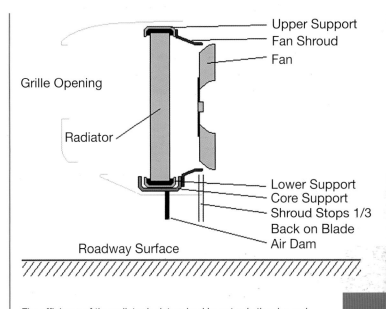

The efficiency of the radiator is determined by not only the size and construction of the radiator but also the airflow across the cooling fins. The best system will ensure adequate low-speed airflow by using a fan and a fan shroud that are matched. Proper high-speed airflow will be assisted by adding an air dam.

at highway speeds, the temperature of the air leaving the radiator will be lower, due to the sheer volume, and the fan clutch will unlock, allowing the fan to freewheel. Also, the fan clutch will slip as rpm increases, preventing the fan blades from being spun too fast. Engines with a fan clutch were usually fitted with a larger, high-capacity fan blade. Air-conditioned cars almost always came equipped with a heavy-duty engine cooling system.

THERMOSTAT

The thermostat is present to ensure that the engine warms up quickly. It also ensures that the engine

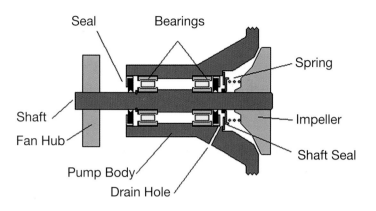

Water pump shaft and seal.

will maintain a minimum operating temperature, regardless of the ambient temperature. As the engine warms up, the thermostat will slowly open once the coolant temperature reaches the rated temperature of the thermostat.

Most factory thermostats are rated at 195 degrees. This means that they begin to open when the coolant temperature reaches 195 degrees Fahrenheit. The thermostat will not be fully open for another 5 to 10 degrees. The quick warm-up is important for engine life, as wear is increased when oil temperature is low. I think the factory 195-degree thermostat is too hot.

I prefer a 180-degree thermostat. Do not run a colder thermostat; engine life is reduced if the cylinder walls are too cool, as the oil will not lubricate the cylinder walls properly.

WATER PUMP

All modern automobile engines, with the exception of air-cooled models such as the original Volkswagen Beetle and the Chevrolet Corvair, use a water pump to circulate the coolant. The water pump must circulate enough coolant to prevent hot spots in the heads or around the cylinders. All muscle cars use an impeller-style pump that is driven by the engine.

One common water leak is at the water pump vent hole. This hole allows water to escape from the rear of the seal area, ensuring that the bearings remain dry. All modern water pumps use a smooth seal rather than a packing-style or lip seal. A smooth seal relies on the two flat, highly polished metals to fit tightly and seal. This seal lasts for a long time, much longer than a lip seal or the old shaft-packing seal. The life of one of these seals is usually 7–10 years or 100,000 miles, provided the coolant is kept clean.

Aluminum water pumps are available for most engines. The aluminum will not improve the cooling efficiency, but it will save a few pounds.

Water pump efficiency can be improved by welding a circular disc behind the impeller blades. This forces all of the coolant to be picked up from the front of the impeller.

Do not operate the engine without coolant. The water lubricates and cools the seal in the water pump. A damaged seal may not leak immediately, but will usually fail in a short time. Also, do not fill the vent hole with RTV or some other type of sealant. This is a misguided attempt to prevent leaks. If the seal fails, the bearings will be flooded with water and destroyed, resulting in not only a leak, but a possible wobbling or thrown fan. If the vent hole is plugged, the small amount of water and vapor that makes it past the seal will not be able to escape and will cause premature bearing failure.

On all muscle car engines, the coolant enters the pump from the radiator and is propelled into the block. The coolant circulates through the water jacket that surrounds the cylinders, enters the cylinder heads, flows out the front of the heads, and is routed to the thermostat. The outlet of the thermostat returns the coolant to the radiator.

A passage allows coolant from the heads to bypass the thermostat and the radiator to enter the water pump. This ensures that coolant is circulated when the thermostat is closed.

MAINTAINING THE COOLING SYSTEM

Proper cooling system maintenance begins by keeping the coolant clean and its antifreeze component fresh. Antifreeze prevents the coolant from freezing and it raises the coolant's boiling point. Antifreeze also helps prevent corrosion and rust, and it also lubricates the water pump seal.

Pure water transfers heat better than almost any other liquid; adding antifreeze reduces the specific heat capacity of the coolant. This disadvantage is far outweighed by the corrosion inhibitors and lubrication properties gained by using antifreeze. If you expect your cooling system to last, you must use antifreeze. If you have an aluminum intake manifold or aluminum heads, it is even more important to use a quality antifreeze to protect the aluminum from corrosion.

Antifreeze does not last forever and the coolant will accumulate dirt and scale. For this reason, the cooling system must be flushed every two years. Before beginning this job yourself, think about how to dispose of the old coolant. Flushing a cooling system uses a lot of fluid, and you can't just dump it on the ground or down a wastewater drain. The best way to flush a cooling system is to take the vehicle to a service center that has a coolant system flushing machine. This will cycle the coolant through the machine, removing the contaminants and sediment and replenishing the coolant.

ELECTROLYSIS—YOUR COOLING SYSTEM'S ENEMY

The flow of electrical current in your cooling system needs to be avoided at all cost. Electrical current flow in the system will cause electroplating. When this happens, the dissimilar metals that make up the cooling system will either be a donor or a receptor. Aluminum and brass are donors, and this means that they will be giving up material. This will result in a leak, as the donor material is eaten away by the electrolysis process.

Electrolysis is caused by current flowing through the cooling system from an outside source or the cooling system generating electricity. Current flowing through the cooling system is always due to a bad ground. This is easy to prevent; just make sure the engine and car body are grounded to each other. Electrical generation can be prevented by keeping the coolant fresh. Since the cooling system is made up of different metals, if the coolant becomes acidic (low ph), it will create a battery. The fluid conducts electricity between the elements and current will flow, resulting in corrosion of the donor materials.

The symptoms of electrical corrosion are pinhole leaks in the radiator or heater core or corrosion around the water passages on intake manifolds, especially near iron cylinder heads or an iron water-outlet neck. To test for this, remove the radiator cap while the engine is cold and place one voltmeter lead in the water in the radiator. Touch the other lead to the engine and check for a voltage of greater than

0.1 volt. A voltage more than 0.1 volt will indicate current flow and a coolant problem. Start the engine. If the voltage rises to more than 0.1 volt, you have a current flow problem that is being caused by a bad ground. If the problem is not corrected, you will experience shorter component life of aluminum and brass parts.

One more tip: mount the radiator so it is insulated from the car body, as this will help minimize the effects of the current flow. Not all cars have a design that allows for this, but this will greatly lengthen the life of the radiator if it is possible. The same is true for the heater core.

PREVENTING COOLANT LEAKS

Diagnosing coolant leaks is similar to finding oil leaks, except the cooling system is pressurized. All joints that seal the system must be smooth and flat, with no warpage or scratches. If you attempt to seal a pressurized coolant joint that is not smooth and flat, the gasket will either be blown out or the fluid will leak around the gasket. These types of failures will usually not be revealed by a pressure test. Once you heat the engine up, however, the leaks appear.

Water leaks from gasket joints are often caused by corrosion, especially on engines that use a removable front cover. Over time, these aluminum front covers

To check a thermostat, place it in a pan of water on the stove. The thermostat must open before the water boils, or it is bad. By the time the water boils, it should be fully open, as this one is.

The fan must be exposed at the edge of the shroud or low-speed cooling will suffer. One major flexible fan manufacturer has an easy tip: Make sure that the fan mounting point is even with the edge of the shroud.

corrode, especially if the former owner did not keep the antifreeze fresh. The corrosion is always around the water passages and water pump. This corrosion will cause insufficient sealing area. If the cover cannot be cleaned enough to yield a smooth, flat surface that is free of corrosion, the cover must be replaced. Aluminum intake manifolds will have these problems around the water passages as well. Don't try to mitigate the problem by using extra sealer or RTV, as the makeshift seal will leak.

On both the intake and front cover water passages, pay careful attention to the areas that are on the inside of the sealed engine. An undetected leak of this kind will introduce coolant to your engine oil and quickly destroy the engine!

The best test for a cooling system is to fill the engine, run the engine until hot, verify that there are no external leaks, and let the engine cool. Once it is completely cool, attach a cooling system tester and pump the system up to the maximum rated pressure

(the radiator cap pressure). Most muscle cars use 15 psi caps, but check your owner's manual or factory service manual.

Leave the system pressurized for 10 minutes and check that the pressure holds. If not, you have a leak. If the coolant is leaking out of the engine it will be obvious—water will drip from the leak. I start by looking under the car for the water, and trace the drip or stream back up to the source. If no trace can be found, it must be assumed that the coolant is leaking inside of the engine. Cracks in the block or heads can cause internal leaks, and it is not uncommon for these to only leak when the system is pressurized. Another source of internal coolant leaks are blown head gaskets.

One final source of water leaks are freeze plugs. Factory engines used freeze plugs for a couple of reasons. First, this is how the core material left over from the casting process is removed. Also, these plugs may save the block by popping out if the water in the

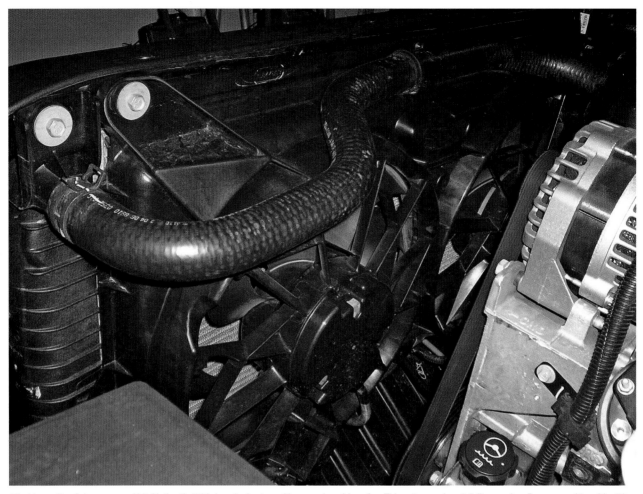

Electric cooling fans on a new V-8. Notice that this is a dual setup with no engine-driven fan. This setup cools a 6.2-liter engine. Be prepared to add a 30 amp or more load to the electrical system for fans such as these.

block freezes, but don't count on it. These steel plugs corrode and leak over time. Most big blocks used three freeze plugs per side. Most cylinder heads also use freeze plugs as well. The only cure for a leaking freeze plug is to replace the plug.

To remove a freeze plug, select a suitable driver that is slightly smaller than the inside diameter of the plug. Place a bushing driver (or a piece of pipe) in the freeze plug and knock it into the block or cylinder head. Tilt the top of the plug out of the block and hook it with a prybar. Pry the plug from the block. Clean the bore thoroughly and inspect it for signs of corrosion.

To install the new plug, coat the bore with high-quality gasket cement (not RTV). Select a bushing driver, or any other suitable tool that is slightly smaller than the inside diameter of the freeze plug. Place this tool in the new plug and drive the freeze plug in until the plug is just below the outside of the block. You can use brass freeze plugs instead of steel. The brass will resist rust, but steel plugs will last if the antifreeze is kept fresh.

DIAGNOSING A HOT-RUNNING ENGINE

An engine that overheats is no fun. Fortunately, the cooling system can be modified to ensure that your muscle car does not overheat. Before performing any modifications, ensure that the cooling system is properly flushed and filled. Also verify that the engine has the proper ignition timing. Retarded timing will cause the engine to run hot, especially at slow speeds. Take note of when the vehicle overheats, such as during slow-speed driving, high-speed driving, or when the car is idling. Also note if there is any operating condition that will cool the engine back down.

If the engine warms up and the temperature gauge keeps on rising until the engine overheats and operating conditions have no effect on this, the likely culprit is the thermostat. A stuck thermostat will result in an overheated engine in less than 10 minutes from a cold start. To verify that the problem is caused by the thermostat, remove it from the engine and place it in a pan of water. Put the pan on the stove on high heat and bring the water to a boil. The thermostat should be open when the water is hot enough to be boiling. If it does not open, or only opens just a little, the thermostat is bad and must be replaced.

If the thermostat is found to be operating as it should and the system has been flushed recently, check the radiator. Remove the radiator cap and inspect the coolant passages carefully. Look for signs of scale or other evidence of obstruction. Run the engine until warm (at least 190 degrees) and turn off the engine. Carefully feel the radiator and verify that the temperature feels uniform all across the core. If there are large areas that feel cooler, this is a sign of an obstructed core.

If the engine has been modified to produce more power, or if the original engine has been replaced with a larger engine, the factory radiator may be too small. Another consideration is that a previous owner replaced the radiator with an improper version. If the radiator is too small for the engine, the engine will warm up normally and slowly heat up until the engine overheats. The system may cool the engine adequately at idle, and perhaps even at low-speed cruising. Once hot, however, it will not be able to recover. Unless a larger factory radiator is available, the only cure is to replace your car's radiator with a high-capacity aftermarket model. Aluminum radiators work well. Copper is better at conducting heat, but aluminum tubes are stronger and allow the use of larger-diameter tubing, which provide better heat transfer.

A larger engine requires more radiator surface area to properly cool the engine. A larger engine generates more heat, and this extra heat has to be removed. This is simple physics. Most automobile engines, regardless of size, are about the same efficiency. In most conditions, a larger engine will generate more heat for the cooling system to get rid of than a smaller one.

Also bear in mind that the cooling passages in the radiator will constrict and plug over time. Part of this is due to deposits from the water and some is due to deposits from the antifreeze additives that turn to gunk as the coolant ages. Cooling system flushes will help but not prevent this from happening. Eventually, the vehicle will begin to exhibit overheating problems. The cooling system on a daily driver will typically last 8 to 10 years before these deposits become significant enough to cause overheating.

When the problem is radiator deposits, the easiest solution is to replace the radiator.

If replacement is not an economical option, a good radiator shop can disassemble and rod the core to clean out the deposits. They can also straighten any bent fins and fix leaks. Cleaning and repairing the radiator is a good option for brass radiators or aluminum radiators with removable plastic tanks such as those found in most new vehicles. Custom aluminum aftermarket radiators are typically welded in place and will cost more to have cleaned and rebuilt.

LOW-SPEED COOLING PROBLEMS

If the vehicle overheats in stop-and-go traffic and runs cool while cruising down the highway, airflow is the problem. First check if the fan shroud is present. If the shroud is missing, the fan will not be able to pull the maximum air through the radiator. Also ensure that the fan and shroud are matched. Most fans will move the maximum air through the radiator if the shroud only covers the forward third of the fan blade. To put this another way, picture a fan mounted to the front of an engine, with a shroud ahead of it. If we slowly move the engine forward until the first third of the fan blade is within the shroud, leaving the rear two thirds of the blade unaffected by the shroud, it will allow air to spill off of the blade more efficiently, enabling the fan to move more air. If the fan is completely inside the shroud, the air exiting from the blade edges will be blocked and airflow will be reduced.

Electric cooling fans usually do not work well on big-block engines. They simply do not move enough air to keep the engine cool at low speeds. This is because most electric fans are designed for smaller displacement engines. Electric fans with enough airflow to cool a big block can be obtained from dedicated cooling specialists, such as aluminum radiator vendors. Also note that most flex fans will not move enough air to cool a big block. The factory fan and fan clutch are usually the best solution. If you use aftermarket cooling accessories, be sure they are up to handling your big block's horsepower output and displacement.

Bear in mind that electric fans capable of cooling a big block, especially if it has air conditioning, draw 30 to 50 amps of power. This is most likely more current than your stock alternator puts out. If you plan on running electric fans on your muscle car, you need to plan on upgrading your charging system as well.

Do not use electric cooling fans that were designed for a smaller engine. These will not move enough air to cool your big block. The cooling fan size will be roughly proportional to the engine size. So your 7.5-liter big block will require almost four times the airflow of one that will cool a 2.0-liter four cylinder!

When testing low-speed cooling performance, make sure you test the worst-case scenario. This would be stopped in traffic on a hot day. Now make this worse by adding a light breeze of 10 to 15 mph blowing in the same direction the car is facing. This creates interference with the fan as it tries to move air across the radiator. If the vehicle has air conditioning, turn this on as well. Doing all these things at once will require the maximum fan performance.

HIGH-SPEED COOLING PROBLEMS

For high-speed overheating, again check airflow through the radiator, except now it is usually not the fan and shroud combination that is at fault, but vehicle aerodynamics. Air always enters the engine compartment from in front of the radiator, but at higher speeds the fan shroud can actually interfere with the total airflow through the radiator. Also, air can be trapped in the engine compartment. This will limit the flow of fresh air into the engine compartment and will also interfere with airflow across the radiator.

Several solutions exist if airflow is insufficient. The shroud itself can be modified to provide a shroud that is round and extends to the radiator, leaving the radiator core area outside the shroud open. This removes the shroud from the airflow restriction.

Old muscle cars are not very aerodynamic, and at higher speeds, not enough air will flow through the radiator due to pressure building up under the hood. One cure for this is to add an air dam under the radiator. A 4-inch dam works nicely, and placing it under the radiator ensures that it will not only function properly, but be far enough back that it should clear most parking blocks. The air dam works by preventing air from flowing back behind the radiator, and helps to create a low-pressure area behind the air dam, thereby pulling the air from the engine compartment and through the radiator when the vehicle is moving. Several muscle cars did have primitive air dams when new, but after 30 years most have been removed (by accident or on purpose).

CHAPTER 8
EXHAUST SYSTEM

Exhaust modification is the most subjective topic covered in this book. Each of us has our own idea of how a muscle car should sound. Keep in mind that overly loud exhaust notes make the stereo hard to hear on the highway and are rarely popular with your neighbors. With loud pipes, those 11:00 PM runs to the market can be annoying.

On the flip side, a high-performance exhaust system can yield excellent performance gains without affecting drivability. Unlike a hot cam, a free-flowing exhaust system will only enhance the performance of the vehicle while leaving drivability unaffected.

EXHAUST MANIFOLDS

For stock vehicles or restorations, factory equipment manifolds may be the only way to go. Manifolds usually seal better than headers. They are also quieter; manifolds do not have that hollow "tsh tsh" sound of headers. Also, manifolds contribute less underhood heat than headers.

This is not to imply that manifolds don't have problems. They crack or warp with age. Since they are usually made of cast iron, repairing a crack will require an experienced welder who knows how to spray-weld cast iron.

If a manifold is only slightly warped, the sealing surface may be able to be milled flat. Severely warped manifolds can affect how one or more of the ports line up with the head and will have to be replaced.

Most vehicles came with cast-iron manifolds. They are usually long-lasting and quiet. They are not the most efficient way to extract the exhaust from your engine. One item to notice: Look at how the factory-installed heat shields keep the heat away from other items under the hood.

Nothing beats a good set of headers and a free-flowing exhaust system for an easy horsepower addition. These are ceramic-coated headers and have been in service for eight years.

EXHAUST SYSTEM

Finding a replacement iron manifold is not as easy as it used to be. Before purchasing a used manifold inspect it carefully. Check the port sealing surfaces with a straightedge, looking for warped surfaces. Check the exhaust pipe connection to be sure that it is smooth. Check all bolt holes to make sure that they are not stripped. Finally, check for cracks.

HEADERS

Upgrading to a good set of headers will enhance both performance and mileage. If the headers are ceramic coated, they will last for years. Headers work by allowing the exhaust gases to flow more easily out of the cylinders. The length and diameter of the primary tubes define the rpm range where the headers are most efficient. Smaller-diameter tubes promote higher rate of exhaust gas flow at lower rpms, while large-diameter tubes work best at high rpms.

To pick the right headers, the engine package must be considered. For large-displacement engines with a high-lift camshaft, large diameter headers are the way to go. For small-displacement engines with a stock or mild camshaft, use small diameter headers. If in doubt, talk with your camshaft vendor; they will be able to recommend the proper headers to match your engine's state of tune.

Most headers can be coated with ceramic. Some are even available from the manufacturer with a ceramic coating. Coating the tubes with ceramic will more than double the life of the headers. They also look better. The coatings hold up well. After several years of service, the headers look almost as good as when they were new.

PREVENTING HEADER LEAKS

One problem with headers is exhaust leaks. These can be eliminated by using copper or aluminum gaskets, which will not blow out like a composite exhaust gasket. Also, use grade 8 nuts and bolts to fasten the header to the cylinder head, and don't forget to use lock washers. The heating and cooling cycles can cause the bolts to loosen, so check them at each oil change. Use anti-seize on all bolts, and only tighten or loosen the fasteners when the engine is cold. These steps will help prevent damaged or stripped threads.

DETERMINING EXHAUST SYSTEM SIZE

Exhaust gases travel at approximately 250 feet per second (fps) in the header primary pipe. This rate slows down to about 125 fps in the collector. The collector volume determines the torque characteristics of the engine below the engine's torque peak. So a larger collector volume in the header will add low-end torque. A smaller collector volume will kill low-end torque. A properly placed crossover pipe flows like a larger collector and increases low-end torque.

As a rule of thumb, headers should be sized so that they match up with the rpm at which the engine produces the maximum torque.

$$\text{Primary pipe diameter} = 2 \times \sqrt{\frac{\left[\dfrac{\text{RPM} \times (\text{CID}/\text{CYL})}{88200}\right]}{3.1416}}$$

Using this formula, RPM is the torque peak. CID is the displacement of the engine and CYL is the number of cylinders. Be honest here, if the primary pipes are too big, power will suffer. It is best to round down. D is the diameter of the primary pipe. Note that changing the primary pipe diameter will flatten the torque curve rather than move the torque peak.

For example, if the headers are sized 500 rpm above the engine's torque peak, then the net effect will be a lower peak torque at the torque peak, with the torque curve not falling as fast up to the header size peak. This only works within a reasonable area. For example, if the engine torque peak is at 3,500 rpm, sizing the headers for a 5,500 rpm peak will yield disappointing results. Tuning with the headers works best within a 500 to 1,000 rpm range.

A better way to broaden an engine's torque curve is to use a stepped header. This is a header with the primary pipe made with two (or more) different-diameter

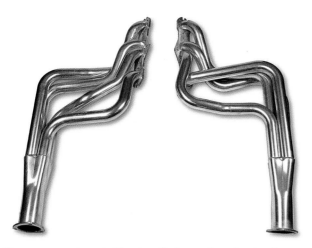

These are ceramic-coated headers. Hooker produces headers for just about any muscle car.

pipe segments. This allows the primary pipe to function across a wider rpm range. Headers like this are usually constructed with the smaller pipe connecting to the exhaust port, then transitioning to a larger diameter pipe 1/3 to 1/2 of the way down.

Once the headers are installed, match the rest of the system appropriately. Begin by sizing the exhaust pipes to match the header collectors. On all big blocks, the exhaust should be no smaller than 2.5 inches. This includes the tail pipes! If the engine makes over 450 horsepower, 3.0-inch pipes should be the minimum. A proper exhaust system will be as invisible as possible to the engine and cause minimal back pressure. Furthermore, if the system is set up correctly, it will help scavenge the system by providing negative pressure waves to the exhaust ports.

Don't buy into the old wives' tale that engines need some back pressure to develop maximum low-speed torque. This is utter nonsense. Maximum power is only achieved when the engine can breathe to its fullest potential. Any back pressure at all interferes with engine breathing.

Don't get the pipes too big, either! You want velocity, not back pressure. The speed of the gas in the pipe will help cylinder scavenging. You want the pipes just right. The table below will help determine the proper pipe size. As with carburetor selection, pipe size should be based on horsepower, not engine size. Also pay attention to the bends; make sure that the bends are made on a mandrel. They should be smooth and the pipe's diameter should remain as close to the original diameter as possible (in other words, do not crush the pipe when you bend it).

$$\text{Duel exhaust pipe diameter} = 2 \times \sqrt{(HP / 288)}$$

$$\text{Single exhaust pipe diameter} = 2 \times \sqrt{(HP / 144)}$$

TABLE 4: EXHAUST PIPE SIZE RECOMMENDATION BASED ON HORSEPOWER

Horsepower	Single Exhaust Diameter (inches)	Dual Exhaust Diameter (inches)
Up to 150	2.00	2.00
150 to 200	2.25	2.00
200 to 300	2.50	2.00
300 to 350	3.00	2.25
350 to 450	3.50	2.50
450 to 650	4.00	3.00

MUFFLERS

Good-quality low-restriction mufflers are vital. The muffler you choose will affect the power output and personality of the car. Be careful here—don't get mufflers that are too loud. The mufflers should be as far back as possible from the crossover pipe. Mufflers are heavy, so be sure to use top-quality hangers.

Mufflers are not usually rated like carburetors, but airflow through the mufflers is just as important. If you want the vehicle to perform as if it has an open exhaust, size the mufflers with this formula:

$$CFM = (2.2 \times HP)$$

HP is the peak horsepower that the engine will develop. So for a 500-horsepower engine, the exhaust system must flow 1,100 CFM at 1.5 inches of mercury (0.75 PSI).

CROSSOVER PIPE

The crossover pipe helps make the exhaust system appear bigger to the engine, as the pressure pulses have two paths to travel. X pipes work better, but they are usually harder to install. Regardless of what style of crossover or X pipe you use, it must be installed the correct distance back from the header collectors to be effective. As a rule of thumb, 12 to 14 inches back from the collectors is a good distance. The overall length from where the primary pipes merge in the collector to the placement of the crossover pipe should be about 18 to 24 inches back.

If you have raced your vehicle and determined the optimum collector length and are now installing an exhaust system, the crossover point should be located as close to the ideal collector length point as possible. The diameter of the collector is critical; it should be approximately 1.75 times the primary tube diameter.

Collector length is critical for maximum performance and placing the crossover or X pipe at the ideal collector termination point will give the headers the effect of the end of the collector. This can be fine-tuned at the drag strip by using just the crossover or X section with a slip joint. Start with a collector length that is too long, say 36 inches, and make runs while sawing 2 inches off of the length until the performance drops off. Then add back the length removed and you are done. Pay attention to the elapsed time as well as the mph. You are not just after peak horsepower here; you also want to broaden the torque curve.

ROUTING EXHAUST COMPONENTS

When routing exhaust pipes, keep them one inch or more from the underbody of the car. The engine will move and the exhaust system will move with it. You don't want the pipes striking the underside of the car, as this will cause an annoying rattle or vibration. Also check the exhaust pipes' clearance from the rear suspension components and the driveshaft. Make sure that as the suspension moves, the control arms, springs, and rear axle do not come too close to the pipes or mufflers.

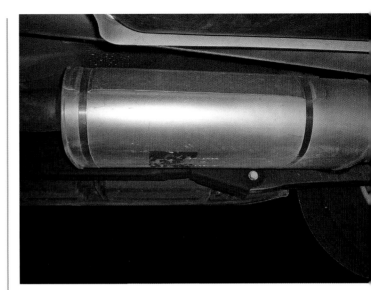

Cadillac Escalade muffler. Notice the size of this thing! Also notice the 3-inch exhaust pipes. The engine in this vehicle is rated at 400 horsepower, and since this is a new car, this rating is with the exhaust flowing through this muffler.

One trick for ensuring proper clearance for the rear axle when using custom tail pipes is to remove the rear springs. For coil spring cars, jack up the vehicle and support the frame with jack stands. Remove the shocks and lower the rear axle. The rear springs will simply fall out. Now place a jack under the rear axle housing and raise the rear axle back up and install the shocks. Now you can raise and lower the rear axle over the full range of travel to verify proper clearance from the exhaust pipes.

Even easier is to take a piece of stiff wire and bend it in a U shape that is as wide as the rear axle tube. Now measure from the bump stop to the frame and then mount the U-shaped wire on the rear axle tube with the curved section 1/2 inch higher above the axle tube than the bump stop is from the frame. For example, with the car up on jack stands, if the top of the bump stop is 12 inches away from the contact point on the frame, mount the U-shaped wire so that it is 12 1/2 inches above the axle housing. Mount this right where the exhaust pipe is passing over the axle. Now check for 2 inches of clearance from the U-shaped wire and the exhaust pipe.

When checking for clearance, don't forget the front and back of the exhaust as well as the top. If the exhaust pipe is too close to the front or rear of the tube, the axle may hit the exhaust pipe even though there is sufficient vertical clearance. Tight clearances can result in damage to the exhaust pipes or to anything mounted to the rear axle. The brake lines for the rear wheels are mounted to the rear axle, usually along the top of the axle tubes or across the rear of the axle tubes. Damage to the brake lines can result if there is insufficient clearance between the axle tube and the exhaust pipe.

Another area to watch is the exhaust pipes that connect the headers to the mufflers. These are usually routed toward the center of the vehicle, close to the driveshaft. As the rear axle moves up and down, the driveshaft does as well. It is imperative to make sure that the driveshaft and exhaust pipes have ample clearance, no less than 2 inches. Watch the mufflers as well.

Headers create several potential areas of interference. When installing headers on certain muscle cars, one or more tubes run extremely close to the steering or suspension. For vehicles where the steering linkage is routed behind the crossmember, it is not uncommon for headers to be fabricated so that one or more tubes are routed around the steering linkage. These headers typically have a removable section for ease of installation.

Also check for interference between the header tubes and the steering shaft. Overly tight clearance

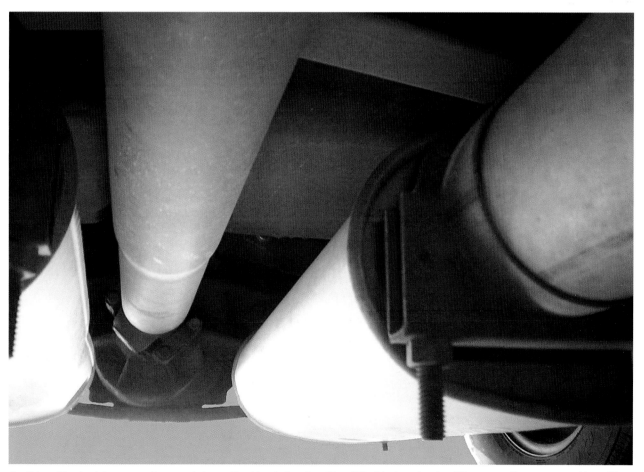

Don't forget to check for proper clearance between the driveshaft and mufflers. This 3-inch system is a little snug on the passenger side muffler.

This 3-inch tailpipe is too close to the rear tire. Notice the rub marks on the pipe where the tire contacts the pipe when the suspension allows the body to move up.

here can cause difficult steering under acceleration. Check for proper clearance with the engine under load. The motor mount will flex, allowing the engine to move. Check for this by using a large pry bar to lift the driver's side of the engine. Verify that the headers do not get within 1 inch of the steering shaft. For steering linkage, consider the engine's torque and the suspension movement.

The clearance between the exhaust and the upper and lower A-arms need to be checked, too. If the header tubes contact the A-arms, they will usually be damaged. Watch out for header tubes that are routed within 1 inch of control arm bushings. The

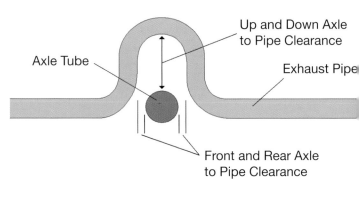

Tailpipe to axle tube clearance.

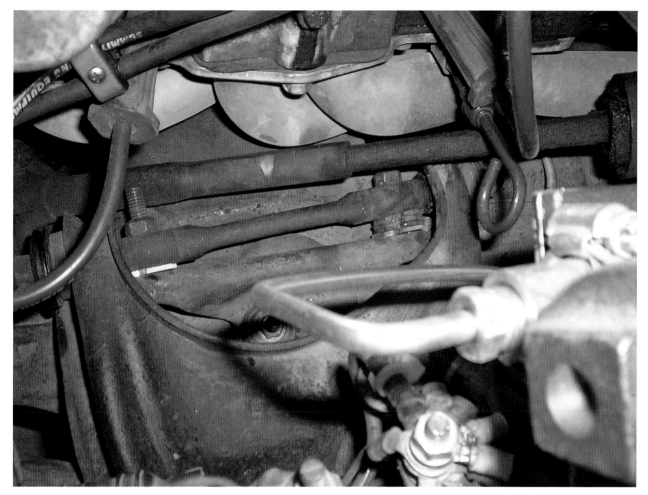

Clearance can be an issue with headers; check carefully around suspension and steering components. These headers clear the steering shaft by a half inch. Also, don't forget that motor mounts can make a difference. With the tight fit, a broken or loose mount may cause problems.

heat can damage the bushings, resulting in shortened bushing life. If clearance is an issue, fabricate a heat shield and place the heat shield an equal distance between the tube and the bushing.

Check the clearance between the header and exhaust pipe and the brake lines. There should be at least 6 inches between any exhaust or header pipe and a brake line, distribution block, or master cylinder. If possible, move the brake line away from the pipe. If the headers are too close to the master cylinder, fabricate a heat shield and place it between the pipe and the master cylinder.

Fuel lines need to be at least 12 inches away from any exhaust pipe or muffler. The fear is not just fuel line

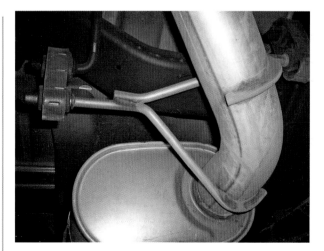

Modern vehicles use tubular steel rods welded to the pipes that are slip fit into a rubber isolation block. This makes factory assembly quick.

This is a terrible way to hang a tailpipe. The muffler shop used a piece of metal that was bolted to the frame with a piece of rubber between the bracket and the frame. Then the clamp was installed in the metal. The holes were even made with a cutting torch!

Tailpipes and exhaust tips should continue at least 2 inches past the bodywork or bumpers. This helps prevent exhaust soot from collecting on the vehicle.

These are two styles of clamps, the U-bolt and band clamp. U-bolt clamps have been around for years. The band clamp is just as effective and usually will fit into a tighter space. This stainless steel band clamp does cost more than the U-bolt style.

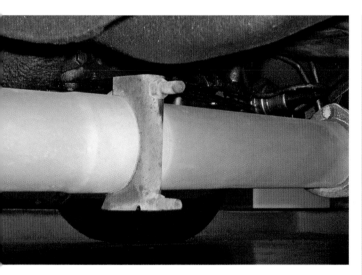

Even though this clamp is oriented properly to provide good ground clearance (not pointing down), it still scrapes on the ground. This is evident because the side of the clamp facing the ground has been slowly ground off due to the occasional contact with speed bumps and peaks on driveways.

damage or fire but also fuel warming and vapor lock. You need to keep the fuel cool by routing lines as far away as possible from any exhaust component. This is especially true if the system has a return line, as the circulating fuel can be slowly heated by the exhaust system if the fuel lines are routed too close to any exhaust system components.

HANGERS

Don't skimp on hangers; they must keep the exhaust components in their proper location as the vehicle travels around corners and goes over bumps. You don't want your exhaust system moving out of position during harsh maneuvers. Excessive movement can rupture seals or gaskets and cause exhaust leaks. Even worse, movement can result in exhaust component failures.

Hangers must have a compliant, sonically dead isolation region to prevent the transmission of exhaust noise into the vehicle. Use hangers with rubber isolation bumpers to prevent the vehicle's body from resonating and vibrating at certain engine speeds.

Using high-quality clamps is also important. While most clamps will perform satisfactorily, there are different types that can make the job look more professional or can solve a clearance issue. Check the clearances of your hangers with the car and the ground, as well. You don't need to be scraping the clamp on the ground over every speed bump.

CHAPTER 9
FUEL SYSTEM

The fuel system (like the cooling system) is one of the most overlooked areas on a muscle car. In most cases the fuel system is either totally stock, or a full-on performance system. Usually, either type of system is inadequate for the true daily driver. If the engine has been modified, chances are good that the fuel system will be unable to meet the fuel demands of the engine. Don't even consider running a nitrous with a stock fuel system.

Be careful when setting up a fuel system. While a racing pump, regulator, and braided lines look trick, most of these high-performance components are not intended for daily operation. The pump motor will quickly burn out when subjected to the rigor of daily

Replace the fuel filter and hoses every 12,000 miles or once a year. A hose failure will result in a fuel leak, the major cause of underhood fires.

operation. This will most certainly leave you stranded on the side of the road. If you use an electric fuel pump, it is a good idea to carry a spare and the tools needed to change the pump.

Also consider ease of replacement when setting up the fuel system. Design the system so that filter and pump changes can be made with a minimum of hassles. Regardless of these concerns, a rear-mounted pump provides the best solution if maximum fuel delivery is the first priority.

Operating pressure is another important factor—limit fuel pressure to reasonable levels or your carburetor will experience fuel creepage and low-speed flooding. For fuel-injected cars, fuel pressure is vital for proper operation and mixture. Also, when running an electric fuel pump, use an oil pressure switch or an ignition monitor to turn the fuel pump off if the engine is not running. For a carbureted street car, limit fuel pressure to no more than 6 psi. Fuel-injected cars should be set according to the factory service manual.

Don't neglect the fuel filter. Carburetors and fuel injectors do not take kindly to dirt. Foreign matter easily clogs small passages, especially in the idle circuit. The needle and seat can be damaged or rendered ineffective by dirt, resulting in flooding. Use a high-quality in-line fuel filter installed right before the carburetor. For electric pumps, a good screen filter should also be installed between the tank and pump to protect the rotors inside the pump. Proper maintenance is required; change the fuel filter(s) every 12,000 miles.

Safety must be considered when modifying or restoring a fuel system. If possible, use only hard line after the fuel pump, as flexible hose can break. Most underhood fires are caused by leaking gasoline.

Avoid using hose for fuel line. If it must be used, keep the length to a minimum and change it every year. Make sure that the hose is routed and properly supported so stress is not placed on any part of the hose, particularly at the ends. If braided hose is used, change it every two years. Braided hose is fairly durable, but the chemical agents in gasoline and the heat of the engine will degrade the hose and it will eventually fail.

DIAGNOSING FUEL SYSTEM PROBLEMS

Even the best-designed fuel system can experience problems with insufficient fuel delivery or problems that are heat-related. The first step is to diagnose the problem. Keep notes. Was the vehicle fully warmed up prior to the problem occurring? At what speeds did the problem occur and how was the vehicle operated just prior to the problem occurring? These notes will help pinpoint the problem.

Vapor lock is a frustrating problem. A daily driver's fuel system must be capable of surviving gridlock on a hot day. Vapor lock occurs when the fuel in the fuel line vaporizes before reaching the fuel pump. This leads to fuel starvation or stalling.

Vapor lock is usually most pronounced at low speeds in stop-and-go traffic. The condition occurs when the fuel in the line before the fuel pump becomes hot enough that the suction of the pump leads to fuel vaporization. This is most likely to occur at low speeds, when heat from the engine and exhaust system warms the underside of the vehicle. At higher speeds, airflow around the vehicle will usually keep the fuel line cool enough to prevent vapor lock.

Do not confuse vapor lock with vapor spewing. This problem is also heat-related, but the hot gasoline vaporizes when it exits the high-pressure fuel line into the atmospheric pressure fuel bowl. Once exposed to the lower pressure, the fuel vaporizes and spews from the bowl vents into the air cleaner. This results in an extremely rich fuel mixture. The effects on performance can range from a mild bog to a complete loss of power. One telltale sign of vapor spewing is that the exhaust will emit black smoke while the mixture is rich (have a friend follow the vehicle to check this). If the problem is vapor lock, there will be no visible exhaust smoke, as there is no combustion taking place due to a lack of fuel.

Here is a fuel pump with a return line. The return line is the smaller fitting on the pump, in this case 1/4 inch.

Another common problem is hot soak. This results in a car that is hard to start after sitting for a short time. Just like fuel delivery problems, this one is also heat-related. For nonreturn fuel systems, when the vehicle is turned off, the heat from the engine warms the carburetor and the fuel in the fuel bowls. This can lead to fuel slowly boiling and filling the air cleaner as well as the intake manifold with gasoline vapors. This floods the engine and makes the car extremely difficult to restart. The throttle typically must be fully depressed while cranking the engine to get the car to restart. This condition can be worsened if the heat from the engine causes the fuel pressure in the fuel line to rise enough that the needle valve in the carburetor is overcome, and additional fuel is pumped into the fuel bowl. In extreme cases, this excess fuel overfills the bowl and drains directly into the engine!

Before assuming a hot soak problem, operate the vehicle until it is good and warm, and then shut the vehicle off. Wait the time that usually passes for the problem to appear. Open the hood, remove the air cleaner, and check to see if the choke is trying to close. Feel the manifold and cylinder heads—if these are warm the choke must be fully open (choke is off). Lightly open the throttle and verify that the choke does not close at all. If the choke does not remain fully open, correct the choke problem prior to trying to fix

the hot soak problem. The choke problem will usually be more pronounced in cold weather.

Fortunately, none of these problems are difficult to solve. The stock vehicle had considerable engineering to ensure that these problems were kept to a minimum. Most manufacturers performed testing at temperature extremes to ensure that their products would not have these types of problems. But that was the stock fuel system, and it is probably a fair assumption that your fuel system is no longer factory stock.

One likely culprit is exhaust components routed to close to the fuel system. The factory fuel setup accounted for the stock exhaust, and any deviation may result in excess heat affecting the fuel system. The factory's first line of defense from excessive fuel heating was component placement; ensure that fuel lines are routed as far as possible from any exhaust or cooling system components. The goal is to minimize heating the fuel. Pay attention to the airflow from the radiator. Try to minimize fuel line exposure to the warm air blown from the fan.

The next line of defense is to add a fuel return from the pressurized side of the fuel system. Most factory air-conditioned cars used some sort of fuel return to combat vapor lock and hot soak. This seems counter-intuitive, but it works by keeping fuel circulating in the lines, which minimizes time for the fuel to be excessively heated. A fuel return results in a reduced tendency for vapor lock or fuel spewing. The return line also eliminates fuel line pressure when the vehicle is turned off, thus minimizing hot soak problems.

To check if your muscle car originally had a fuel return line, check for a 1/4-inch line at the tank, usually next to the fuel line from the tank. To connect the return, the factory either used a fuel pump with a smaller return line (GM applications) or a fuel filter with a return line (Chrysler applications). For custom fuel systems, the Chrysler fuel filters allow an easy way to get the return fuel. Also, a custom return can be fabricated that flows fuel through a 0.0625-inch orifice back to the fuel tank. Install a tee fitting in the line between the fuel pump and the carburetor, and run the line back to the tank from there. This will allow fuel to circulate, which will keep it cooler than if it were just sitting in the line. Watch the placement of the filter and return line, as the goal is to minimize the heating of the fuel. The worst place for the fuel filter is in the hot air stream from the fan, which is typically where the factory placed it.

If a fuel pressure regulator is used, connect the return line after the regulator. This will allow the regulator to provide a more realistic pressure to the carburetor, as the regulator will "see" the fuel return as additional fuel demanded by the engine. Setting the fuel pressure will be easier due to less pressure creepage. A final benefit will be that the regulator will run cooler, as fuel will always be circulating through the regulator.

If your fuel system did not originally have a return line, you can add one. You can obtain a fuel tank that has the appropriate fittings, or you can add them yourself. Finding a factory tank with the appropriate fittings will usually require that you contact one of the many suppliers of restoration parts. When searching for the appropriate tank, remember that the air-conditioned big-block cars usually had the return line.

To add a line, attach it to the gas gauge sending unit. Drain and remove the fuel tank. Always keep the tank on a concrete floor, as this will minimize the danger of sparks from static electricity. Before touching any tool to the tank, touch the concrete with the tool immediately before contacting the tank. If the tank must be worked on above the floor, connect a heavy copper wire to the tank and then to a good ground. The idea here is to prevent static buildup. You must discharge yourself and any tools prior to touching the tank.

Next, remove the sending unit. This will require a brass sending unit spanner or wrench. I do not recommend using a steel or iron tool to remove the sending unit as either can spark when striking the steel retaining ring. Sparks are the one thing that must be avoided when working around a gas tank. Don't assume

that washing or boiling out the tank will eliminate the explosion hazard; gasoline vapors will still be present. Never use any type of welding or brazing equipment or any electrical tool around a fuel tank as the sparks created by them can cause an explosion.

You can either order a replacement sending unit (one from a model that has a return line) or you can add the return line to the sending unit you already have. The latter is a simple procedure. First remove the filter (sock) from the fuel line. Thoroughly wash the sending unit to remove as much residual gasoline as possible. Verify that the sending unit float is empty. A small leak in the float can fill it and cause erroneous fuel gauge readings. Thoroughly dry the sending unit.

Study the top of the sending unit assembly and pick a suitable location to mount a return line fitting. Secure a length of 1/4-inch steel tubing, drill a tight clearance hole through the sending unit top, and braze the line into place. You can have an experienced welder or radiator shop perform this task. Just make sure that you inform them that this is a fuel sending unit and that it has been in a gasoline tank. Make sure that the return line is routed down to the bottom of the tank, and route the inlet to run parallel with the fuel feed line. Slightly flare the end to facilitate clamping the fuel return hose.

Next, a return line must be routed from the engine to the tank. Route a 1/4-inch steel return line next to the fuel feed line. Mount it securely to the frame. Ensure that the line will not rub against any other objects, and make sure it is not in contact with any sharp edges or corners. At the tank end, route the line so that it is in a straight line with the return line fitting at the tank. Stop the hard line 1 inch from the tank fitting. A short piece of 1/4-inch fuel hose will be required to make the connection; this is to allow for vibration and movement of the tank. At the end of the line that terminates in the engine compartment, securely mount the end of the return line near the filter or fuel pump. Use a short section of 1/4-inch fuel hose to make the connection to the filter or fuel pump return barb. Both sections of hose must be changed every two years.

If the return line does not eliminate the heat-related fuel problems, insulate the fuel lines and fuel filter, especially those mounted at the front of the vehicle. The fuel leading to the fuel pump must be cool, which is another reason that the fuel pump should be at the rear of the vehicle in an all-out performance vehicle. This isn't vital on modestly modified cars if you carefully route your fuel lines. I have seen several 11-second street cars that were equipped with front-mounted factory or aftermarket mechanical pumps.

FUEL STARVATION

Fuel starvation is another problem with modified engines. This condition results when the engine's power output rises above the fuel system's ability to supply fuel. Keep in mind that as power is increased, more fuel is required. The stock system has limitations—if enough modifications are made the vehicle will run lean while accelerating. If you use a power adder such as nitrous oxide, don't even think about using the stock fuel system. Most stock muscle car fuel systems are adequate for engines that produce 400 horsepower or less.

To feed your modified engine, you need to determine how much fuel you need. Fuel pumps are rated for output measured in gallons per hour (gph). Most engines will consume about 0.5 pounds of fuel per hour for every horsepower produced. Assuming that gasoline weighs 6.33 pounds per gallon, a 400-horsepower engine will need a fuel supply capable of delivering 31.6 gph to the engine.

Now consider that all fuel pumps on the market are rated with no load. Your stock pump's 50 gph rating may seem like it will supply enough fuel, but this is the amount it can supply through an open line with no resistance. This is not how much fuel it is capable of supplying when dealing with the fuel lines, filters, and needle and seat of the carburetor. You need a pump that can supply enough fuel at a

high enough pressure to ensure that you get enough fuel into the carburetor float bowl. This usually means that your fuel system must be able to hold 4 to 6 psi pressure at the carburetor with the needle valve fully open. The following formula will help you determine how much fuel your engine will need.

$$GPH = \frac{(HP \times 0.5)}{6}$$

So how do you go about picking a pump? Most experts will agree you need a pump capable of handling two times the computed needs at the desired inlet pressure when measured at the carburetor. For our 400-horsepower example above, the engine needs 31.6 gph of fuel at 5 to 6 psi at the carburetor. Therefore the pump should deliver 63 gph at 6 psi. But remember, pump flow numbers are usually rated at zero pressure, so the safe bet is to select a pump that is rated at five times what the formula shows you need.

For a 400-horsepower engine, this means the pump should flow 158 gph (31.6 x 5), so a pump with a minimum rating of 160 gph should be considered. Most pumps that are capable of supplying over 80 gph will also have an outlet pressure of more than 6 psi when the vehicle is not using a large amount of fuel. This means a pressure regulator must be used. For high-horsepower applications (more than 400 hp), use a bypass-style regulator. This style returns excess fuel to the tank. But a bypass regulator may also require a fuel cooler to prevent heating the fuel in the tank. Install the cooler in the return line, after the regulator. Mount the cooler in front of the radiator and any other coolers.

For fuel-injected engines, the pump must be able to supply fuel while maintaining 30 to 50 psi fuel pressure throughout the system. Fuel-injection fuel pumps are rated the same as regular fuel pumps, at no load or output pressure. So the same rules apply: the pump should be rated to flow more than the vehicle needs. Also, the higher the deadhead pressure, the more efficient the pump is.

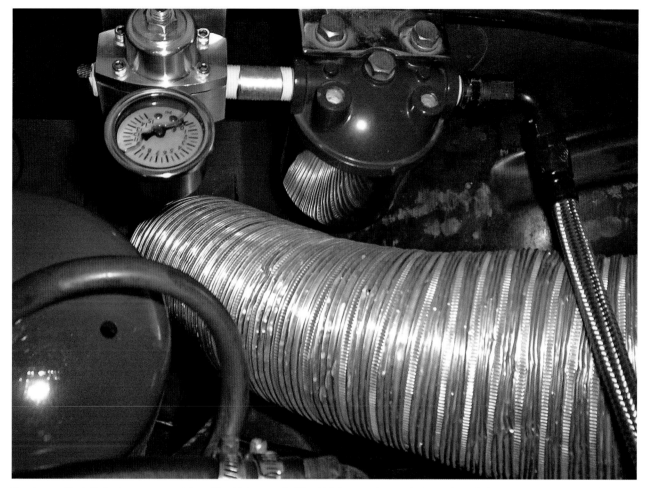

Here is an adjustable fuel pressure regulator with a high-capacity filter. This is a restrictor style; it regulates fuel pressure by closing down the opening in the regulator as the pressure rises to the set point. The fuel enters the regulator from the bottom and then flows to the filter and finally to the carburetor by the braided line.

Most pumps will not advertise their deadhead (no flow) pressure rating.

To set up a good high-performance fuel system, mount an electric fuel pump back by the fuel tank. Run a 3/8-inch steel fuel line from the pump up to the engine compartment. Route this line away from the exhaust and suspension components. Also, make sure that the line is properly secured. Connect this line to a good-quality high-flow filter and then to a pressure regulator. Now tee the fuel line from the stock fuel pump and use a piece of braided hose to connect the tee to the outlet of the pressure regulator (as with all fuel-line hose, this piece needs to be replaced every two years). This completes the plumbing.

Next, the electrical power for the pump can be connected. Install a ring terminal on the negative wire for the pump and connect this to the frame. Run a 12-gauge wire from the positive terminal on the pump up to the engine compartment. Protect the wire in a plastic sleeve and mount it securely to the vehicle. Keep the wire away from the exhaust, driveline, and suspension components. Mount a relay under the hood and connect the positive wire from the pump to one of the relay's contact terminals.

Run another 12-gauge wire from the relay's other contact terminal either to the main junction or directly to the battery. The main junction block is the point in the electrical system from which battery power is tapped for all of the vehicle's accessories. On some cars, this is the starter solenoid, on others it can be at the positive battery terminal. The wire must have a 20-amp fuse installed in it. Do not skip the fuse. Connect one of the relay coil wires to a fused power feed that is hot when the ignition switch is on. Ground the other coil lead.

FUEL TYPES

The fluctuations in gasoline prices have created a renewed interest in alternative fuel sources. One of these is E85. This is a blend of gasoline (15%) and ethanol (85%). This fuel has a bright spot for performance automobiles; namely, it has a higher octane than gasoline.

As with any alternative product, there are good points and bad points. First, the good points. E85 burns cleaner than gasoline, and E85 has a higher octane level that allows for higher compression.

Now the bad points. Since E85 is made from corn, it is available mainly in the Midwest, where corn is grown. Also, since this is a relatively new product, the production and distribution infrastructure is not fully established. Therefore, availability, even in the Midwestern states, is spotty. The BTU content is lower, so you must burn more of it to travel the same distance. Finally, the federal government and some state governments are subsidizing E85 right now, but this could change at any moment, resulting in higher prices for ethanol.

Below is a table that shows octane ratings for E85, straight ethanol, methanol, and gasoline. Note that the octane number shown is for premium gasoline that is available in Texas. Also, the energy content for all of the fuels is also shown. As for fuel mileage, expect a 25 to 30 percent drop in fuel economy when running E85. This means that you will use 1.4 times as much E85 as you would conventional gasoline.

TABLE 5: FUEL COMPARISON CHART

	Octane	BTU	Fuel mixture ratios	
			Stoichiometric	Power
Gasoline	93	114,000	14.7:1	12.5:1
E85	103	83,000	9.7:1	6.9:1
Ethanol	115	76,000	9.0:1	6.0:1
Methanol	119	57,000	6.45:1	4.5:1

You can make up for some of the economic loss by increasing the compression ratio. Increasing the compression to 11.5:1 will increase combustion efficiency, thereby offsetting some of the loss due to the lower BTU content. Also, this will increase the engine's power output.

Due to the changes in the mixture ratios, your carburetor or fuel injection will have to be calibrated to run E85. This is not a minor jet change. The volume increase is about 30%, and this may require that the internal passages in the carburetor be modified as well. Also, your power valve circuitry will need to be modified; the step up for full power is also increased for E85 over gasoline. If this is not set correctly, when the full power mixture is correct, the light load mixture will be too rich.

SELECTING A CARBURETOR

Selecting a carburetor is not hard. First, consider what type of engine you are building. If you are interested in a period-correct restoration, you will have to search for an old carburetor that is rebuildable. Most muscle car original equipment carburetors are no longer available new. This is especially true for OEM carburetors, like the Rochester and Autolite carburetors. For cars that used Holley or Carter carburetors, you have a much better chance of finding a new model that is similar to the original carburetor. The exception

This is the famous Holley 4150 series "double pumper." These have mechanical secondaries with accelerator pumps for the primary and secondary sides, hence the name "double pumper."

here is the Carter Thermo-Quad that was used on several Chrysler products. These have been out of production for several years now.

For higher-performance engines, an aftermarket carburetor is required. It is important to select the proper size and type to mach your engine. For starters, the carburetor needs to be the proper size. Do not select a carburetor that is too big, or low-speed responsiveness will suffer. Also, if the carburetor is excessively too big, even high-rpm power levels will be down, even if the mixture is correct, due to poor atomization.

Watch the type of gasket that is used on your manifold. For an open intake like this, don't run a gasket that is exposed to any part of the opening. It will slowly deteriorate, dropping gasket parts into the intake (and the engine!).

Selecting the correct carburetor size is easy. There is the old tried and true formula:

$$CFM = \frac{(CID \times rpm)}{3,456}$$

CFM is the carburetor size (the amount of fuel-air mixture it will flow), CID is the displacement of the engine in cubic inches, and rpm is the engine rpm at maximum horsepower. This formula will select a carburetor that will not be oversized. Notice that the efficiency multiplier has been omitted. This is because most modern true performance engines will approach 100% VE at peak torque. For stock engines with small camshafts and older original-equipment cylinder heads, multiply the results by 0.8:

$$CFM = \frac{(CID \times rpm \times .08)}{3,456}$$

There is a more accurate way to select a carburetor. This formula uses power, not engine size or rpm. For a naturally aspirated gasoline engine, the following formula should be used. Do not include the added horsepower of a nitrous system in these calculations as the additional oxygen and fuel is supplied by the nitrous system.

$$CFM = HP \times 1.4$$

CFM is the carburetor size and HP is the peak engine power in horsepower. This formula relies on the fact that horsepower requires fuel, and a good rule of thumb is .49

Don't run this type of gasket on an open-plenum manifold.

pounds of gasoline per hour per horsepower. Now that the fuel required can be found, the airflow must be the proper ratio in order to develop maximum horsepower. This means that the airflow for a given horsepower is the same, regardless of the engine size.

Since the calculations will almost never exactly match an available carburetor size, round up or down to the closest available size. If you are building a high-performance engine, err on the larger size, as a carburetor that is slightly too big will benefit maximum horsepower by minimizing the pumping loss as the air flows through the carburetor. Notice the "slightly" in slightly larger; don't use a 1,050 CFM dominator if the calculations show that a 730 CFM

Other items to consider are screws that are exposed to the plenum. If one of these were to come loose and fall into the intake, that would most certainly spell disaster.

Using a heat shield has a secondary benefit; it will also ensure that any bolts on the underside of the carburetor are prevented from entering the intake if they happen to work loose.

carburetor is required; instead, round up to the next available size, or 750 CFM.

Selecting a carburetor that is too large will result in sluggish performance and poor low-speed response. Also, if the carburetor is too big, once the throttles are opened to the horsepower potential of the engine, any further increase in opening will have little to no effect. Finally, if the carburetor is too large, fuel atomization may suffer, resulting in a reduction in horsepower.

Always use two return springs, and, if possible, mount them to different locations. This ensures that you will always have at least one spring in the event of a failure.

Be sure that your carburetor linkage and throttle cable match. Also, the cable (or rod) is usually retained by a special clip; don't lose it!

By using a small funnel attached to one of the bowl vents, the carburetor can be prefilled with gasoline prior to starting. This saves wear and tear on the starter. Don't go overboard: You need only a half cup to get the engine started.

Don't forget to properly install the carburetor. Pay attention to the linkage; make sure it moves freely and does not bind. Always use two return springs, and if possible, anchor each spring to a different point. Also, use the correct gasket. Don't use a full gasket on an open plenum. Once installed, verify that the throttles open and close properly, with no signs of binding. Next, verify that the carburetor is fully open when the accelerator is floored, and when the accelerator is released, that the throttles close properly.

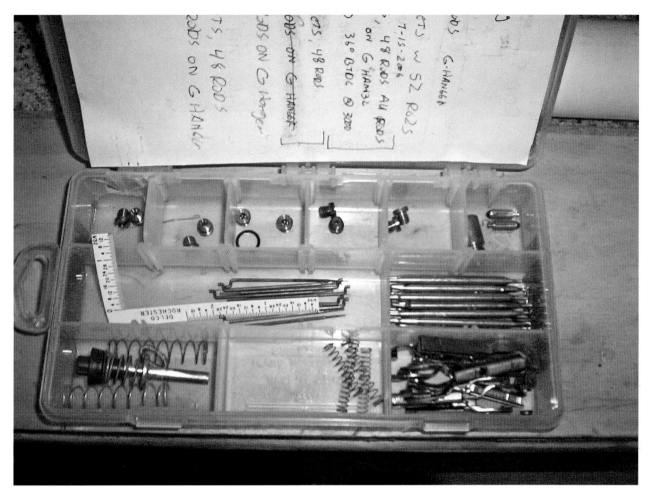

You will need metering components such as jets and metering rods to tune your carb. Also, keep notes that show your current setup. Besides jets, you should have accelerator pump parts and different power valves (or power valve springs).

After the carburetor is installed, prime the float bowls prior to starting. This will save wear and tear on your starter. If you have an electric fuel pump, switch the pump on and check for fuel leaks. If you have a mechanical pump, you will have to fill the fuel bowls through one of the vents.

CALIBRATING YOUR CARBURETOR

This is one of the most important aspects if you expect your car to run properly. This includes cruising as well as full-throttle operation. Properly tuning and jetting a carburetor is a slowly dying art. It is not that difficult, with the primary requirement that you keep good notes and most importantly, *only make one change at a time*! If you change two or more things, you'll never know which change had what result. Then the following three things can happen:

1. Both changes result in a performance decrease, but you don't know how much performance each one cost you.

2. Both changes result in a performance increase, but you don't know which one had what amount of effect.

3. One change results in an increase, one change results in a decrease, so you think that both changes had no effect and therefore you lose the benefits that the positive change could have given you.

First, obtain a book that details how to set up and

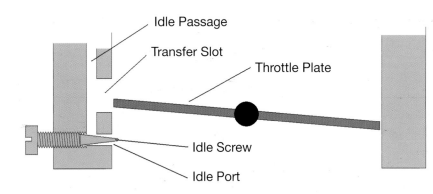

Idle Passage

Transfer Slot

Throttle Plate

Idle Screw

Idle Port

These are the key idle discharge points, the transfer slot, and the idle port.

tune your carburetor. There are several good books for all of the muscle car–era carburetors. These books go into great detail on what changes to make to solve the various problems that you are likely to encounter. For that reason, this book will only outline the basic procedure and not get too deep into the actual changes that will work best for your carburetor. Also, I strongly recommend that if you are anticipating a major change, such as a camshaft or intake manifold, that the carburetor tuning be done after the change is made.

The order in which you make changes is just as important. First, get the vehicle to idle. This will make the engine easier to work on. The second is the WOT (wide open throttle) mixture. Don't even mess with cruise or off idle until the WOT mixture is correct. Third is cruise, and this may require that the WOT be re-checked. Last is off-idle, and this may affect cruise. Also understand how the idle circuit overlaps and provides part of the fuel during off-idle and low-speed cruise speeds. For engine speeds between 1,000 and 1,800 rpm during low engine loads, both the idle and main jets play a large part in setting the proper mixture.

Before you begin, you will need jets for your carburetor; without jets, you cannot change the mixture. Depending on your carburetor, you may need metering rods or power valves in order to set the cruise mixture. You also need some way to evaluate the changes. The best is an engine dyno, where the operator can make a pull and show you the horsepower. If you don't have a dyno, then a drag strip is the next best option. Make two back-to-back passes and average the

This shows the idle discharge port and the transfer slot. This carburetor also has air bypass ports.

mph at the end of the run. Don't use elapsed time, as this is affected by tire slippage. The mph indicates horsepower, so use the mph. Do not change any other aspect of the tune, such as ignition timing.

NOTES ON FUEL ECONOMY

This section is being written while premium unleaded gas is selling at $4.00 a gallon here in Austin, Texas. While your big-block muscle car will never get 20+ mpg in town or 30+ mpg on the highway, it can be made to do better than it did when it was new. First, consider that all cars get 0 mpg when idling, and your 450 CID big block will use 3.5 to 4.5 times the fuel as a 2.0-liter engine while idling. This is assuming that it is not running an aggressive cam and that the carburetor is properly tuned. Also, if the idle speed is increased,

The screwdriver is pointing to the idle-speed-adjusting hole that has been drilled in the primary throttle plate. This allows the throttles to keep most of the transfer slot covered while at idle.

this number will only go up. So for a start, the engine is using roughly four times the fuel as an economy car. Things do get better once you get moving, but this baseline fuel consumption is always present.

Exactly what is the reason for the increased baseline fuel consumption? For starters, consider the pumping loss while the throttles are closed or nearly closed and the engine is developing vacuum. The energy required to pull the piston down against this vacuum is not recovered on the compression stroke. For a 7.5-liter big block, this is 3.75 times as much energy as a 2.0-liter engine! Also, the frictional loss is greater for the big block than for the smaller engine. Bearing surfaces are larger and the piston-to-

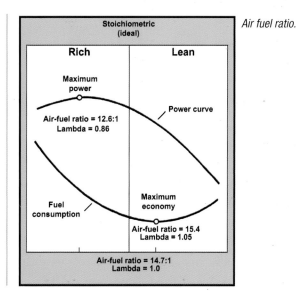

Air fuel ratio.

Stoichiometric (ideal)

Rich   Lean

Maximum power

Power curve

Air-fuel ratio = 12.6:1
Lambda = 0.86

Fuel consumption

Maximum economy

Air-fuel ratio = 15.4
Lambda = 1.05

Air-fuel ratio = 14.7:1
Lambda = 1.0

wall contact area is greater. Together, these add up to increased baseline fuel consumption. Now when you add in the extra power required to accelerate and move the heavier car, you lose again!

IDLE SPEED AND MIXTURE

This should be done first, as the jet changes will have minimal effect. Verify that the idle mixture screws can roll the rpm down both rich and lean. If not, verify that the throttles are not too far open by removing the carburetor and ensuring that no more than 1/3 of the transfer slot is uncovered. If it is, back off the idle speed screw. Re-install the carburetor and re-check the mixture screws. If the engine will not idle, note if the screws have any effect at all. If not, then you will need to perform surgery on your idle circuit before you attempt to set the idle speed. This is not recommended without a good blueprint manual for your carburetor. It is not difficult, but you will need to follow the instructions or you could end up with a car that is too rich at cruise.

SETTING THE IDLE SPEED

Begin by removing the carburetor and setting the idle speed so that the throttle plates uncover 1/4 of the transfer slot, no more. Now re-install the carburetor and start the engine. If the idle speed is too slow, the carburetor will need bypass holes drilled through the throttle plates. Before performing this, check the cruise mixture, and if you are going to provide bypass air, then this should be done instead of drilling holes through the throttle plates. Also, some carburetors, such as the Demon series and the Carter AFB, have idle air bypass screws that are used instead of drilling holes in the throttle plates. On these carburetors, set the idle mixture screw to uncover no more than 1/3 of the transfer slots. Then use the bypass screw to set the idle speed.

If your carburetor needs bypass holes, start small, usually a 1/8-inch hole to begin with. Drill this hole in each primary throttle plate, halfway between the throttle shaft and the idle needle and transfer slot. Retest, and if the idle speed is OK, you are done. If it is too slow, then increase the size of each hole by 1/16 of an inch. Don't get the holes too big or the idle speed will be too high. Get the idle speed close and then adjust the idle speed with the throttle opening, but do not allow more than 1/3 of the transfer slot to be uncovered.

Once this is complete, the idle speed will be correct and the transfer slots will be properly related to the throttle plates. This is important if you expect to have crisp throttle response. Again, if carburetor surgery is required, make sure that you have a good book that details how to set up your carburetor. Changes like these are usually hard to undo, but when done correctly, they can tame all but the wildest camshafts. If the idle is rough, don't drill the holes to obtain the correct idle speed until you have read the next section.

IDLE CONSIDERATIONS

A common problem is that cars with large camshafts have to be set rich at idle so that the car will keep running. As the engine speed increases, the mixture goes extremely rich because the engine vacuum is increasing. Most engines, even with large cams, will easily pull 16 to 18 inches at 2,000 rpm, even though the engine may idle at 900 rpm at 11 inches or less. You can see that to get the mixture rich enough with a low vacuum signal is surely going to result in too much fuel flow at light-throttle cruising when the vacuum goes higher.

The reason the idle performance is so poor is due to what the large camshaft is doing to the engine at idle. First, the piston speed is slow. As the exhaust stroke finishes up, the intake valve opens. Since performance camshafts have a large amount of overlap, and because the exhaust velocity is slow, as the piston starts back down on the intake stroke, it actually pulls some of the exhaust back into the cylinder. Next, with the large overlap, while the intake and exhaust valves are both open, the vacuum in the intake manifold actually pulls some of the exhaust back into the intake, further diluting the mixture and lowering the intake vacuum. This also decreases the signal that the carburetor sees. Finally, at the end of the intake stroke, the piston starts up on the compression stroke and pushes some of the charge back into the intake manifold.

Because of the items mentioned above, the vacuum is low and the signal that the idle circuit is presented with is low. To get the engine to idle, the idle circuit has to be modified or adjusted to flow enough fuel. Unfortunately, this results in the engine going excessively rich once the engine speed is increased. Be careful if modifications are made that increase the size of the idle feed restrictions. If changes like this are required, make them in extremely small increments, just enough to get the idle correct. Modifications such as these can result in the engine going too rich at cruising speeds, resulting in poor fuel economy and excessive exhaust emissions. Again, before making such changes have a good manual in hand that describes how to modify your carburetor. For a large camshaft, shoot for a 13.5:1 air-fuel mixture during idle.

Once the ideal cruise mixture is attained, the transition point must be found. This is the vacuum where the mixture starts to richen up. For this, set up a vacuum gauge so that the idle and cruise vacuum can be monitored. The cut-in point should be 2 inches lower than either of these. You don't want the power circuit kicking in during idle or cruise. Once the cruise mixture is set properly, fuel economy will be maximized and emissions will be low. Don't eliminate the power valve or enrichment circuit; the car will be too rich during cruise. Take the time to set these up correctly and you will be rewarded with a car that is responsive, does not foul its plugs, and gets the best possible mileage. A side benefit is that the cylinders will not be washed clean with excessive fuel while cruising; therefore the oil will stay cleaner longer.

A good indicator of cruise mixture is the color of the inside of the exhaust pipes. If the mixture is correct, the inside color should be medium to dark gray and should also appear smooth and dry. If it is dark gray to black, the mixture is too rich. Also, the texture will roughen up as the mixture goes too rich. If the inside is wet or greasy-looking, the mixture is excessively rich or the engine is burning oil.

SETTING THE AIR-FUEL MIXTURES

For your car to run properly and yield the maximum performance and fuel economy, the air-fuel mixture must be correct. See the narrow-band 0_2 sensor voltage graph for the air fuel ratios required for best performance and best economy. The carburetor should be tuned to achieve these. Begin the tuning by setting the full-throttle mixture first and then set the part-throttle mixtures.

Remember, carburetors can be set up to meter fuel quite accurately, but they cannot compensate for air density variations. Once you have calibrated the carburetor, it will be correct for the atmospheric conditions under which the carburetor was tuned. So if you tune the car on a hot day, when you drive it on a cold day, the air will be denser and the mixture will, therefore, be leaner. The reverse is true if the vehicle is operated on a hotter day than when the vehicle was tuned. Barometric pressure is just as important as temperature, so just as you try to avoid days that are extremely hot or cold when tuning, the same applies to air pressure. Keep a record of the temperature and barometric pressure under which the car was tuned.

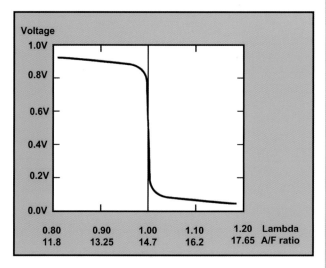

Narrow-band 0_2 sensor voltage.

Here is a wide-band oxygen sensor installed in the exhaust pipe, just behind the header collector. Note that the O2 sensor is angled up.

After the idle speed has been set, the main-jet air-fuel mixture can be set. You will usually have to make slight adjustments to the idle mixture once the main jets have been changed, but it is much easier to work with the vehicle if it will idle, which is why we set the idle first. This also helps prevent fouling the plugs while tuning the vehicle.

Another way to look at air-fuel mixture is to consider how much fuel is required for each mixture ratio. For example, if your vehicle is cruising with an air-fuel ratio of 12.5:1, it is drawing in 92.5% air and 7.5% fuel. Change this to 15.4 to 1 and the engine will now be drawing in 94% air and only 6% fuel. This is a reduction in fuel usage of 20%. Even considering the slight drop in power,

the vehicle would likely see a 20% increase in fuel economy while cruising.

So if your car is getting 12 mpg on the highway, and it is running at 12.6:1, this change will increase your mileage to over 14 mpg, all from a simple carburetor tune! Another consideration: For idle mixture, a stock cam should have an air-fuel mixture of around 14.5:1, while a performance cam will idle better with a mixture of 13.5:1. You want as lean an idle mixture as you can get without sacrificing idle quality.

SETTING FULL-THROTTLE MIXTURE

The first order of business when setting the main-jet air-fuel mixture is to set the full-throttle mixture. Begin by running two passes down the strip. Record the trap speed, as this indicates horsepower. Now increase the jet sizes in the primary side of the carburetor. Make two more passes. Note whether mph increased, decreased, or remained the same. As long as it is increasing, keep changing up, one size each time. Once it stops increasing, back up one size. If the first change results in a drop in mph, then decrease the jet size and retest. As long as the mph keeps increasing, keep decreasing the jet sizes until the mph falls off, and then increase it by one.

Now do the secondary jets (or metering rods) just as you did the primaries: increase one size and retest. Continue increasing jet size and retesting until the mph starts to drop off, then back up one size. If the mph falls with the first change, decrease the jet size (increase the metering rod diameter) by one and test. Again, if the mph keeps increasing, keep going down in jet sizes until the mph falls off, then increase jet size by one.

Now go back and retest the primary jets. Try one size leaner, and then one size richer in order to verify that changing the secondary jets did not affect the primary mixture. If the change did affect the primary mixture, you will have to repeat the primary jetting procedure, which means you will also have to repeat the secondary jetting procedure. In fact, you might have to repeat the procedures several times. Now record the primary and secondary jet

When tuning most carbs, the idle air bleeds are not removable jets and will have to be drilled. Make changes carefully and slowly. You can always make the hole larger; going smaller will require some epoxy. You will also need a collection of numeric drill bits and a handheld pin vise; no power tools here!

Just like the idle bleeds, most carburetors use a fixed-size orifice for the high-speed or main circuit bleed. Changes require caution; go slowly while increasing the size. You can always drill larger.

sizes you settled on as well as the temperature, barometric pressure, and humidity readings during the test runs.

SETTING PART-THROTTLE MIXTURE

After setting the full-throttle air-fuel mixture, the part-throttle air-fuel mixture can be set. This is important, as the part-throttle mixture will affect fuel economy and feel of the car while cruising. If the mixture is too rich, the engine will feel lazy. If it is too lean, the engine will stumble. Either way, if the part-throttle mixture is wrong, fuel economy will be poor and emissions will be high.

Another benefit of a properly set cruise mixture is improved engine life. If the mixture is too rich,

the excess fuel will wash the oil from the cylinder walls and cause excessive cylinder wear. Modern fuel-injected engines have improved engine life due to the fact that the air-fuel mixture is usually right on, which prevents the cylinder walls from being exposed to an overly rich air-fuel mixture.

A CO or O_2 sensor is by far the easiest tool you can use to set the part-throttle mixture. These are inexpensive and an O_2 meter can be installed in one of the header collectors. This is the most accurate way to measure the fuel mixture while cruising.

You can find wide- and narrow-band O_2 sensors. Most computer-controlled vehicles use narrow-band O_2 sensors. If you are attempting to tune using a

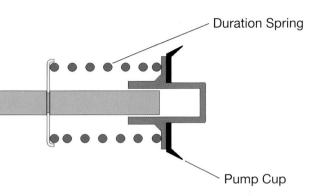

Duration Spring

Pump Cup

Accelerator pump piston. The duration spring actually moves the pump cup down. It also determines how long the pump shot will last. If the spring is stiff, the fuel is delivered in a shorter amount of time. Making the duration spring weaker will cause the pump shot to take more time to be delivered.

narrow-band O_2 sensor, remember that the sensor reads from about 0.1 volt to 0.9 volt. The curve is not linear, and a 14.7:1 reads as approximately 0.25 volt to 0.7 volt. See the graph for the curve that a typical low-cost O_2 sensor will produce. Most low-cost O_2 monitors you can buy will show the mixture

Most carburetors use some sort of clip to retain linkage. This accelerator pump rod is retained by a harpin clip. Also note that while working on the carburetor, it is not set down on the bench. The linkage extends below the carb base, and if the carburetor is not properly supported, the linkage can be damaged.

Holley carburetors use a cam to apply the accelerator pump. This cam can be changed to alter the delivery curve.

incorrectly. Do not use them to tune; instead connect a voltmeter to the O_2 sensor output and tune for 0.85 to 0.9 volt at full throttle. At crusing speeds, tune your car so the output is 0.1 volt.

While cruising, monitor the O_2. If it is low (indicating a rich mixture), increase the diameter of the primary metering rods. For carburetors that do not use primary metering rods, the air bleeds will have to be changed.

If after changing jets and power valves the ideal power mixture is found but the car is too rich during cruise, the next step is to change the air bleeds. These provide fine control of the curves. For example, installing a larger main jet air bleed will delay the start of the fuel curve, and the flow will start out leaner and then richen up as flow rates increase. The overall mixture will be leaner as well. If the main jet air bleeds are going to be changed, the main jets will usually need to be changed as well. Larger engines will usually draw harder on the carburetor, resulting in the mains coming in too soon. They usually require larger air bleeds to delay the start of the main circuit under cruise conditions.

Engines with large-overlap camshafts will radically increase vacuum as rpms increase, and this can cause the motor to run rich. This occurs because an idle circuit calibrated to supply sufficient fuel to an engine with low manifold vacuum will supply excess fuel when it experiences higher vacuum during cruise. By increasing the size of the main-circuit air bleeds, the mains will be delayed and the overall air-fuel mixture will lean back out.

To properly tune air bleeds, use either a wide-band O_2 or a CO sensor to measure the mixture.

Here is the duration spring that is responsible for actually working the pump. On a Holley, the spring pressure works against the discharge (shooters) holes, and this determines the duration of the pump shot. "Shooters" with larger holes will deliver the pump shot more quickly. The volume of the pump shot is determined by the pump size (Holley has two, a 50cc and a 30cc) and the accelerator pump cam.

Full-throttle air-fuel mixture is easy for drag racers: monitor the trap speeds through the quarter-mile and tune for the best mph. Setting part-throttle cruise mixture requires a sensor. When tuning the air bleeds, take care not to run your engine too lean, especially at highway speeds. Internal damage can result if the mixture is too lean.

Most OEM carburetors use fixed bleed sizes; the only way to change them is by drilling. If you purchase a replacement carburetor, select one that has changeable air bleeds if this level of tuning is going to be attempted. Modifying the bleeds on a carburetor that does not have changeable air bleeds is a slow and sometimes painful process.

Idle air bleeds work the same way as main jet air bleeds; increasing the size of the bleeds will lean the overall mixture, particularly at lower vacuum and lighter throttle openings. For light-throttle mixture problems, start with the idle circuit. If the engine is going rich just off idle, decrease the idle restriction to limit the total fuel available. This will result in the engine being too lean at idle, which can be corrected by decreasing the idle air bleed. When this is done properly, the engine will idle smoothly and light throttle openings will be properly metered.

The correct way to set the idle and transition air-fuel mixture is to reduce the idle fuel restriction size until the air-fuel mixture in the 1,200–1,600 rpm range under no load is in the 14.5–15.5:1 range. This will usually result in a car that cannot be made to idle. The next step is to decrease the idle air bleeds until the idle mixture screws can be adjusted to make the car idle. This may require you to change the idle fuel restrictions. Go back and forth until the car idles around 13.0–14.5:1, depending on the camshaft overlap. Cams with large overlap should shoot for the 13.0:1 end of the spectrum, while cams approaching stock overlap should shoot for a 14.5:1 ratio at idle. Also, verify that the no-load mixture at 1,200 to 1,600 rpm is between 14.5 and 15.0:1.

Ideally, you want to see a 15.0 to 15.5:1 mixture during light cruise, with 15.3:1 as the perfect cruise mixture, slowly richening up as the throttle is opened and engine load is increased. Adjust the tip-in point of the mains by changing the main air bleeds. These can be changed to tailor where the main circuit comes in. If the idle and light-cruise mixture is fine, but the engine goes too rich as the rpm is increased, open up the main air bleeds. This may require an increase in main jet size to keep the wide-open throttle mixture correct.

At higher cruising speeds, a 15.0:1 mixture will result in a more responsive engine. A richer high-speed cruise mixture will also protect the engine from excessive heat. Regardless of what the meter tells you, any surging is a sign of a too-lean engine. Richen up the mixture until surging is eliminated. If you tune the cruise mixture on a dynamometer, use a 45-horsepower load at 60 mph and a 60-horsepower load at 70 mph as the load power at which to set the mixture. By 75 mph, the mixture should be no leaner than 14.7:1.

ACCELERATOR PUMP TUNING

Now that the mixture is set, the accelerator pump can be tuned. If the pump shot is too weak, the vehicle will stumble. If the duration is too short, the vehicle will take off, immediately stumble, and go again. Don't set

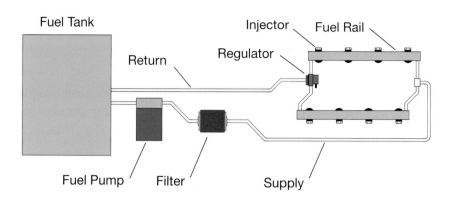

Fuel Tank

Return

Injector   **Fuel Rail**

Regulator

Fuel Pump   **Filter**   **Supply**

the pump shot too strong or the vehicle will be lazy. Bear in mind that the accelerator pump operation doesn't adjust to rpm or conditions. At slow speeds more pump shot is required, while at high speeds you want less. This is why the pump shot tuning is always a compromise. You will have to consult the appropriate book for your carburetor on how to tune the pump.

If you quickly open the throttles and the engine stumbles or backfires through the carburetor, the pump shot is too weak. If the engine is lazy or sluggish, there may be too much pump shot. If there is a puff of black smoke but the engine seems to respond correctly, then the pump shot may be supplying just a little too much.

The best way to tune the pump is at the drag strip. Watch the 60-foot times. Keep making changes that result in 60-foot time improvement, but watch for traction problems. Most pumps can be tuned for both discharge and duration.

Another point: all carburetors use a spring to apply the accelerator pump. The linkage does not directly push the pump. It may appear that it does, but it does not. This allows the pump shot to continue after the linkage has stopped moving. Under no circumstances should the pump be modified to override this spring. The result will be bent and damaged linkage and pump parts! Fuel is a liquid and is not compressible. When the throttles are slammed open, something has to give.

For Rochester and Carter carburetors, the pump is usually a rod with a sliding end and a pump cup. There will be a spring that forces the cup down when the rod is pressed down into the carburetor. This spring is called the duration spring. By changing this spring, the pump shot can either be quickened or slowed down. This does not change the total amount of fuel delivered, but it does change how quickly it is delivered. These carburetors also have more than one hole in the accelerator pump linkage, usually on the pump lever. These holes allow the rod that actuates the pump to be moved. This is what will change the volume of the pump shot.

Holley carburetors use a diaphragm accelerator pump mounted under the fuel bowls. These are more adjustable, giving you control over how much and when additional fuel is delivered as the throttles are opened.

There are three items that tune the pump shot on a Holley carburetor, the first of which is the discharge nozzles or squirters. These are mounted in the carburetor bore. The larger the squirter's set of holes, the quicker the fuel will be delivered.

Next, the volume of fuel delivered is tuned by an adjusting screw in the linkage arm. Just like the Rochester and Carter carburetors, the accelerator pump is actuated by a spring, and this is where the adjusting screw is located. By tightening this bolt down, the volume of fuel delivered is increased.

Finally, Holley carburetors have a cam that actuates the accelerator pump linkage. Unlike

FUEL SYSTEM

Rochester and Carter carburetors, the Holley accelerator pump delivery curve can be changed. The cam allows you to have a bigger or smaller accelerator pump shot delivered under part throttle maneuvers. For drag racing, it does not matter much, as the throttles are mashed wide open. But for street driving, these can make a big difference by allowing you to tune for the correct amount of pump shot under various driving conditions.

ELECTRONIC FUEL INJECTION

Modern electronically controlled fuel injection systems can easily be fitted to any muscle car–era engine. You will need an intake manifold with a throttle body, fuel rails and fuel injectors, a computer, a new fuel pump, assorted sensors, and a wiring harness. It may seem like a lot of work, but the tuning options are much broader than a carburetor could ever allow. Unlike a carburetor, fuel injection can adjust the air-fuel mixture to account for temperature and air pressure variations.

Fuel injection can eliminate those seemingly impossible carburetor tuning issues. A good example is setting the idle mixture with a big cam. Since the vacuum is low at idle, a carburetor has to flow more fuel in order to idle properly. This can be accomplished easily enough, but the downside is that the deceleration or light-cruise mixture is now too rich. With fuel injection, you can simply tune the fuel map to solve this problem. The result can be a car that performs to the best of its ability under all conditions, including behaving well in traffic.

The downside to electronic fuel injection is its cost and complexity. Plan on spending three to four times the cost of a good high-performance four-barrel carburetor and manifold combination. Also, the added complexity means that you are more likely to have a failure. Carburetors require constant tuning and maintenance that fuel injection eliminates, but most carburetor problems will not result in a stranded vehicle. Fuel injection system failures can result in a stranded vehicle. The car may be down for several days

if you use an aftermarket system and have to wait for replacement parts to arrive.

The intake can be either a standard aluminum four-barrel-style intake with injector bungs welded at each intake port, or it can be designed for fuel injection only. The latter is usually only available for commonly modified engines such as the big- and small-block Chevys and Windsor small-block Fords. For the rest, a converted four-barrel-style intake is the only option. Fuel injection systems can be obtained from a variety of sources; be sure to obtain the custom fuel rails that match the intake as well.

This book will not detail how to install a fuel injection system. This is a subject that could fill a book and a lot of what is required will depend on what type of system is being installed. Follow the recommendations that the manufacturer of your system provides. If you are building your own system, you will still have to obtain a manifold, throttle body, computer, injectors, regulator, and sensors, not to mention a wiring harness. Follow the recommendations of the manifold and computer suppliers. This book will describe changes that will have to be made to the car to accommodate the fuel injection system.

There are also several good books on fuel injection; the key point is to do your homework. By doing some careful research, you will be able to design a system that will work for you and you will be rewarded with a vehicle that starts and idles like a stocker but uses all of the performance the engine is capable of providing under any environmental condition.

FUEL SUPPLY CONSIDERATIONS FOR ELECTRONIC FUEL INJECTION

Before you begin a fuel injection conversion, plan out how to supply highly pressurized fuel to the engine. All fuel injection systems require a high-pressure fuel supply. Most factory injection systems use a pump mounted in the fuel tank. For a conversion, a high-pressure pump mounted at the rear of the vehicle is the best plan. See the Fuel Pump section of this book for details on how to mount and plumb a rear-mounted fuel pump.

Fuel injection systems also use a bypass-style pressure regulator, so a return line will have to be routed from the engine to the fuel tank. Be careful to not route either of these lines near any hot components, or the fuel in the tank will be heated excessively as the fuel travels from the tank and back to the tank.

The pressure regulator should be mounted at the opposite end of the fuel rails from where the pressurized fuel enters. This helps ensure that the fuel pressure at each injector is correct. Also, the regulator must connect to the intake manifold vacuum. All fuel injection systems operate with the expectation that the injector will be supplied with consistent fuel pressure. This means that the fuel pressure at the inlet is always the same relative to the discharge nozzle. By operating this way, the computer does not have to figure out the difference in volume of fuel flow as the manifold vacuum changes.

For example, say an injector is rated at 30 pounds of fuel per hour at a pressure of 40 psi. This pressure rating is measured between the fuel rail and the discharge nozzle. Considering that the discharge nozzle is inside the intake manifold, when the vehicle is cruising down the road with a manifold vacuum of 15 inches, the fuel pressure must be reduced by 7.4 psi (15 inches of vacuum is the same as 7.4 pounds per square inch) in order to keep the injector "seeing" 40 psi of pressure from the fuel rail to the injector outlet. The regulator does this by connecting a diaphragm to the intake manifold vacuum and having it work against the pressure regulator spring.

There are also fuel-pressure regulators for engines that have a turbocharger or supercharger. These regulators work just like the regular vacuum-only regulators, but they also raise the fuel pressure while the engine is under boost. There are 1-bar and 2-bar versions, with 1-bar for engines that will see up to 14 psi of boost, and 2-bar for engines that will experience boost pressures up to 29 psi.

The typical operating pressure is 43.5 psi above the manifold pressure. Your pump must be able to maintain this pressure at all required flow rates or the system will not be able to provide the proper amount of fuel.

Consider an 850-horsepower turbocharged small block that runs a maximum boost of 20 psi. This will require a fuel system that can provide 425 pounds of fuel per hour and maintain 63.5 psi while doing so. This is almost 68 gph while maintaining the 63.5 psi. It will not be a stock fuel pump.

Units of measure commonly found when dealing with or tuning a fuel injection system are the pascal and the bar. A pascal is the metric measurement for pressure, with 101,325 pascals being equal to one standard atmosphere, or 14.696 psi. Most systems will deal in kilopascals or KPa, so one atmosphere is equal to 101.325 kPa. A bar is 100,000 pascals, so one atmosphere is roughly one bar (actually, 0.98692 bar = 14.696 psi).

It is a good idea to check for excessive fuel heating by driving the vehicle for at least one hour in stop-and-go traffic. If the fuel is getting too warm, a fuel cooler will be needed. This looks just like an oil cooler and should be mounted in the return line from the regulator. Mount the cooler in front of the radiator. Ensure that the fuel lines you add are routed as far as possible from any exhaust components.

All of the lines should be formed stainless steel lines with flare fittings. If any flexible hose is going to be used, use only high-quality aircraft-style hose and AN fittings. As with all hose in the fuel line, if flexible hose is used, it needs to be replaced every two years. Remember, the fuel will be under considerable pressure, and any leak will spray large quantities of fuel and will most likely result in a fire.

Finally, the fuel pump should have some sort of cutoff in the event that the engine dies. All factory computers handle this, and this is why the computer controls the fuel pump relay. If you are adding a fuel injection system, the computer you are using should have a fuel pump control relay. Use it.

SIZING FUEL INJECTORS

Injectors are sized based on fuel flow, which is rated in pounds per hour. A 35-pound-per-hour injector will flow 35 pounds of fuel per hour if it is open 100 percent of the time. This is not practical; the injector needs to be sized such that the engine control module (ECM) can accurately control the mixture. This requires that the full capacity of the injector is not required; otherwise, the engine may run lean. If the injector is sized so that at 100% flow it just meets the engine's fuel requirements, the ECM no longer has any extra capacity, and if the engine is operated in colder air or higher density (pressure) air, the engine will go lean because the injector is already open all of the time. Furthermore, a decrease in fuel pressure will also lean the engine if there is no extra injector capacity available to adjust to the conditions. Finally, the injector is an electromagnet, and off time allows the injector coil to cool.

At this point, it may seem that you should just select injectors that are way too big and use the computer to limit the fuel flow. This is also not a good idea; the system will be more accurate and easy to tune if you size the injectors properly. Here's why: the fuel flow is controlled by limiting the open time, but the computer does not have the ability to move down in infinitely smaller steps to restrict the fuel. Most work with a standard binary value, like an 8-bit field for the injector-open value. This allows only 256 steps, so if the injector is too big, the upper steps cannot be used.

To size injectors, use the following formula:

$$\text{Pounds per hour} = \frac{(\text{HP} \times 0.5)}{(\text{CYL} \times 0.85)}$$

This formula allows for 0.5 pounds per hour per horsepower. Also, CYL is the number of cylinders. Finally, 0.85 is the injector's maximum-duty cycle. This allows the injector to have some headroom and also to have some guaranteed minimum off time to allow the coil to cool. If the engine develops 500 horsepower it will need a 36.76 pound per hour injector (allowing for 85% maximum duty cycle), so round up to a 40-pound-per-hour injector, as they are usually sized in 5-pound increments.

Fuel injectors are typically either high-impedance and low-impedance. This refers to the coil in the injector. Most OEM systems use the high-impedance type. The electrical resistance of a high-impedance injector is roughly 12 ohms. The fuel flow rates for high-impedance injectors range from 15 to 45 lb/hr. A low-impedance injector uses a coil with a resistance of roughly 2 ohms. This means that the injector will require more current to open, but low-impedance injectors usually have high flow rates. So if you need injectors that flow above 45 lb/hr, you will most likely be getting low-impedance injectors. Most throttle body injectors were also low-impedance. This is important: the fuel injection controller must be matched to the injector coil type. A controller that is designed to drive high-impedance injectors may be damaged if low-impedance injectors are connected to it.

Almost all fuel injection systems use a return-style fuel delivery system, with the pump mounted at the rear of the vehicle. Most OEM systems mount the pump in the fuel tank. The fuel is pumped forward, through a filter, into the fuel rails and then to the fuel pressure regulator. The regulator controls the pressure by sending excess fuel back to the tank. This continuous fuel circulation can expose the fuel to hot underhood air. If you are adding a fuel injection system, pay close attention to where and how you route the fuel supply and return lines. Keep these far away from exhaust components and other warm components in order to avoid heating the fuel.

ELECTRICAL SYSTEM CONSIDERATIONS FOR ELECTRONIC FUEL INJECTION

If you plan on converting your vehicle to fuel injection, you will need to update your electrical system.

Your original muscle car electrical system was not designed to handle an electronic fuel injection system. The stock alternator or generator cannot supply enough power to run the fuel injection system, headlights, and stereo while keeping the battery charged.

The old points-style regulator on early alternators and all generators will create excessive electrical noise and voltage spikes that may interfere with proper operation of your electronic fuel injection system, and in severe cases may even damage or destroy the computer or active sensors such as a mass airflow sensor.

The increased electrical demand comes from two primary sources. The first is the fuel injection computer, which requires power and drives the fuel injectors. A typical computer and its injectors will require 20 amps of continuous current. Also, the computer will need a constant battery connection in order to preserve the computer's memory while the vehicle is off.

The best way to power the computer is to connect the computer to the battery through a dedicated circuit using 12-gauge wire and a relay, but check with the manufacturer of your ECU for their recommendations. The ignition switch turns on the relay, connecting the battery to the computer. This ensures that the computer receives a clean, uninterrupted supply of power. There will usually be two power connections, one that connects directly to the battery, and one that connects to the ignition switch.

Grounding for the computer is critical. The computer must have a ground circuit that is just as good as the power. But don't connect it to the battery! For fuel injection to function, it gathers inputs from several sensors mounted on and around the engine. Some of these readings are analog. This means that the computer is reading a voltage level across the sensor. To read this voltage correctly, the computer and the sensor must be connected to the same ground.

High-current flow—like the charging current from the alternator—can cause 0.1 to 0.3 volt of error between the engine block and the car battery. Prevent this from interfering with the computer by grounding it to the engine block with 10-gauge wire, preferably at the intake manifold. If possible, ground all sensors to the same point.

The next electrical draw is the fuel pump. Fuel injection systems require a continuous, high-pressure fuel source that is much more powerful than stock. The typical selection is an electric pump. Budget at least 20 amps for the pump. High-performance racing pumps can draw more than 30 amps.

The fuel pump's power should come straight from the battery and be switched through a high-current relay. This relay is controlled by the fuel injection computer, allowing the computer to switch off the fuel pump if the engine stalls. Also, some race pumps are available with a controller that monitors engine vacuum or throttle position and can scale back the power that is sent to the pump. This allows a high-volume pump to be used on the street by scaling back the power while cruising, which extends pump life and reduces the heating effect of circulating the fuel.

These powerful fuel pumps will most likely be mounted at the rear of the vehicle. This will require that the power wire be run a long way. It will have to be carefully routed to prevent damage. The gauge of the wire will have to be chosen with the length in mind to prevent excessive voltage drops.

If you plan on adding an electric cooling fan, this will add another 20 to 40 amps or even more. Several fuel injection computers have a provision to control the cooling fan. The fan output on the computer is intended to control a relay rather than be connected directly to the fan. This relay should be set up to connect the fan to the battery.

Add up all of these requirements and you are looking for a system that produces 60 amps or more! This is the main reason modern cars have 100-amp and larger alternators. Your stock original equipment 37-amp alternator simply will not cut it. Also, modern alternators are designed to be more efficient at low rpm. Even though the fuel injection system draws almost the same power at low speeds as it does at high speeds, at low speeds (idling in traffic), it is more likely that the cooling fan will be on. If the alternator is not designed to keep up, the battery will discharge while sitting in traffic.

A modern alternator will usually be able to supply 70 amps while the engine is idling. This is to keep up with the engine computer, fuel pump, and cooling fans as well as the normal accessories.

It is mandatory that you convert your muscle car to a modern high-current alternator before adding fuel injection. You will also be extremely sorry if you don't remember that the wire that connects the alternator to the battery has to be 6 gauge or larger.

TROUBLESHOOTING FUEL INJECTION

Fuel injection systems can be intimidating, but they are not actually that hard to work on. Before you dig out the wallet and start replacing sensors and the computer, check the basics. The problem probably comes down to just one part. The trick is how to be able to find the bad part!

Begin with the obvious. If the car will not start, check for fuel and spark. This will divide the system down the middle, and you should focus on the section that is not working. If the car starts but runs poorly, again, check the basics. No matter what you think is wrong, check the four fuel injection basics first. These items are:

1. Fuel pressure
2. Static ignition timing
3. Throttle position sensor (TPS) voltage
4. Idle speed (car must be running for this)

Always check the fuel pressure first. If it is low, the car will either run poorly or not start. There is a pressure-test fitting on the fuel rails or at the regulator for this. Get a good-quality fuel pressure test gauge and connect it to the test fitting. Turn on the ignition switch and observe the gauge reading. Most computers will only run the fuel pump for a couple of seconds if the starter is not engaged, so check the gauge reading just after the ignition switch is turned on.

If the reading shows no pressure, find the fuel pump relay before replacing other parts. Remove the relay and test it. If the relay is good, connect a voltmeter or trouble light to the line that goes to the pump. Turn the key on. If the voltmeter or test light indicates 12 volts, the pump needs to be replaced. If no voltage is present, check the line from the computer that activates the relay. Before replacing the computer, check for a vehicle collision switch—these turn off the fuel pump in case of an accident. Several newer cars have these. The owner's manual will usually show the location of the switch.

All modern electronic fuel injection systems control ignition timing. If the input reference to the computer is off, the car will run poorly or not at all. Earlier fuel injection systems used a distributor with fixed timing (these had no advance weights) and the computer signaled the distributor when to fire the coil. The distributor sent a fixed reference pulse to the computer. If the distributor is set incorrectly, the computer will have problems getting the timing correct. For cars with a distributor, there is a connector that you disconnect in order to set the timing. Follow the instructions for your particular fuel injection setup. If the car is not running, time the engine statically by following the instructions in your fuel-injection system installation or service manual.

Next, check the throttle position sensor voltage. This tells the computer how far open the throttle plates are. Proper adjustment of this sensor is vital for proper operation of the fuel injection system. This sensor is adjusted by monitoring the voltage from the sensor with the throttles closed. Each manufacturer will have its own recommended setting, but it is usually around 0.5 volt at idle.

After the idle setting is verified, open the throttles all the way (with the engine not started) and verify the full throttle voltage. Next, move the throttles slowly from idle to full throttle and observe the voltage reading. It should be a smooth increase from the idle voltage setting all the way up to the voltage the manufacturer lists for full throttle. Any jumps or dips indicate a bad TPS that needs to be replaced.

The idle speed is checked by disconnecting the idle speed controller and starting the car. This gives you the idle speed that is set by the throttle stop, just like on a carburetor.

Idle speed is regulated by the computer, which controls a motor called the idle air controller (IAC). This servo-style motor opens or closes a bypass valve that lets additional air into the engine. Since the computer "knows" whether it is letting additional air in or keeping air out, it then also adjusts fuel supply accordingly, thereby maintaining a steady idle speed.

Test the IAC by disconnecting it with the ignition off and then starting the car. Set the idle to the manufacturer's recommended idle speed for a warm engine. If the idle adjustment is set too low, the car may have a tendency to die, particularly right after you remove your foot from the gas pedal while traveling slowly. If it is set too high, the computer may set a trouble code and light up the Service Engine Soon or Check Engine light. The car may also surge when idling. Note that before adjusting the idle setting, the base ignition timing must be correct and the engine must be fully warmed up. Once adjusted, turn the car off and reconnect the IAC. Start the car and drive it for a few miles to recalibrate the IAC.

EMISSIONS CONCERNS

Emissions controls have been around since 1966, so you will most likely have to deal with them. While the early devices were crude and simple, the year of your vehicle will determine what devices were installed and may still be required by your state law. Each state, and in some cases county or city, will have its own restrictions and testing requirements.

It makes no sense to have a daily driver that is incapable of passing the required smog check. Several states are implementing mobile smog check stands that measure exhaust emissions from vehicles traveling down the road, and photograph the license plates of vehicles suspected of being in violation. And a clean-running vehicle can deliver improved drivability and mileage.

Even with a fairly radical camshaft, it is possible to properly tune the engine so your vintage muscle car can easily pass a yearly smog inspection or roadside vehicle emissions test. Pay particular attention to the off-idle and cruise air-fuel mixtures and you should have no trouble with smog inspections.

It used to be that only harmful emissions were what everyone was worried about. The assumption was that if combustion was perfect, the only chemicals emitted would be water and carbon dioxide. Now we know this is not true! Carbon dioxide is a greenhouse gas. So even if the combustion process is perfect, carbon dioxide emissions are still a problem. The amount of CO_2 emitted is related to fuel mileage, and the following formula will approximate the levels emitted.

$$\text{Lbs per mile} = \frac{19.5}{\text{MPG}}$$

In the formula listed above, Lbs per mile is the pounds per mile of CO_2 emitted, and MPG is the fuel economy in miles per gallon. This formula works for gasoline-powered vehicles. It should be obvious that CO_2 emissions are directly related to the amount of fuel burned.

CHAPTER 10
IGNITION, CHARGING, AND ELECTRICAL SYSTEMS

Most muscle cars are getting by with either a stock ignition system or a racing ignition setup. Neither is ideal for a reliable daily driver. Considering when these vehicles were built, the stock ignition system was most likely breaker-point based. Chrysler owners are luckier than most, as the factory switched to electronic ignition sooner than the other manufacturers, and replacement components are still available new or from the aftermarket. GM and Ford owners will probably find a set of breaker points underneath the distributor cap.

Don't fret—points may not be the perfect performance solution, but they can be made to be reliable. I have seen several 12-second cars that use points.

The first requirement for reliability is to use a good set of points. Accel still makes points for all GM, Ford, and Chrysler muscle car applications. Don't even try to use a cheap set of no-name or house-brand points in your distributor. You will be faced with a car that falls on its face as rpm increases.

To reliably tune a points-based ignition system, start by replacing the points and condenser. When the old points are removed, check the distributor shaft for side-to-side wobble. If you detect any, replace or rebuild the distributor, as this is the sign of a worn upper shaft bearing or bushing. It is impossible to set your points properly if the distributor shaft does not run true. After installing the new points and condenser, use a feeler gauge and set the gap to the manufacturer's recommended setting. GM cars do not have a recommended gap setting, only a dwell setting. Set the gap on these cars to .017 inch in order to start the car so you can set the dwell. It is important to set the gap with the points fully open. This means that the rubbing block on the points arm will be on the high point of the rotor cam. This can be hard to see on GM cars with the distributor located at the rear of the engine.

Once the points have been initially set, replace the rotor and distributor cap. Connect a dwell meter to the negative lead of the coil and fire up the engine. Don't adjust the timing just yet. Check that the dwell is between 28 and 30 degrees. For all V-8 engines, a setting in this range allows for maximum coil charge time while allowing sufficient time for the coil to discharge across the spark plug at high rpm. I set points at 28 degrees because it favors the coil charge time, which is especially helpful if the engine is a high-revving small block.

For Chrysler and Ford applications, if the dwell needs to be changed, the cap and rotor must be removed. If the dwell is too high (above 30 degrees), decrease the gap slightly; if the dwell is too small (below 28 degrees), increase the gap slightly. For GM cars, points adjustments can be made with the engine running. Slide open the window in the distributor cap and insert the appropriate adjustment tool (Accel points can use either an Allen wrench or a small regular screwdriver). Just be careful not to contact anything other than the adjustment screw, or you will be in for a nasty shock. Remember, even a points-style ignition system can generate 300 or more volts on the primary side.

All GM, Ford, and Chrysler muscle cars can be converted to electronic ignition. Accel, Mallory, and other major aftermarket companies produce electronic ignition distributors for these cars. If you prefer the stock look, companies such as Pertronix make conversion kits that fit inside your original points-

Most modern vehicles use coil on plug ignition systems with a separate coil for each spark plug. This allows maximum coil saturation time. There is also no cable crosstalk. This is the 400-horsepower Cadillac Escalade powerplant.

style distributor. Regardless of the method chosen, carry a spare ignition module. Several companies also make later-model high-energy electronic ignition conversion kits for earlier muscle cars. These kits use the factory electronic ignition systems that became available in the mid 1970s, usually with enhanced ignition modules.

When considering an aftermarket ignition, don't fall for the higher-voltage-is-better trap. A system that puts out 10 to 20 kilovolts will usually be sufficient to fire your plugs. Any excess capacity is wasted. Regardless of its capacity, a coil only charges to the voltage required to strike the arc, then falls to whatever is needed to sustain the arc. What is important is the intensity and duration of the spark. Higher intensity (current) will result in a fatter spark. A longer spark duration will help prevent misfires.

If you add an aftermarket ignition that connects directly to the battery for power and uses a smaller wire that connects to the ignition switch to turn the ignition on or off, you may find that, once started, you cannot turn the ignition off. This is because the sense wire for the ignition draws very little current and the current that back-feeds from the alternator indicator lamp is sufficient to keep the ignition turned on. To fix this, the alternator indicator wire must be opened and a diode must be installed that allows current to flow into the alternator indicator

This shows the cam that actuates the breaker points.

terminal but prevents current from flowing back out of the alternator indicator line. Your ignition system should have instructions.

Regardless of what ignition system you use, carry a spare set of points or ignition module. These components are small enough that you can easily fit them in a small toolbox in the trunk. Considering how easy these are to change, why would you want to risk being stranded due to a failure? Also, as time marches on, these parts may be hard to find.

DISTRIBUTOR

All muscle cars use a distributor to trigger the ignition coil and distribute the spark to the proper spark plug. Since each cylinder in a four-stroke engine has one power stroke every two revolutions of the crankshaft, the distributor must rotate at one half the crankshaft speed. Because the camshaft also must rotate at one half the crankshaft speed, all muscle car engines drive

the distributor from the camshaft. Therefore the camshaft has a gear that drives the distributor.

All muscle car engines drive the oil pump from the distributor drive gear as well. To accomplish this, a shaft extends from the bottom of the distributor gear down to the oil pump. This means that the distributor and oil pump are at the same end of the engine. All General Motors V-8 engines except Cadillac and Buick have the distributor at the rear of the engine, while all Ford V-8 engines have the distributor at the front. Chrysler uses both styles, with the LA series (273, 318, 340, 360) distributor located at the rear while the B and RB (361, 383, 400, 413, 426W, and 440) engines have the distributor located in the front. AMC V-8 engines also place the distributor at the front.

The distributor is responsible for accurately firing the ignition coil. It does this by opening the breaker points or turning off the transistor that serves as the electronic "switch" for an electronic ignition system.

This sudden interruption in current flow is responsible for the creation of spark in the ignition coil. This event must be accurately timed so that the spark occurs at precisely the correct time. Mechanical breaker points-style distributors have a machined cam at the upper end of the distributor shaft. A V-8 engine's cam has eight flats and, therefore, eight rounded corners or lobes that work against the movable arm of the breaker points unit to open the points.

ENGINE TIMING REQUIREMENTS

Since gasoline has a slow combustion rate, time is required for the flame to travel across the packed air-fuel mixture in the cylinder. Therefore, the ignition system is timed to generate the spark before the piston has reached top dead center (TDC) on the compression stroke. This ensures that combustion pressure will rise to its peak when the piston and crankshaft are able to convert the released energy into motion as efficiently as possible.

Fire the plug too early and the increasing pressure will actually work against the engine as the piston is still traveling up toward TDC. Even worse, the increasing pressure caused by the combustion process plus the increasing pressure caused by the piston traveling up and decreasing the combustion chamber's volume can cause detonation. This occurs when the unburned air-fuel mixture is ignited before

These are the mechanical advance weights. As the engine rpm increases, centrifugal force swings them out, moving the rotor and the points cam ahead of the distributor driveshaft. The springs return the weights as engine rpm decreases.

the spark event by the rapid pressure (and, therefore, heat) increase of the power stroke. Again, this works against the engine, but in a much more dramatic fashion. Detonation needs to be avoided at all costs; it can damage pistons, break rings, and cause other internal engine damage.

If the timing is too late or retarded, the pressure peak will occur too late, resulting in a loss of efficiency in converting the energy released by the combustion process into motion. If the timing is retarded, it will also pass additional heat energy into the exhaust. Retarded ignition timing can cause the engine to run hot or even overheat.

To further complicate things, engine speed and throttle opening change the ideal ignition timing. At low speeds, less ignition advance is required, with a setting of 12 degrees before top dead center (BTDC) of crankshaft rotation as a typical setting. Refer to your factory service manual for the actual timing parameters you should use. As engine speed is increased, the timing must be advanced to accommodate the shorter time required for the piston to finish the trip to TDC. Most engines will run best with a timing that fires the plugs around 34 to 36 degrees before TDC when rpm is 2,500 rpm and above. Finally, at light engine loads, due to the low cylinder pressure, additional advance will make the engine more efficient. Usually 5 to 15 degrees of additional timing is required.

DISTRIBUTOR TIMING MECHANISMS

In order to accommodate the engine's timing requirements, the distributor must be more than a simple switch. By using centrifugal weights that are counterbalanced by springs, the actual cam that actuates the points (or the trigger for an electronic ignition) can be advanced. This is accomplished by having the weights set up in a lever arrangement so that as they swing out at higher rpm, they rotate the points cam or ignition trigger ahead of the distributor driveshaft. Conversely, the weights have springs that pull the weights back as the distributor driveshaft rotation speed is reduced at lower engine

rpm, resulting in the points cam or electronic ignition trigger returning to its original position relative to the distributor driveshaft. This is called a mechanical advance system.

The other type of timing adjustment system most distributors have is vacuum advance. This is a vacuum canister with a diaphragm that is activated by engine vacuum. A rod connects the diaphragm to the plate in the distributor on which the breaker points, or electronic ignition trigger, are mounted. As vacuum is applied, and the diaphragm moves the plate so the firing point is advanced relative to the distributor rotation. When the vacuum is removed, a spring pushes the plate back to the original position, retarding the timing. This allows the engine to have a higher vacuum when cruising down the highway. Also, most engines that use a vacuum advance are set to only apply the vacuum when the throttles are opened past idle. This prevents vacuum advance at idle, as this increases hydrocarbon emissions and may make the idle slightly rougher.

When purchasing an aftermarket performance distributor, check for vacuum advance. Several performance distributors do not have vacuum advance. While this will not cause any performance loss, it can result in a fuel economy decrease. Vacuum advance can give you a 5% to 10% economy improvement, especially if you take any highway trips.

CHECKING DISTRIBUTOR OPERATION

Begin by setting the engine timing. Refer to your service manual for the proper timing specifications and adjustment procedure. Once the initial timing has been set, timing accuracy, vacuum advance operation, and mechanical (rpm) advance can be checked.

Begin by checking accuracy. Remove the hose from the vacuum advance and plug the end of the hose to prevent a vacuum leak. Connect the timing light and start the engine. Monitor the timing, making sure the reading remains steady and does not appear to move. If the engine has a rough idle, increase the idle rpm to 1,200 to 1,500 so that the engine operation runs smoothly. Again, check for a timing reading that remains steady and does not appear to change. Now increase the rpm to 2,500 rpm and check for a steady reading. Any indication of erratic timing or timing that appears to change while engine rpm remains steady indicates that something is loose or worn in the distributor.

The mechanical advance system is checked by recording the timing at idle with the vacuum advance hose detached from the intake manifold and plugged. Now increase the engine rpm to 3,000 and read the timing. Most engines do not have timing marks that will allow an accurate timing reading, so you must use a timing light that has a dial-back adjustment. This is a knob on the timing light that, as you turn it, changes when the strobe is flashed. It allows you to adjust the strobe until the line on the balancer is aligned with the 0 degree marker on the timing tab. Then the actual

distributor advance is read from the timing light. Refer to the instructions for your timing light. If the timing does not advance as rpm is increased, the mechanical advance mechanism is sticking. If the advance does not move the timing to at least 28 degrees BTDC, the mechanical advance needs to be checked or the distributor should be replaced.

Finally, to check the distributor's vacuum advance, you will need a vacuum source. Since most engines use a ported vacuum for the advance, there will be no vacuum when the engine is idling. I prefer to use a hand vacuum pump, just like the one used to bleed brakes. Remove and plug the vacuum hose that connects to the distributor. Now connect the hand vacuum pump to the vacuum advance canister on the distributor. Connect the timing light and start the engine.

This is a dial-back timing light; the readings are in crankshaft degrees.

With the engine idling, read and record the timing. Now pump the vacuum pump up to 15 inches of vacuum. Check the timing; it should be at least 5 degrees more advanced. Now release the vacuum and be sure that the timing returns to the original reading. If the timing does not advance and retard, either the vacuum advance canister is bad or the breaker points plate is stuck. Usually if the vacuum advance canister is bad, it will leak and you will not be able to pump up and maintain a vacuum.

A good vacuum advance canister should not begin to add advance until the manifold vacuum is above 8 inches. This helps to prevent part throttle pinging, especially when going up a light grade. By the time vacuum reaches 15 inches, the vacuum advance should be all in.

Checking vacuum advance with a hand-operated vacuum pump. As vacuum increases, the breaker points mounting plate should move, advancing the timing.

DISTRIBUTOR MECHANICAL PROBLEMS

If erratic timing is detected, something is loose in the distributor. Begin by checking the distributor driveshaft. If the bushings that support the shaft are worn, the shaft will be free to move from side to side, which can result in inconsistent timing. The only cure for this is to replace the distributor.

The next issue is improper advance operation. For proper operation, the advance weights must be free to move without binding and the return springs must not be broken or missing. As corrosion and oil and grease and other contaminants build up, the weights can stick, resulting in no mechanical advance or a distributor that is stuck at full or an intermediate level of advance. The result is that the timing will be incorrect unless the engine is operating at the exact rpm that matches where the distributor advance mechanism is stuck.

For example, if the advance weights are stuck in the idle speed position, the distributor will not provide timing advance at higher engine speeds, resulting in poor performance and reduced fuel economy. Likewise, if the advance mechanism is stuck in the advanced position, the engine will have too much

ignition timing at low speeds and will idle roughly and might ping under acceleration.

Finally, if the mechanical advance weights are slow to respond, usually due to grease buildup or excessive corrosion, the timing will be slow to respond. This will usually affect acceleration from a stop. The mechanism will be slow to respond, resulting in no or little ignition advance as the engine accelerates. This will make the vehicle feel sluggish, but a steady-state test with a timing light might not show the problem if the mechanical advance is able to attain the proper timing advance during the test.

The best way to check for sticking advance weights is to use a timing light to carefully observe the timing mark on the crank pulley, then blip the throttle open and immediately release it so engine speed rapidly increases to about 3,500 and then returns to idle. Remove and plug the vacuum advance hose from the distributor before performing this test. The timing mark should move as soon as engine rpm increases and then return to the idle setting as the engine settles back down to idle speed. If there is any apparent hesitation, carefully inspect the advance mechanism—the weights, springs, and the outer

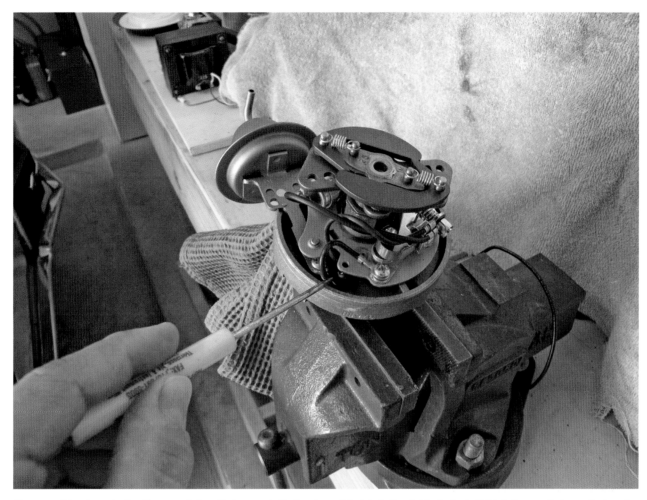

The screwdriver is contacting the ground strap that connects the breaker point plate to the distributor body. If this is loose, missing, or broken, the engine will run rough or may not run at all.

shaft to which the rotor mounts—for signs of damage, corrosion, or gunk buildup. These components should move freely by hand.

DISTRIBUTOR ELECTRICAL PROBLEMS

Besides a failure with the points or electronic ignition sensor or module, there are other items that can malfunction. The plate that mounts the breaker points must be grounded or the engine will not run. This grounding is accomplished by a short wire that connects the points plate to the inside of the distributor body. If this wire breaks or one of the screws becomes loose, the engine will misfire and run rough, or may quit running altogether.

To check for proper grounding of the breaker plate, use your ohmmeter and test for zero ohms from the breaker points plate to the engine block. While testing, locate this wire inside the distributor and gently move the wire while testing for 0 ohms. The meter reading should not change as the wire is moved. If it does, check for a loose mounting point or replace the wire.

Check the wire or wires that lead from within the distributor to the ignition coil or ignition system. Verify that where the wires pass through the distributor body the insulation is not damaged or rubbed off. This can lead to shorting and misfiring. Also check the routing of the wires inside the distributor to be sure that they will not be contacted by the rotating components within the distributor.

The distributor cap must be checked. Be sure that it is clean, and check for any signs of cracking. If the vehicle is hard to start on a damp or rainy day, remove the distributor cap and check for signs of moisture. Especially if there is any dust buildup inside the cap, moisture can condense on the inside of the cap, causing the ignition spark to be routed to several plugs at the same time. In a pinch, the cap can be removed and cleaned and then dried thoroughly.

Cracks in the distributor cap can result in misfires as well. They will attract dust and moisture, which will form a track that the spark energy can follow. Also, check the rotor carefully. The tang that passes the spark from the center coil terminal to the spark plug towers needs to be clean and free of pitting, and the edges should be straight with sharp corners. A sharp edge is better at passing a spark than a smooth, rounded edge. Also check the rotor for any signs of arcing from the tang through the rotor body to the distributor shaft. This was a common problem on the GM H.E.I. ignitions. When it happens, the engine will begin to misfire and will usually quit running.

DISTRIBUTOR REMOVAL AND REPLACEMENT

Since you will want to re-install the distributor and have the engine start, before the distributor is removed, you need to record a few things. First, find the number one spark plug wire and note what tower in the distributor cap it is connected to. Next, remove the distributor cap and record the position that the rotor is pointing. Finally, record how the distributor body is oriented. If it has a vacuum advance canister, note what direction it is pointing; if not, use the distributor cap locating notch in the housing. These three items will allow the distributor to be re-installed close enough that the engine can be started so that it can be timed.

Removing the distributor is usually easy. Remove the spark plug wires from the distributor cap, loosen and remove the distributor hold-down bolt and clamp, disconnect the wire or wires that lead from the distributor, and remove the distributor by pulling it straight out. Immediately stuff a rag into the hole to prevent any foreign objects from entering the engine. Do not rotate the engine with the distributor out or you will not be able to use the notes taken to re-install the distributor.

When re-installing the distributor, first remove the rag from the hole. Insert the distributor body partway into the hole, orienting the housing so that it is positioned the same way as it was when it was removed. Rotate the rotor so that it is pointing the same direction that it was when the distributor was removed. Slowly continue inserting the distributor until the drive gear engages with the camshaft drive gear; you will know when this happens because the rotor will move as the housing is lowered.

Pay attention—if this causes the rotor to move so that it does not match the position when it was removed, raise the housing back up and rotate the rotor approximately 30 degrees in the opposite direction and re-install the housing. Pay careful attention to see that the housing is fully seated in the block; in addition to the camshaft gear, the distributor-drive gear must also engage the oil pump driveshaft. If it does not correctly engage, the distributor will not seat fully in the block, but will remain about a half inch too high. If this happens, gently twist the rotor back and forth while pushing down on the distributor. In extreme cases, have an assistant rotate the engine crankshaft back and forth by hand while you gently push down on the distributor body.

If the engine was rotated after the distributor was removed, or if the orientation was not noted before removal, the engine will have to be timed. Begin by removing the number one spark plug. Now place your finger over the spark plug hole and rotate the engine in the correct direction (clockwise if viewed from the front). As soon as pressure is felt at the spark plug hole, stop and note where the timing mark on the harmonic balancer is.

Continue rotating the balancer until the timing mark is aligned with the timing tab marker that corresponds to 12 degrees before TDC. Now orient the distributor housing so that it faces the correct position. Refer to the factory service manual; it will specify where the number one spark plug wire is located on the distributor cap and the general position that the housing should be positioned. Now rotate the rotor so that it is pointing toward the number one spark plug.

Insert the distributor with the housing properly oriented. Note if the housing seats fully in the block; if it does not, the distributor drive gear is not engaging with the oil pump driveshaft. Remove the distributor and examine the orientation of the distributor gear and the oil pump driveshaft, and, using a suitable tool, rotate the oil pump driveshaft so that it will align with the distributor gear. Now repeat the installation process.

Install the hold-down clamp and bolt. Do not fully tighten, as the timing will need to be set. Install the distributor cap, re-install the number one spark plug, and reconnect the spark plug wires. Connect any wires that were removed when the distributor was removed, usually the wire from the points to the coil terminal. Connect the timing light, start the engine, and verify that you have oil pressure. Now set the timing to recommended timing value in the service manual. Don't forget to tighten down the distributor clamp bolt and re-connect the vacuum advance hose.

DISTRIBUTOR UPGRADES: ELECTRONIC IGNITION

Converting from breaker points to electronic ignition is definitely a good idea. Chances are that either you or a previous owner have already done this. There are several options. You can replace the stock distributor for an aftermarket high-performance distributor; there are probably several electronic ignition options available for your car. Most factory big-block engines were available at some point during their production lifespan with electronic ignition, so retrofitting with a later-model distributor and ignition

system is also an option. Almost all of these systems will require that the distributor be removed and replaced with a new electronic-ignition distributor.

Don't forget the camshaft. If you convert your engine to a roller lifter camshaft, the new camshaft will most likely be made of steel. Unless the new camshaft has a special gear, your original iron distributor gear cannot be used. Check with your camshaft manufacturer for their recommendation for the type of distributor gear that you need to use.

DISTRIBUTOR UPGRADES: TUNING THE MECHANICAL ADVANCE

One upgrade is to tune the mechanical advance. Generally, it is a good idea to have the mechanical advance all in by 2,600 rpm. This means that the advance mechanism is fully operational by 2,600 rpm. This is easiest to set on a distributor machine. With the distributor removed from the engine, the distributor machine will spin the distributor shaft while allowing the timing to be monitored.

Since most of us do not have access to a distributor machine, the timing procedure will have to be done the hard way: modifying the advance mechanism. Start the engine, and using a timing light, check the advance mechanism operation. Before making any changes, verify that the advance mechanism is working properly. Record the total amount of advance provided and the rpm where it is all in. Do not go above 3,600 rpm.

In order to tune the advance mechanism, you will need weights and springs for your distributor. These can be purchased in kits, which are available for most stock and aftermarket distributors. If you are using an aftermarket distributor, get the kit from the same manufacturer that made your distributor. Follow the instructions provided with the kit. Generally, to make the advance come in sooner (at a lower rpm), change to heavier weights and lighter (weaker) springs. To slow down the advance rate and make it come in later (at a higher rpm), change to lighter weights and stronger springs.

SETTING THE OPTIMUM IGNITION TIMING

Once the mechanical advance mechanism has been tuned, you can then work to set the optimum timing. This can be done on a dynometer or at the drag strip. For both procedures, all of the following timing numbers will be listed assuming the vacuum advance has been disconnected, so when you are setting initial timing or checking and setting total-advance timing, be sure to have the vacuum advance disconnected and plugged. After setting total advance at 2,600 rpm (or whatever rpm your maximum advance is all in), allow the engine speed to return to idle and check and record the idle rpm timing. This way, once you find the optimum setting, you can then check and set the timing using the idle rpm timing number that you have recorded.

For dynometer tuning, start with 32 degrees total and make a pull, noting the horsepower peak. Advance the timing by 2 degrees and perform another pull. Keep doing this until the horsepower begins to fall off. Now back up one degree at a time until the horsepower begins to decrease. Go back up one degree and you have your optimum setting. Don't forget to record the idle timing value so that you can easily check and set the timing.

If you are not using a dynometer, the drag strip can be used. Start with 32 degrees total and make a pass down the strip. Record the miles per hour at the end of the run. When tuning on the dragstip, miles per hour is the indicator of horsepower; elapsed time can be affected by wheelspin. Now advance the timing by 2 degrees and make another pass. Keep doing this until the miles per hour begin to fall. Now back the timing up 1 degree at a time until the miles per hour begin to drop. Advance 1 degree and you should have your optimum setting. Don't forget to record the idle timing value so that you can easily check and set the timing.

SETTING THE OPTIMUM IGNITION VACUUM ADVANCE TIMING

Now that the ideal full throttle timing has been found, you can tune for vacuum advance. This is more subjective, since there is no clear indicator such as trap speed. Also, adjusting the total vacuum advance can be harder, since there are no readily available kits as there are for the mechanical advance system. There are adjustable vacuum advance canisters available for some distributors.

What you are watching for are signs that the timing is being overadvanced while under light to moderate engine loads. Any signs of surging or pinging can be signs that the vacuum advance is adding too much additional timing. Verify by temporarily disconnecting and plugging the vacuum advance hose and repeating the driving maneuver that exhibited the symptoms.

All testing should be done on a fully warmed-up engine that has been driven for at least 5 miles. Cool engines are less likely to ping. You need to test both low-speed acceleration and highway speed acceleration. Also, look for signs of surging while maintaining constant speeds, both on level roadways and also going up light-grade hills. Test for steady-state surging at various speeds, from 35 through 70 miles per hour. Again, if there are signs of pinging or surging, disconnect the vacuum advance and repeat the test. If the pinging or surging is gone, the vacuum advance is adding too much additional timing.

SPARK PLUGS

Sparks plugs are not all created equal. There are several different brands, some of which use different electrode configurations and materials. All claim to give you the edge. The bottom line is if the fuel mixture is being properly ignited, with no pre-combustion due to the spark plug, changing to a different type of plug has no benefit.

NITROUS AND SPARK PLUGS

Do not use platinum plugs with nitrous oxide. Most platinum plug manufacturers will not recommend their plugs for use with nitrous. There are concerns that the platinum tip may detach from the base metal. Platinum can take the extra heat, but the joint where the platinum tip is welded to the base electrode may fail, and a hard platinum tip could enter the cylinder. One manufacturer warns that a chemical reaction could take place and cause deposits to form on the plug that may bleed off some of the spark energy, resulting in misfire. Use only copper or iridium plugs with nitrous.

Engines that burn nitrous oxide produce extremely high cylinder temperatures that could degrade the spark plug electrode and tip. A side-ground electrode style of plug has a much shorter ground electrode, which makes for a cooler-running ground electrode.

Try to find a plug that does not project the center electrode into the chamber. Most modern plugs are projected, as this helps ensure complete combustion at low speeds. When running nitrous, a projected plug will subject the center electrode to the combustion process, and this can result in excessive heating or even damage. A nonprojected plug will have a shorter ground electrode.

The ignition system might have to be upgraded. Nitrous-burning engines create high cylinder pressures that require a higher voltage to ensure that the mixture is ignited. Iridium spark plugs use a smaller tip, and this usually requires a lower voltage.

IGNITION WIRE ROUTING

This sounds simple enough—route the wires so that they look good. It's not that simple, however. How are the wires constructed? Are they original equipment resistor, aftermarket solid wire, or spiral core? Selecting the proper insulation type and thickness is also important.

Original-equipment resistor wires are awful. These are usually a fiberglass strand coated with a carbon powder and encased in a rubber or silicone-based insulator. The fiberglass is an insulator and does not carry electricity; that job is left to the carbon coating. The carbon also forms a resistor, so these wires have

a resistance of around 10,000 to 50,000 ohms per foot. This results in a considerable loss in ignition power. They are not very reliable, and they are the thinnest type of spark plug wire, typically 7mm or less in diameter.

Aftermarket wires come in all types, with the cheap ones being the same or even worse than stock wires! There are also solid core wires. These consist of a solid copper center covered with a 7, 8, or 9mm insulating jacket. While these wires deliver spark energy with the least amount of loss, the resulting interference can cause serious problems, especially with fuel injection systems. Whenever a high-energy current pulse travels down a wire, it radiates electrical interference. This electronic noise causes problems with car radios, electronic ignition, and fuel injection systems. Do not run solid core wires.

The better wires are spiral core. These use a low-resistance steel wire wound in a tight spiral, creating a wire with considerable inductance. This reduces the amount of radiated emissions, or EMI. These wires will work with high-energy ignition systems without generating harmful levels of interference.

Another concern is crossfire, which occurs when the ignition pulse in one wire induces a current flow and a resulting spark in a neighboring wire. This is especially troubling for neighboring cylinders that are adjacent in firing order. For example, be careful when routing the plug wires for cylinders 5 and 7 on GM V-8 engines. These two cylinders are one after the other in the firing order (1-8-4-3-6-5-7-2), and since they are next to each other (1, 3, 5, 7) on the driver's side, the wires exit the distributor and are routed next to each other.

Improper routing can result in crossfire. If cylinder 5 causes 7 to fire, it will be 90 degrees too soon. This results in a serious case of preignition. It is not uncommon to find broken rings or a damaged piston, usually in cylinder 7, on GM V-8 engines. If you find this in your engine, investigate how the ignition wires are routed. As a rule of thumb, keep the wires at least 1 inch away from each other.

Remember, the amount of induced energy decreases exponentially as the separation distance is increased. Doubling the distance between the wires will reduce the amount of induced energy by four.

BASIC WIRING TIPS

Before working on the electrical system, you need to know what size of wire to use and how to replace a broken wire. Wires must be sized properly in order to handle the current flow. For example, using an 18-gauge wire to connect the alternator output to the battery will prevent the alternator from charging the battery properly. Also, the wire will get extremely hot and will most likely melt, since wire resistance varies with size—the smaller the size of the wire (larger gauge number) the larger its resistance, therefore the hotter the wire will get. This increased resistance results in less current flow. Think of a wire as a hose: just as a larger-diameter hose carries more fluid, a larger-diameter wire can carry more current.

In the table below, maximum currents are shown both for wires bundled in a harness and for wires routed alone. Notice that the current rating decreases for bundled wires; this is because each wire adds heat to the bundle, and therefore the allowable maximum current for each wire in the bundle must be decreased.

A wire's current rating is determined by two factors. The first is the maximum temperature rise that the wire can handle. The amount of current flowing through the wire determines this rise, and the wire must not heat up beyond the insulation's temperature rating. In addition to the heat from current flow, the ambient temperature of the operating environment also plays a part in defining a wire's maximum allowable current.

The second factor that determines the wire's current rating is the allowable voltage drop created by the wire itself. The wire's resistance can be calculated from the gauge and length of the wire. Once the resistance is known, multiply the current by the resistance to get the voltage drop across the wire. For most circuits, a 0.95

TABLE 6: WIRE SIZE AND CURRENT CAPABILITY

Wire Size (gauge)	Max. Current (amps): Bundled	Max. Current (amps): Single	Resistance per Foot (ohms)	Typical Use
18	10	15	.00639	Single small light bulb, gauge wiring.
16	13	19	.00402	Single taillight or parking light.
14	15	25	.00253	Ignition coil, windshield wiper motor, taillights.
12	23	35	.00159	Headlights, horn, starter solenoid, fan motor, ignition switch.
10	30	50	.001	Power feed from junction block to fuse box, alternator charge wire (stock), power feed and ground wires for high power amplifiers.
8	45	70	.00063	Alternator charge wire for high output alternators. Main power feed wire from battery to junction block.
6	60	100	.0004	High output alternator (80A) charge wire to battery.
4	80	130	.00025	Battery cables on smaller cars, high output alternator (100A) wire to battery, ground straps.
2	100	180	.00016	Battery cables on small V-8 engines.
1/0	130	210	.0001	Battery cables on large V-8 engines.
4/0	220	360	.00005	Battery cables and arc welding cables.

percent drop is the maximum allowed. For example, a 20-amp headlight circuit using an 8-foot length of 12-gauge wire would see a 0.25 volt, or 2 percent, drop from the light switch. This is not including the voltage drop from the battery to the light switch or the voltage drop due to the resistance of the switch's contacts.

The wire used should have a 125-degree C temperature-rated insulation, such as TXL Polyethylene. Do not use ordinary hook-up wire, as its low 80-degree C temperature rating will quickly harden and crack when subjected to the high-temperature environments. In a pinch, 105-degree C temperature-rated PVC wire can be used, but it should be replaced as soon as you get the chance. Most factory wiring in muscle cars was 105-degree C PVC.

Don't forget to check connectors. Most old wiring problems are usually due to bad connectors. As the vehicle ages, the connectors oxidize and increase the resistance at the connector. This increased resistance causes the connector to get hot. The heat increases the speed at which the connector oxidizes, which adds still more resistance and heat. This downwardly spiraling destructive process continues until the circuit fails. Replacement inserts are available for the original factory-style connectors. Or you can do what I do, which is to replace the connectors with newer weather-tight connectors like those used on modern vehicles. These seal out moisture and help prevent oxidation.

Existing connectors can be cleaned if the damage is not too severe. Older cars use a blade-style connector. The blade can be removed from the connector housing by inserting a small pick into the open end of the connector, behind the solid side of the blade. This will release the tang that holds the terminal in the housing. Once removed, brush the blade with a wire brush. If the terminal does not clean up and become shiny again, the terminal should be replaced. If the terminal is loose and does not grip the mating terminal tightly, it should be replaced.

To replace the blade, cut off the old blade at least an inch back from the old terminal. Install the new terminal using the proper style of crimpers. Do not use pliers, as the connector will not properly connect to the wire. Solder the wire where the crimp is the tightest. Do not use excessive heat. Ensure that solder does not run up into the active area of the female connector. Once the soldering is done, immediately cool the terminal. I solder all connectors, as this seals the air away from the wire where the connector mates with the wire, preventing oxidation at this point.

To repair a broken wire, strip the insulation back at each end approximately 3/4 of an inch. Next, cut a 2-inch long piece of heat-shrink tubing that is slightly larger than the diameter of the wire and slip it over one of the wires. Push the heat shrink tubing far enough down the wire so that it will not shrink when the wire is soldered. Now hold the two wires parallel to each other, with the bare ends overlapping. Twist the two wires around themselves so that a tight connection is made. Solder the joint. Once the soldering is complete and the joint has cooled, slide the heat-shrink tubing up to cover the joint. Heat it with a hot air gun or soldering iron to shrink the tubing.

MAINTAINING AN OLD ELECTRICAL SYSTEM

A muscle car's original electrical system is not complicated and maintaining it is not that difficult. The electrical systems on these cars are, however, at least 30 years old. The parts used were never really intended for such extended service. Furthermore, factory electrical systems were not designed to support much more than a set of headlights, so any additional accessories can quickly exceed the system's output capacity. Fortunately, complete stock replacement or upgraded aftermarket wiring harnesses are available for most cars. The aftermarket versions provide extra fuses and circuits to support added accessories.

In order to maintain your system, you'll need to understand the terms used to describe electrical system problems. *Short circuit* defines a circuit that has an unintentional connection to something else. For example, if a taillight wire rubs against the body until the insulation is damaged and the bare wire

To splice two wires together properly requires a soldering iron. I do not use the crimp splices, as the wires will oxidize and the joint will fail. Begin by stripping the wire back about 1 inch. Also, at this point, cut a 2-inch length of heat-shrink tubing and slip it on one of the wires. Push it far enough back so that it will not be affected by the heat of soldering.

contacts the body of the car, the wire is shorted and the current goes directly to ground. The result is that the taillight will not work, and the fuse that protects the taillight circuit will blow. If the circuit is not protected by a fuse and the wire shorts, the wire will melt. This is why a fuse should never be bypassed or replaced with a larger value fuse.

An *open circuit* occurs when a wire breaks or a connector fails. Once the wire breaks, the current can no longer flow through to the destination. The result is that the device no longer works. Unlike the short circuit, no fuse blows. A short circuit can cause an open circuit, as the disproportionate current flowing as the result of the short can cause the wire to melt or the fuse to blow. Another potential cause of an open circuit is a wire that is stretched or flexed excessively. This can result in a wire that looks okay but has a

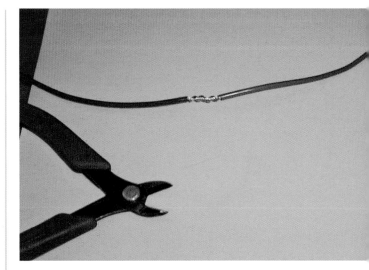

Cross the wires about halfway on the stripped sections and then twist the two wires tightly together. This is what determines the length to strip the insulation back; the thicker the wires, the farther back the insulation must be stripped.

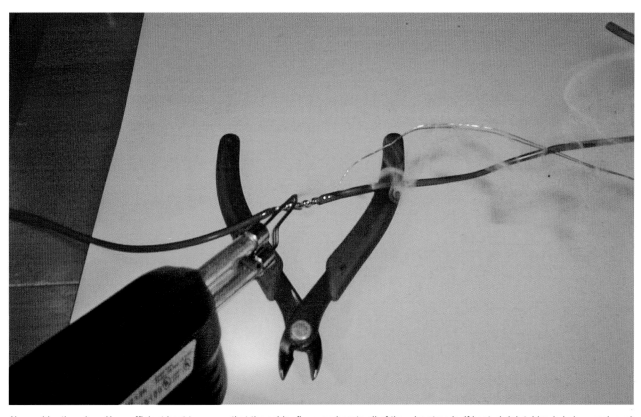

Now solder the wires. Use sufficient heat to ensure that the solder flows and coats all of the wire strands. If heat-shrink tubing is being used, push it far enough back so that it does not shrink due to heat conducting up the wire while soldering.

broken internal conductor. For example, a wire that is subjected to excessive current levels may fail inside the insulation. Overloaded wires usually develop a "French fry" look; the typically smooth insulation will become slightly crinkled in appearance.

Both short and open circuits can be intermittent. This is when the failure comes and goes. In the short circuit example above, this would occur if the wire rubbed against the body until the insulation was gone and allowed the bare wires to contact the body and short out. As the wire moves, it may only occasionally come into contact with the body. Therefore, the short will only occur once in a while. This is usually the cause when you are faced with a fuse that blows every so often, and the system seems to function normally after the fuse is replaced.

Open circuits also result from components that need a ground. For all circuits, current must be able to flow to the device and back to the battery. On a car, this return path is the body. If the part that mounts to the body has corrosion under it or if the mounting bolts are loose, the connection to ground might be lost and the device will not function properly.

For example, a taillight socket is often grounded with a metal clip that connects the shell of the light bulb to the car body. This clip will be part of the taillight socket. If the clip is corroded or missing, or if the car body is rusted at the point of contact, the taillight will not function properly.

To check for proper grounding at the bulb, connect a voltmeter between a known good ground point and the metal of the taillight bulb. This reading can be obtained by pushing the probe tip between the socket and the bulb. Turn on the taillights and the turn signal. The voltage should read no more than .2 volt.

CIRCUIT PROTECTION DEVICES

Muscle cars use three types of circuit protection devices. The most common is the fuse. A fuse is basically just a piece of wire with a low melting temperature. It is sized so that when the current flow exceeds a certain value, the wire will melt. The rating of the fuse is the maximum current that the fuse will allow to flow for a given period of time. When overloaded, the fuse will melt and open the circuit in order to protect the wiring. How long the fuse takes to open depends on the current level. For example, a 20-amp fuse will not fail instantly if 25 amps pass through it. However, if a fuse is used at the maximum rating for a long time, the wire inside it will heat and eventually fail.

For the maximum reliability, the circuit should be designed to flow no more than 66 percent of the fuse rating. The wire size is typically what dictates the rating of the fuse needed. Refer to the wire size chart earlier in this chapter. The fuse size is the maximum current shown for the wire size. For example, a 14-gauge wire must be protected with a 15-amp (or less) fuse when the wire is bundled with other wires, or a 25-amp fuse if the wire is single. Never use a fuse with a rating higher than that which is recommended; damage to the wiring or the vehicle can be the result. Worse yet, you could end up with a wire fire!

The next circuit protection device found on muscle cars is the fusible link. This is a short piece of wire—usually two gauge sizes smaller than the wire used in the circuit—that is covered with a special flameproof insulation. This wire is designed to melt and protect the rest of the wiring harness in the event of a serious overload. Fusible links are located in the main power-feed wires, such as the battery-to-alternator wire, the battery-to-headlight switch, and the battery-to-vehicle power. They are easy to check. Use a voltmeter to see if power is present at both sides, or simply give a gentle tug on the wire. If the internal wire has separated, the wire's casing will stretch like a rubber band.

TABLE 7: FUSIBLE LINK RATINGS

Fusible Link Size	Circuit Rating	Wire Size Protected
12	100 amps	6 gauge
14	75 amps	8 gauge
16	55 amps	10 gauge
18	40 amps	12 gauge
20	30 amps	14 gauge

The values on the table are approximate; ambient air temperature and air circulation around the wire will change them. These numbers should not be taken as the working current for the circuit. For example, according to our circuit rating table, a 12-gauge circuit should be designed for a maximum continuous current of 20 amps, so use an 18-gauge fusible link. For that 10-gauge alternator charge wire on a stock vehicle, use a 16-gauge fusible link.

The fusible links are located at the main junction block. On Fords, this is at the starter solenoid mounted on the fender well. GM cars usually had this junction at the starter solenoid as well, but the solenoid is located on top of the starter. Chryslers and some GM cars usually had

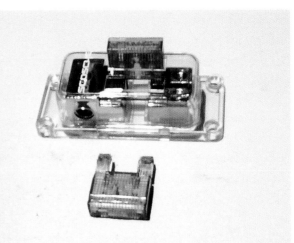

Fusible links can be replaced with a Maxi-fuse. These fuses range from 30A to 80A. This holder has two Maxi-fuse slots. These are easy to find; any place that carries automotive audio equipment will sell these.

the junction on one of the fenders, where it is a separate connector block, or at the horn relay. Refer to the service manual for exact location on your car. If a fusible link fails, do not replace it with a regular link of wire. Replace it with another fusible link or you run the risk of a wiring catastrophe! A car battery can deliver hundreds of amps of power in the event of a short circuit. Fusible links will protect heavy-gauge wires that take power directly from the battery.

The final protection device used on muscle cars is the circuit breaker. Muscle cars use the self-resetting type. A circuit breaker is a switch that turns itself off when excessive current flows. One example is the headlight switch. Most muscle cars use a headlight switch with a circuit breaker. If the headlight circuit overloads the wiring, the circuit breaker will open and protect the wiring. After a few minutes, the circuit breaker will cool and reconnect the circuit. This will continue until the fault is corrected or the circuit breaker fails. Using a circuit breaker has the advantage that a momentary overload will not blow a fuse and require user intervention.

Most convertible tops, power seats, and power windows are protected by circuit breakers. This way, if the motor is operated past the stop or becomes overloaded for some other reason, the excessive current drawn will trip the circuit breaker, protecting the wiring and the motor. Once the circuit breaker cools, it can be reset, restoring power to the device. If a fuse had been used, you would have had to replace it. So if your power windows, power seats, or convertible top are not operating properly, first clean the mechanical slides to ensure that excessive friction is not overloading the motor. If this does not solve your problem, replace the circuit breaker. Only replace a circuit breaker with another one of the same current rating. Using a circuit breaker with a higher current rating can result in damage to the motor of whatever device the circuit breaker is protecting. Or worse yet, a wire fire.

THE BATTERY

The battery stores electrical energy used to run the starter and start the car. Besides voltage, batteries are rated for cold-cranking amps and amp-hour rating. The cold-cranking amps rating is the amperage that the battery can supply for 30 seconds at 0-degree F. This rating determines how much power is available to the starter to get the engine turning. The amp-hour rating tells you how much power the battery can provide. For example, a 60-amp-hour battery can provide 60 amps for one hour, or one amp for 60 hours. The higher the amp hour rating, the more power the battery is capable of storing. For a typical muscle car, you need at least 750 cold-cranking amps and a minimum of 50 amp hours.

Automobiles use lead-acid batteries and the charge level can be determined by testing the specific gravity of the electrolyte in each cell with a hydrometer, or by measuring the voltage across the terminals with a voltmeter. If you charge the battery, wait eight hours before ascertaining the charge level with a voltmeter. A freshly charged battery can show 13.1 to 13.2 volts across the terminals right after charging, even if, in reality, the battery needs to be replaced. This is called a surface charge, and will dissipate on its own in about 8 hours, or it can be removed by turning on the lights for one minute.

A fully charged lead-acid cell has 2.11 volts. A 12-volt automobile battery consists of six cells connected in series. The resulting voltage for a fully charged 12-volt battery is 12.65 volts, and a 6-volt battery has a full-charge voltage of 6.33 volts. The following table shows the specific gravity and voltage for a lead-acid cell at various states of charge. Note that once the cell voltage drops below 1.98 volts, the battery is fully discharged. Automotive batteries are not deep-cycle designs, and operation below 50 percent should be avoided, as battery life will decrease dramatically.

For vehicles that are regularly stored for one week or longer, a float charger is a must in order to preserve battery life. A float charger is a special battery charger that maintains a constant voltage across the battery of 2.3 volts per cell, or 13.8 volts for a 12-volt battery.

TABLE 8: LEAD-ACID BATTERY CHARGE

Charge	Specific Gravity	Cell Voltage	12-Volt Battery Voltage
100 percent	1.265	2.11 volts	12.65 volts
75 percent	1.225	2.075 volts	12.45 volts
50 percent	1.190	2.04 volts	12.24 volts
25 percent	1.155	2.01 volts	12.06 volts
Dead	1.120	< 1.98 volts	< 11.90 volts

This float charger prevents sulfation by maintaining the battery at 100 percent charge. Do not use an unregulated or standard charger to maintain a battery.

Voltages in excess of 2.3 volts per cell will cause the battery to overheat and lose electrolytes, eventually destroying the battery.

Most muscle car starters will develop around 2 horsepower at around 60 percent efficiency; this translates into 2,500 watts. A properly charged battery will deliver roughly 10 volts to the starter once the engine is cranking—this is 250 amps! You cannot carry this kind of current through the typical parts store 4- or 6-gauge battery cables. I run 4/0 (0000) battery cables. These usually have to be purchased from the better restoration parts houses or built by you. 4/0 wire is used for making welding cables.

One good place to attach the negative battery cable is at the alternator. Note the size of this cable. To start a big block reliably requires large cables. This one and the positive battery cable are both 4/0 cables. Also notice the clamp that secures the cable to the lower alternator bracket to protect the cable end from vibration as the engine moves.

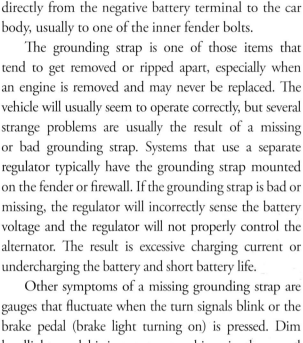

Here is a ground strap from the battery to the car body. This application uses a 6-gauge wire to connect the vehicle body to the battery. Also note the 4/0 negative battery cable. The remaining 10-gauge green wire is the ground for the stereo system.

High-quality battery cables are important. The current required to get the starter turning can exceed 500 amps. If the battery cable is too small, you will waste a considerable amount of power warming up the battery cables rather than cranking over the engine. A good battery cable will not drop more than 0.2 volt while the engine is cranking.

All of the electrical current in the vehicle must travel back to the battery through the ground circuit. The negative cable is usually connected to the engine block. For the gauges, lights, and other electrical accessories to operate correctly, the vehicle's body must also be properly connected to the negative terminal. On most cars, this was accomplished with a grounding strap that connects the engine block to the car body.

The grounding strap on most GM muscle cars was usually located at the back of the engine, running from one of the rear intake manifold bolts or a bolt on the back of a cylinder head to a bolt on the firewall. This wire is an uninsulated braid that is approximately 3/4 of an inch wide and roughly 1/8 of an inch thick. Most

Chrysler cars run the strap from one of the engine motor-mount bolts to the frame. Just like the strap used on GM cars, this strap is also a flat uninsulated braid. Several Ford vehicles used a connection running directly from the negative battery terminal to the car body, usually to one of the inner fender bolts.

The grounding strap is one of those items that tend to get removed or ripped apart, especially when an engine is removed and may never be replaced. The vehicle will usually seem to operate correctly, but several strange problems are usually the result of a missing or bad grounding strap. Systems that use a separate regulator typically have the grounding strap mounted on the fender or firewall. If the grounding strap is bad or missing, the regulator will incorrectly sense the battery voltage and the regulator will not properly control the alternator. The result is excessive charging current or undercharging the battery and short battery life.

Other symptoms of a missing grounding strap are gauges that fluctuate when the turn signals blink or the brake pedal (brake light turning on) is pressed. Dim headlights and hissing, pops, or whines in the sound system, and a starter motor that turns over very slowly are other symptoms of a missing or damaged ground strap.

To check the strap, start the engine and turn the headlights on. Connect a voltmeter from the negative battery terminal to the car body. It should not read more than 0.1 volt. If it does, this indicates that excessive resistance is present in the engine-to-body grounding strap circuit. Find the grounding strap and check for signs of damage, such as torn or frayed wires or corroded terminal ends. Also make sure that the strap is present.

If the strap is missing or damaged, replace it. If a factory-style strap is not used or available, a replacement strap can be made from a short piece of six-gauge wire. Crimp on the appropriate large-ring terminals and solder the crimp. Remove a bolt from the body and one from the engine block. Use a small piece of sandpaper to clean the area under the removed bolt heads. Install the strap and test the integrity of the body-to-battery negative terminal circuit.

The charging system is on the vehicle to charge the battery and power the car when the engine is running. The alternator is the anchor of the charging system on most muscle cars. Unlike the alternators on modern cars that produce 120 amps or more, the typical muscle car came with a 37- or 40-amp alternator or a heavy-duty 55- or 65-amp alternator. Muscle cars typically used separate regulators rather than the built-in solid-state regulator on modern alternators.

An alternator is an AC generator. This is more efficient than the generators used on pre-1960s vehicles, as the main power is generated in the stator (the nonrotating part), and the high-charging current does not have to flow through brushes. The alternator creates AC voltage, and requires a rectifier to change the AC to DC. Most alternators are three-phase systems, which use six diodes. A generator-equipped vehicle will have 30 to 35 amps charging current maximum, with poor charge output at idle.

Alternators require a regulator to handle varying engine speeds and electrical loads. The regulator varies the strength of the electromagnet that is rotating inside the alternator (the armature). The more powerful the electromagnet, the higher the output from the alternator. Thanks to the regulator, the alternator is able to maintain a constant voltage output regardless of engine speed or demand placed on the electrical system.

TROUBLESHOOTING THE CHARGING SYSTEM

When a charging system has problems, it either fails to charge the battery when the engine is running or the battery drains down when the engine is off. If the problem is insufficient alternator output, the car will start and run fine if the battery is charged, but quit and refuse to start after three to four hours of driving. If the issue is a battery drain with the engine off, the car will start and run fine as long as the vehicle does not sit for any length of time.

In order to test a problematic system, place a voltmeter across the battery terminals. Start the car

Use bolts on the intake manifold or cylinder heads for attaching grounds instead of valve cover bolts.

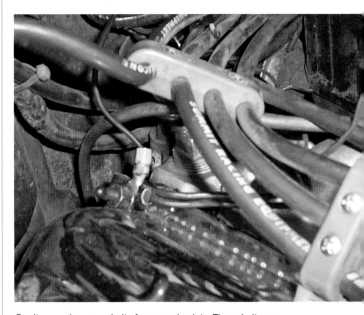

Don't use valve cover bolts for ground points. These bolts are notorious for working loose, resulting in an intermittent or no ground.

and observe the voltage. If it does not rise to 13.8 to 14.5 volts, the alternator may not be working. Before replacing the alternator, ensure that the battery is charged, and test it again. On a severely drained battery, the alternator may be running at maximum

Most muscle cars came with 37- to 63-amp alternators. This one was originally a 63-amp model that has been converted to provide 80 amps.

output and therefore the voltage may appear low. If the voltage rises to 13.8 volts when the engine is running, but the car fails to start several hours or a few days later, check for a battery drain with the engine off.

If the voltage is above 14.5 volts during the test, the regulator is defective or the sense wire is broken. In either case, the excessive voltage will damage the battery, shorten bulb life, and can damage gauges and electronic equipment. For excessive voltage, check the wiring around the regulator and the battery-to-body grounding strap. If the wiring is good, replace the regulator.

TESTING THE ALTERNATOR

To see if the alternator is attempting to put out power, connect the positive lead of the voltmeter to the stud on the rear of the alternator where the large wire connects. Next, connect the black wire to the positive terminal at the battery. With the vehicle off, the meter should read 0.00 volt. Start the car. The meter should read between 0.01 and 0.1 volt. If the reading is slightly higher, excessive resistance in the charging circuit exists. If the reading is higher by one or more volts, the wire between the alternator output and the battery is open and must be replaced.

Most muscle cars used a fusible link in the battery-to-alternator output. Check it, too. If the reading is 0, then the alternator is not driving much current.

To verify alternator output under load, turn on the headlights with the engine running at idle and recheck voltage to verify that the output at the battery remains above 13.2 volts at idle. If the voltage falls off when the headlights are turned on, check to see if the fan belt is tight. If the alternator is slipping, it will not be able to maintain maximum output, even though it seems to be charging the battery. This will cause the battery to gradually run down and not have enough juice to start the car after a few days of operation.

If the alternator fails either of the above tests, the alternator or regulator wiring will need to be checked. If the alternator passes these tests, go to the battery drain section. Verify that the alternator has a good ground. Check this by connecting a voltmeter between the alternator body and the battery negative terminal. With the car running and the headlights on, the voltmeter should read 0.05 volt or less. If the reading is higher, remove the alternator and clean the mounting bracket contact areas. This is a common problem when the car has freshly painted or severely corroded brackets that fail to provide a good ground connection. The alternator bracket must contact the engine block and the alternator. I always connect my negative battery cable to the alternator bracket.

After the ground circuit has been verified and the main output wire has been shown to be good, the rest

Checking the alternator output voltage at the battery. Do this with the headlights on and the heater fan running at maximum speed. Measure the voltage across the battery terminals. The voltage at idle should be above 13.5 volts or you may have a charging system issue. If the voltage is 12.6 or less, the alternator is not functioning properly. Also, if the voltage is 15 volts or more, the regulator is not doing its job and the excess voltage will result in short light bulb and battery life.

This is a modern 160-amp alternator. With fuel injection and electric cooling fans, increased alternator output is required on new vehicles. By the way, while delivering maximum output, this alternator will draw around 3.5 horsepower!

of the wiring can be checked. All Ford and Chrysler muscle cars used an external regulator, as did most GM cars built until 1972 (Oldsmobile 442s were equipped with internal-regulator alternators on 1969 and later cars). Regardless of whether the alternator was equipped with an internal or external regulator, three wires typically lead from the alternator. On an alternator that uses an external regulator, one of these wires is the battery charging wire (the 10-gauge wire that we checked above). The remaining two wires connect to the regulator. For cars that use an alternator with an internal regulator, the same battery charging wire is present, and there will also be one or two wires that connect to the vehicle, one at the alternator warning light and one at the junction block where the positive battery power is distributed, the same point where the fusible links originate from.

TROUBLESHOOTING A SEPARATE REGULATOR AND ALTERNATOR SYSTEM

Before troubleshooting a separate regulator and alternator charging system, check the engine-to-body grounding strap. The two wires that connect the alternator to the regulator are for the armature and stator sense. The armature wire allows the regulator to increase or decrease the alternator electromagnet's strength, thus the alternator's output voltage, by supplying power to the armature. On GM and Chrysler cars, this wire will usually read around 3 to 4 volts when the car is running, and as the electrical load is increased, or the engine rpm drops, this voltage will increase. If this wire is broken, the alternator will not put out any power.

The stator sense wire feeds a small portion of the alternator output to the regulator. The function of this feed is to allow the regulator to turn off the alternator if the engine speed is too slow to allow charging. This way, the armature current will not be driven excessively high. If this wire is broken (creating an open circuit), the alternator will never be switched on by the regulator.

At the regulator, the connector usually has four wires. Two are the ones just described that connect to the alternator. The next two are the ignition feed and the battery sense wire. The ignition feed originates from the ignition switch and routes through the alternator warning light. This informs the regulator to switch the alternator on. The battery sense wire is used by the regulator to monitor battery voltage. If the line from the ignition switch is open, the alternator will not begin to charge. If the battery sense line is open, the alternator may not start to charge. On some models the alternator will start to charge, but the output voltage will be too high.

Finally, check the connection to ground under the regulator itself. Just like the alternator, the regulator must have a good ground. Remove the bolts that hold the regulator mounting bracket to the firewall or fender and clean the back of the bracket and mounting point on the fender or firewall where the bracket is attached. If in doubt, connect a grounding strap between one of the regulator mounting bolts and the negative battery terminal. This connection can also be made at the alternator case and the wire can be concealed in the alternator-to-regulator wiring harness. Use a 10- or 12-gauge wire—nothing smaller.

To check the alternator, start the car and check for 12 volts at the battery sense wire and the ignition feed lines at the alternator. If the proper voltage is present, check for 3 to 6 volts on the armature lead. If this terminal shows 12 volts, check the other end of the wire at the alternator. If the wire is open, it will show 0 volts at the alternator. If the wire shows 12 volts at the alternator, the brushes are worn or the armature is open. Either a 0- or 12-volt reading indicates you need to replace or rebuild the alternator.

If the alternator is replaced, replace the regulator as well. Most muscle car–era regulators used mechanical relays and the contact points pit and wear. Most replacement regulators are solid state and much more reliable.

TROUBLESHOOTING AN INTEGRAL REGULATOR ALTERNATOR SYSTEM

All modern vehicles use an integral regulator alternator. The regulator is a solid state and is part of the alternator. There are usually one or two wires in addition to the main charging output lead wire. The remaining wires sense battery voltage and turn the alternator on. The battery sense wire is usually a 12-gauge wire that connects to the battery. This wire is how the regulator senses the voltage at the battery. The second wire connects to the ignition switch through the alternator light or a resistor.

These alternators are easy to test. Begin by following the charging system diagnostic procedures in the previous section. If these do not pinpoint the problem, check the two secondary wires. Turn the ignition on and verify that the sense wire shows the same voltage as the battery. The indicator line should be low, reading less than 2.0 volts, and the alternator light should be on. Next, start the car; the indicator light should go out and the indicator light wire should show the same voltage as the battery.

Note that the indicator light also serves as the enable mechanism for the alternator. Cars equipped with an amp meter will also have either an alternator warning light or a resistor because the enable mechanism is required to tell the alternator to start charging. This signal prevents the alternator from applying armature current when the engine is off, as this would discharge the battery. If the indicator line does not show voltage with the ignition switch on, check the bulb and the associated wiring. A burned-out indicator light can result in an alternator that does not charge. On cars without a charging system warning light, find the resistor and check it. It should measure around 10 to 20 ohms. If it is being replaced, use the factory resistor, or purchase a 20-ohm/20-watt resistor.

TROUBLESHOOTING BATTERY DRAIN PROBLEMS

When the alternator is charging but the battery goes dead after several hours or days, begin the system test by disconnecting the battery's negative terminal. Connect an amp meter between the battery's negative terminal and ground. With everything switched off and the doors closed, the reading should be .05 amps or less. If not, you have a current draw and this is draining your battery. Consider this: a 55-amp-hour battery will be dead after 55 hours of sitting with a 1-amp load connected across its terminals. Also consider that depending on the vehicle, most cars will no longer start once the battery is down to 1/4 or less charge capacity. So a 1-amp load will drain the battery to the point that the car will not start in less than two days!

If the drain is excessive, begin by removing each fuse in turn and repeating the battery drain test just described. Once you find the fuse that eliminates the drain, find out what is connected to the fuse. Don't forget to check glove box lights, underhood lights, and trunk lights, as these draw enough power to drain a battery in one or two days if the switch is bad and the light remains on.

If removing fuses did not eliminate the drain, disconnect the wires from the alternator. Check the amperage draw at the battery again. If the draw is less than 0.5 amp, replace the alternator. If the leakage is still present, disconnect the regulator and recheck. If draw is less than 0.5 amp, replace the regulator. Finally disconnect accessories such as the stereo, amplifiers, radio equipment, the power antenna, alarm, fog lights, and so on until draw is less than 0.5 amp—in other words, until the problem is found.

Most auxiliary amplifiers are connected directly to the battery, with a feed wire from the radio that turns the amplifier on. Power antennas are also typically connected directly to the battery, and a feed wire from the radio tells the antenna to go up or down. These sorts of accessories should not draw power when the radio is turned off. Troubleshoot them by disconnecting the feed wire from the radio. The amplifier and/or antenna should turn off; if not, one or both are defective. Don't forget power seats and power door locks. Sticking or defective switches can result in battery drains.

When diagnosing electrical problems, check any aftermarket or added wiring carefully. Depending on who added the accessory or wiring, the job may have not been performed properly.

TROUBLESHOOTING THE STARTER

A car that will not start is simply a driveway weight. The starter wiring is rather straightforward, and troubleshooting the starter is simple. Just like any other system, the symptoms will direct the repair efforts.

The first problem is no starter action at all. This occurs when the key is turned to the start position and the result is no noise, not even a click. Begin by verifying that the battery is fully charged. There should be at least 12.6 volts present at the battery terminals. Next, turn on the headlights and try to crank the engine. The battery voltage should drop some with the lights on, but stay above 12 volts. When the key is turned to the crank position, note what happens. If the battery voltage does not change, the starter solenoid or the wiring that activates the solenoid has an open. If the voltage falls to below 9.0 volts and no clicking or other sounds of activity are coming from the starter, either the battery or battery cables are defective.

STARTER PROBLEMS, NO BATTERY VOLTAGE DROP

Begin by attaching a clip lead to the starter solenoid. Be careful to not short this to the battery cable. The clip lead should be a tight-clamping insulated test clip with a 12-gauge wire at least 3 feet long. With the ignition off, touch the other end to the battery positive terminal. A safer way is to use a clip-on remote starter button, with one end attached to the solenoid and the other to the positive battery terminal. Either way, if the engine now cranks, the problem is with the wiring. If not, the problem is with the solenoid.

If the solenoid responded to a direct connection but does not respond to the ignition switch, find the starter solenoid crank wire on the back of the ignition switch. Probe here for 12 volts when the ignition switch is in the crank position. If you don't see 12 volts, the ignition switch is most likely bad. If the switch is passing the battery voltage, the next step is the neutral safety switch, or, for manual transmission cars, the clutch switch.

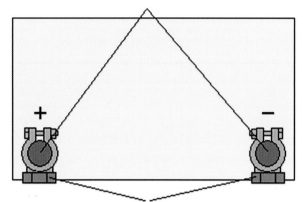

Probe Here for Battery Voltage

+   −

Probe Here for Terminal Voltage

Probe points for checking the battery and the battery terminal connectors. These two test locations per terminal allow the terminal and the terminal connectors to be checked. Corrosion between the two will be evident by a voltage drop.

For all of these next tests, it is important to remember that the voltage must be either 0 when the key is not in the crank position or full battery voltage when cranking. If a switch or connector is bad, it may have higher than normal resistance, and this may prevent the solenoid from activating. If you discover that the voltage on the other side of a switch or connector is more than 0.1 volt below the battery voltage, you have a damaged or corroded contact and it is incapable of passing the current that the solenoid needs to operate. The result may be a vehicle that sometimes does not crank or never cranks.

To check the neutral safety switch, you have to find it. Look near the shifter first. For example, cars with the shift lever on the console often have the neutral safety switch mounted on the console, too. Be careful, as the back-up lights also connect to the shifter. These two switches are usually in a single housing that has four connectors.

The switch can also be mounted under the dash and connected to a column shifter. This can even be true for floor-shifted cars; there will be a solid linkage that connects the transmission to the steering column shifter. This is especially true for 1969 and later cars that

have a steering wheel lock. This feature requires that the transmission be locked in park before it will start, so even for a console-shift car, the linkage to the steering column will be in place. If this linkage has been removed, then there will be nothing to prevent the column ring from turning, which will prevent the car from starting.

Once the neutral safety switch is located, check the starter wires for continuity while the transmission is in park and neutral. The switch should show 0 ohms of resistance, or should pass the battery voltage through when the key is in the crank position. If it does not, verify that it is properly adjusted by removing the switch and reconnecting the wires, and then, while holding the key in the crank position, move the switch lever through its full range. If the engine cranks, re-install the switch and adjust it. If the switch does not pass the voltage, connect a jumper wire across the two starter terminals and see if the vehicle cranks (make sure that the car is in park). If it now cranks, replace the safety switch.

For vehicles with a manual transmission, there is usually a clutch safety switch, and these are almost always mounted under the dash on the clutch pedal linkage. To test this switch, run a jumper wire across the two terminals on the switch and see if the vehicle will start. Make sure the vehicle is in neutral first. If the engine cranks, make sure the switch is properly adjusted before replacing it.

After the clutch or neutral safety switch, the wire should pass through to the starter solenoid. If the safety switch is good and there is battery voltage present on both sides of the safety switch while the key is in the crank position, the problem is with the wiring between the safety switch and the starter solenoid. You know this because you also checked the starter directly as your first test.

Find the starter solenoid wire where it passes through to the engine compartment. Carefully probe the wire to check for battery voltage while cranking. If no voltage is present, the bulkhead connector or the wire under the dash from the interlock switch to the bulkhead connector is bad. If there is voltage

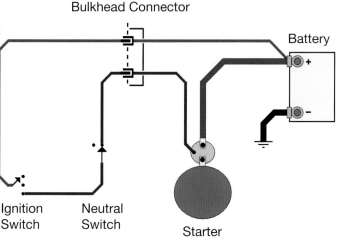

Typical starter circuit. Note that the current that activates the solenoid must pass through the bulkhead connector, the ignition switch, and the neutral safety (or clutch) switch and then back through the bulkhead connector. Each of these can introduce a voltage drop that causes erratic, intermittent, or no operation of the starter.

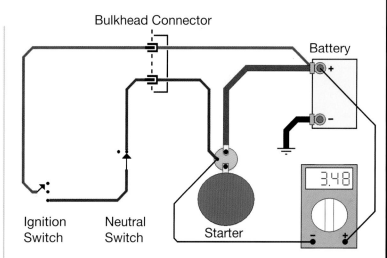

This is what you don't want to see: With the ignition switch in the start position, the meter should be reading 0.2 volt or less, not 3.48 volts, as in this example. On this vehicle, the car would start when cold, but after driving around, the vehicle had a "dead" starter. You would turn the key to crank and nothing happened, not even a click.

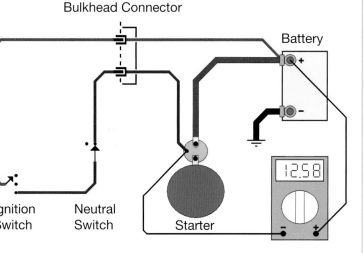

Begin the test by verifying with the key off that you can see the full battery voltage across the circuit. With the starter not engaged, the low resistance of the solenoid to ground will "appear" to the voltmeter as a direct connection to ground.

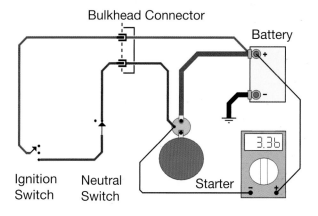

Moving back to check the neutral safety switch. Check both sides of the switch to see if the voltage drop is due to the switch. In this example, the problem is still present at the input to the switch, so the neutral safety switch is not to blame. Moving back to the ignition switch revealed that the source of the problem was a bad ignition switch. Replacing the switch cured the problem

present here, trace the wire to the solenoid; you will probably find that it is broken or damaged. Also, check the connector at the solenoid; if it is a crimp-style connector, it may be damaged or corroded.

STARTER PROBLEMS, VOLTAGE DROP BUT NO CRANK

If the battery voltage drops but the engine does not crank, there are a couple of areas to explore. Begin

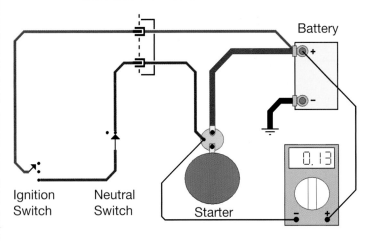

Bulkhead Connector

Battery

0.13

Ignition Switch

Neutral Switch

Starter

This is what you should see: The voltage drop is less than 0.2 volt when the ignition switch is in the crank position. This indicates that there is not excessive resistance in the starter solenoid activation circuit.

with the battery and battery terminals. Place the voltmeter probes in the center of the battery post itself, not on the terminal connectors at the end of the positive and negative battery cables. Next, crank the car. If the voltage drops to below 9.0 volts and there is no noise from the starter, the battery most likely has a dead cell. This is usually the case if after turning on the headlights the battery voltage drops to 10.8 or lower, but with everything off, the battery shows 12 volts.

If the battery maintains good voltage, move the probes to the battery terminal connectors. Place the probes on the body of the connector, or if your terminal connectors have a clamp that holds the wire, place the probes on the clamps. Next, attempt to crank the engine. If the voltage falls off, the clamps need to be removed and cleaned or replaced. You can check each one by probing one voltmeter lead between the center of the battery post and the other on the body of the terminal connector, where the battery cable comes out. If one is showing a high voltage drop, the other most likely needs attention as well.

If the previous tests were passed, check the cables by connecting the negative (black) lead of the voltmeter

to the center of the negative battery terminal and the positive lead to the engine block. Now attempt to start the engine; if the reading is more than 0.25 volt, the negative battery cable is bad.

Check the positive cable the same way. Begin by connecting the voltmeter's positive lead (red) to the center of the battery positive terminal. Now connect the negative voltmeter lead to a test lead that is clamped to the bolt on the solenoid where the positive battery cable is connected. Make sure that the clamp will not short to anything. Now attempt to crank the engine. If the reading is over 0.25 volt, this indicates a bad positive battery cable.

STARTER PROBLEMS, ENGINE WILL NOT START WHEN HOT

If the vehicle starts fine when cold or after a short trip but will not start after being driven for any length of time, suspect a solenoid problem. This is not uncommon, and it might not even be that the solenoid is bad. Before you start replacing parts, perform a few tests to determine what is really wrong.

Begin by checking for voltage drop in the solenoid feed from the ignition switch. Since the starter causes the voltage to drop, these tests are done by connecting a voltmeter between the positive battery terminal and the solenoid supply terminal on the ignition switch. This allows you to measure the voltage drop in the solenoid circuit without the voltage drop of the starter motor interfering.

To make this test, use clip-on test leads with your voltmeter. Connect the negative lead to the solenoid terminal that activates the solenoid; this is the lead that comes from the ignition switch and it will have battery voltage when the key is switched to the start position. Connect the voltmeter positive lead to the battery positive terminal. The voltmeter is now showing the voltage drop across the circuit. With the key in the off position, the voltmeter should be showing the full battery voltage, as the ignition switch is not completing the circuit. When the key is moved to the start position, the voltmeter allows us to check for excessive voltage drop; the meter should not show more than 0.25 volt.

The vehicle does not have to be at operating temperature to perform this test, and it is easier if you don't have hot engine components to work around. Also, it is easier if you deactivate the starter motor so the solenoid circuit can be checked without the starter turning or engaging. On most vehicles, this is easy to accomplish. For Ford vehicles that have the starter relay on the fenderwell, disconnect the heavy cable that leads from the relay to the starter. For GM vehicles, there is a small bolt that connects the solenoid output to the starter. This is the copper strap that comes out of the top of the starter and connects to the back of the solenoid, directly under the battery cable connection on the solenoid. If this bolt is removed, the starter will not run. For the Chrysler camp, the solenoid is fed from the starter relay, and this is usually a brown wire that leads from the relay to the solenoid. Disconnect the brown wire to deactivate the starter.

This same procedure can be used for any circuit on the vehicle, from weak horns to dim lights. For accessories such as lights, don't forget to check not only the power to the accessory but the connection back to ground as well. The device does not care if the

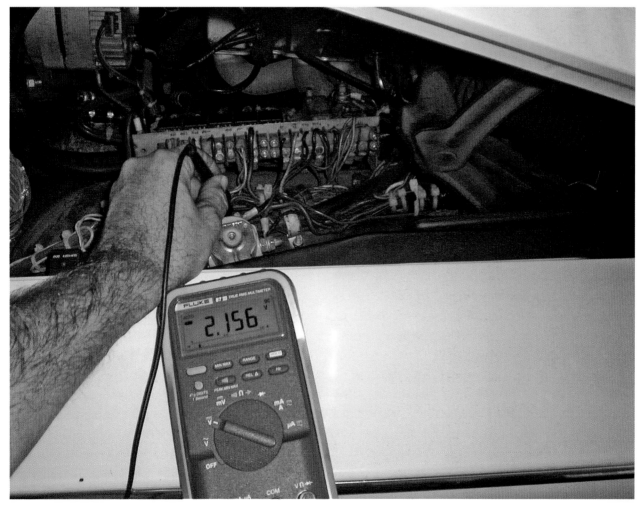

This is not good. The voltage drop in the solenoid feed circuit is 2.156 volts in this example. The result of this is a car that will not start when hot. This was traced back to a faulty ignition switch. On a good circuit, this reading would have been 0.2 volt or less, not 2.156 volts.

voltage drop is on the supply or return side; it only sees the voltage that crosses it.

STARTER PROBLEMS, ENGINE CRANKS SLOWLY

If the engine cranks slowly whether it is hot or cold, check the voltage at the starter motor. Perform the same tests listed previously for voltage drop but no crank. If the engine cranks fine when cold but slowly when warm, or if the starter will not fully engage when the engine is warm, perform the battery cable drop tests listed previously. Also, verify that the starter solenoid crank signal wire is delivering the battery voltage to the solenoid. There should not be more than a 0.25-volt drop from the battery to the solenoid.

Check the battery voltage at the battery terminals while cranking. The voltage must not fall below 8.5 volts on initial crank, and should rise to 10 volts while the engine continues cranking. If the voltage is low, check at the center of the battery terminals. If the voltage is still too low, have the battery load tested. The difference from measuring across the starter and from the center of the battery terminals must not be more than 0.5 volt. If the voltage checks pass and the battery passes the load test and is rated for 750 cold cranking amps or more, then the starter is drawing excessive current and should be replaced.

The average starter motor will develop a peak of 2 horsepower (about 250 amps at 10.0 volts). These current levels are developed when the starter motor is turning at its designed speed, which usually occurs when the starter is turning the engine at about 200 rpm. If the engine is not turning or is turning slowly, the current levels required to turn the starter will be two to three times normal! Consequently, starting to turn the engine may require 500 to 700 amps! This is why the cables and connectors must be up to the task and properly maintained.

Starter problems can also be caused by incorrect starter-pinion-to-flywheel alignment. If the pinion gear is too far away from the flywheel, the starter might emit a whining noise during cranking. If the pinion is too close to the flywheel, the starter might emit a whine after the starter is disengaged or the starter might sound like it is grinding while it cranks the engine over. If the starter is too close, it may hang in engagement after the engine starts.

Improper starter alignment can result in damage to the starter, flywheel, or flexplate. If the starter sounds clean and it engages and disengages crisply without grinding or making other strange sounds, the alignment is probably fine. Also, the hot cranking performance should be the same as the cold cranking performance.

Before verifying starter alignment, check the bolts to make sure that the correct ones are used. Most starter bolts have some sort of shoulder or knurled pattern that correctly locates the starter. Also make sure that the bolts are not bent or damaged in any way. If in doubt, replace the bolts. This will save untold grief if your mysterious starter problems are due to a defective bolt. Also, tighten the bolts to the correct torque value; the starter must be properly supported and held so that it does not move.

The only way to properly check for alignment is to disconnect the negative battery cable and then manually move the starter pinion into the drive position. Don't attempt to move the pinion into position with both battery cables connected; on GM vehicles, the solenoid will be moved as well and the starter might engage. Once the pinion is moved into position, measure the clearance between the valley of the pinion gear and the top of the ring-gear tooth. Check this against the recommended clearance given in the factory service manual. It should be around .020 inch. If it is not close to the recommended value, shims can be added to move the starter farther away to increase the clearance. If the starter is too far away, remove a shim, or if no shim is present, shim the outside bolt only. Each .015 inch shim has roughly a .005 inch effect on the clearance in this case.

Finally, check if you have the correct starter. Most factory muscle cars with high-compression engines came with high-torque starters. These typically look identical and fit the same as the standard-output starter. The problem is that most replacement starters you get from auto parts stores are the standard rather than the high-torque version. This problem's symptoms will usually include slow cranking when the engine is warm.

TROUBLESHOOTING THE HEADLIGHTS

The lighting circuits on a muscle car are pretty simple. Most muscle cars do not use fuses for the headlights. The headlight wiring is protected by a circuit breaker on the light switch. In most cars, a 10- or 12-gauge wire connects the headlight switch to the battery feed. Then a 16-gauge wire is run from the headlight switch to the dimmer switch, which is usually mounted on the floor. From the dimmer, two 16-gauge wires feed current to the headlights. On the typical muscle car the headlights consume more power than other accessories.

If the headlights turn on and off by themselves, the circuit breaker on the light switch might be tripping. Test this by removing one of the headlight bulbs. If the problem is solved, the circuit breaker is bad and the light switch needs to be replaced.

If the lights do not come on at all, remove the connector from the dimmer switch and check for battery voltage at one of the three wires with the headlights on. If all three wires show 0 volts, remove the light switch.

To remove a light switch, the knob must be removed. On most muscle cars, the knob is part of the shaft and the shaft will have to be removed. Usually the shaft is retained by a spring-loaded tang on the switch body. Check the replacement switch carefully to see how the shaft or knob is retained. Once the switch is removed, verify that battery voltage is on the feed wire. This is usually a red 10- or 12-gauge wire. It routes to the fuse box, but does not pass through a fuse. This feed wire typically connects to another feed wire that passes through the firewall connector. The wire in the engine compartment is usually a separate 10- or 12-gauge wire that runs back to the main power junction point. The feed wire should have 12 volts on it at all times. If it does, replace the light switch. If it does not, check the wire from the headlight switch, through the firewall connector, and back to the main power junction. This wire may have a fusible link installed at the power junction point.

TAILLIGHT PROBLEMS

The taillights on a muscle car are wired to turn on with the parking lights and the headlights. Most cars have the dash lights and the taillights on the same fuse. This alerts you if the taillight fuse blows, as the dash lights will go out as well. A singe 14- or 16-gauge wire is run from the passer compartment to the trunk to power the taillights and the license plate lamp.

One common problem with taillights is a bad or missing ground. A typical sympton of a bad ground is a taillight that works fine except that it goes out when the turn signals or brake lights are switched on. This is an easy problem to fix.

In order to fix a bad taillight ground, remove the light socket and determine the socket's ground path. The ground will be either a third wire that connects to the car body or a metal finger that touches the housing directly. Check these for signs of corrosion or damage. Replace the socket if it is corroded. If the socket is clean and it relies on a metal contact for ground, check the taillight housing to ensure that it is grounded.

CHECKING TURN SIGNAL
AND BRAKE LIGHTS

Turn signals are set up on four separate circuits. Each bulb has a separate feed from the turn signal switch. The brake lights are routed through the turn signal switch. Most muscle cars use an 1157 bulb for the front running and rear taillights. The turn signals and brakes use the high-intensity side of the 1157 bulb.

Here is how the indicator circuit works. There are two power feeds to the turn signal switch, one from the brake light switch and one from the ignition switch through a fuse and then through the flasher. The turn signal indicators on the dash are connected to the front turn signal bulbs. When the turn signal switch is off, neither front indicator is connected. The rear bulbs are connected to the brake light switch. This allows the brake lights to work.

When the turn signal switch is moved to enable the turn signals, the front bulb on the turn side is connected to the flasher power feed. The corresponding rear bulb is disconnected from the brake light switch and connected to the flasher power feed. Current flows through the flasher and to the bulbs, causing the lights to illuminate.

As current flows through the flasher, a bi-metal strip in the flasher gets hot and bends away from the internal contact, opening the circuit. This causes the current flow to stop and the lights go dark. The bi-metal strip cools and the flasher re-connects the power. This process repeats and the lights blink. Most modern flashers are solid state and do not rely on a bi-metal strip, but the end result is the same. Current flows intermittently, causing the lights to flash.

The factory flasher was designed to work with the number of bulbs on your vehicle. If you have two taillight bulbs per side and one parking lamp (front) bulb per side, you need to use a three-bulb flasher. These flashers blink at an abnormal rate (usually twice as fast) when a bulb fails. Most replacement flashers do not work this way and will flash correctly with only one functional bulb per side. This means you need to check your signal lamps on a regular basis to make sure that you don't have any bad bulbs if you have an aftermarket flasher.

Most problems with the turn signals are caused by a bad turn signal switch. You can purchase new turn signal switches for most muscle cars. Changing one is not that difficult. First remove the steering wheel. Next, unplug the turn signal connector that connects to the wiring harness at the base of the steering column. Remove the turn signal stalk and the screws

that hold the turn signal switch in place. Carefully pull the wires, with the connector, up through the passage in the steering column.

Disconnect the old switch and connect the new one. Carefully feed the connector down the passage in the steering column and put the new switch in place. Install the screws that hold the switch. Install the turn signal stalk. Connect the switch to the dash wiring harness. Next, turn on the ignition switch and verify proper operation of the turn signals. Install the steering wheel.

The brake lights are routed through the turn signal switch, so it is possible for a bad turn signal switch to cause the brake lights to work on one side only or not at all. Also, the brake lights may work fine when the turn signal switch is centered, but when switched on, the brake lights on the other side may not function anymore. Check the brake lights with the turn signals off. Also verify that with the turn signal switched for each side that the other side still has a functional brake light.

If the brake lights are not working at all, check the brake light switch. For GM and Chrysler vehicles, the switch is usually located under the

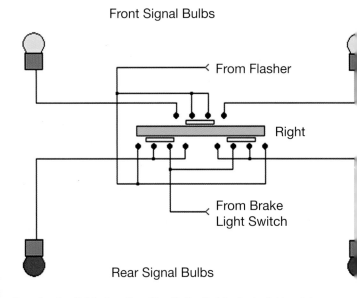

Turn signal switch in the off position. Notice that the brake light switch feed is connected to each rear bulb.

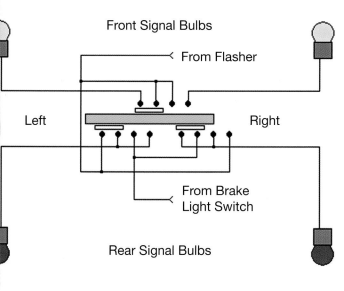

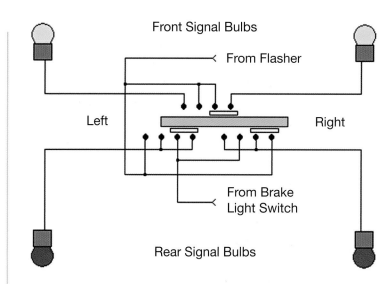

Turn signal switch set for a left turn. Note how the front left and rear left bulb are connected to the feed from the flasher. The right rear is still connected to the brake light switch.

Turn signal switch set for a right turn. Note how the front right and rear right bulbs are connected to the feed from the flasher. The left rear is still connected to the brake light switch.

dash, around the brake pedal. One side of the switch comes from the fuse block, and it is hot all of the time, even with the ignition switch off. The other side will go hot when the brake pedal is pressed. On some Fords, the switch is in the brake system and is activated by hydraulic pressure. This kind of switch is usually located under the hood, around the master cylinder or distribution block.

TROUBLESHOOTING THE HEATER FAN

All muscle cars with a heater had a multiple-speed fan. The switch in the dash that controls the fan is connected to the ignition switch. The wires from the fan speed switch are routed to a connector that appears to go into the heater air duct. This is the fan-speed resistor block. As the switch is moved, the voltage must pass through one or more resistors before being routed to the fan. It is quite common for one or more of these resistors, or the switch itself, to be defective. The result is that one or more of the fan speeds do not work.

To check the resistor block, unplug the connector and measure the resistance between each of the terminals on the resistor block. It should read extremely low (less than 5 ohms) between all of the terminals. Any high reading (over 10 ohms) indicates a bad fan-speed resistor and the whole resistor block needs to be replaced.

To check the switch, leave the fan-speed resistor disconnected and measure the voltage from each terminal of the wiring harness connector to ground.

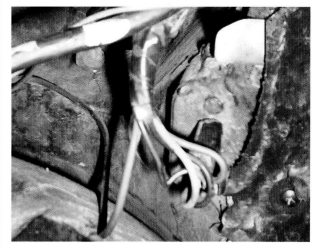

This is the fan-speed resistor. The resistance elements are coils of resistance wire. They are always mounted in the airflow from the fan to keep them cool and prevent failure.

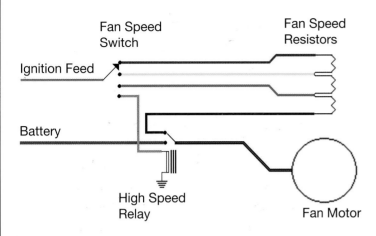

Fan Speed Switch

Fan Speed Resistors

Ignition Feed

Battery

High Speed Relay

Fan Motor

Typical fan-speed circuit. The ignition feed comes from the fuse box, usually the heater fuse. The battery feed to the relay is protected by either a fusible link or a 30-amp fuse.

As the fan-speed switch is moved, a different wire in the connector should indicate 12 volts. When high speed is selected, the fan should run, even with the fan-speed resistor disconnected. If one or more speed selections do not result in a terminal in the connector showing 12 volts, the switch or the wiring is bad.

On GM and a few other cars, the high-speed fan setting does not connect the ignition switch directly to the fan motor. For the slower speeds, the fan speed switch connects the ignition switch to the fan motor through one of the fan-speed resistors. But when the high-speed setting is selected, the fan switch connects 12 volts from the ignition switch to a relay coil. This relay is located under the hood and it connects the fan motor directly to the battery. There is a 30- or 25-amp fuse in the wiring from the battery to this relay. So if you have a GM car and the fan does not run when the fan-speed selector is moved to the high position, check this fuse and the relay.

If the fan-speed fuse blows with the fan speed set to high, chances are that the fan motor is bad. Usually the fan will run, but the fuse will fail within a week. If the fan motor squeals, it should be replaced. When replacing the fan motor, make sure that the cooling tube is present. Most fans have a rubber tube that routes air across the winding of the motor. If your car originally had this tube and it is missing, the fan motor will overheat and burn up. You can check whether your car had one of these cooling tubes by looking for a 1/2 inch hole in the side of the fan motor. You'll find a similarly sized hole in the air duct, usually right next to the fan motor, aligned with the hole in the motor.

ELECTRICAL GAUGE PROBLEMS

Electric gauges have a coil that uses electromagnetic force to move an armature connected to a gauge pointer. One side of this coil is connected to the ignition switch and the other to the sending unit. The sending unit is a variable resistor. As the sending unit directs more or less current through the coil, its electromagnetic force moves the needle of the gauge accordingly.

Most modern gauges add a second electromagnet that counteracts the one that is connected to the sending unit. This counteracting coil is connected from the ignition switch to ground. The purpose of this second coil is to damp voltage fluctuations. This makes the gauge accurate across a wider range of operating voltages. Gauges with a counteracting coil will have three terminals: one for ignition, one for the sending unit, and one for ground.

Gauges can be problematic on older cars. If a stock gauge is not functioning, check the sending unit. Measure from the terminal on the sending unit to ground. The resistance should be 200 ohms or less. If the sending unit reads higher, replace it. An open sending unit will typically cause the gauge to read 0 or whatever the lowest indication is. One exception is GM fuel gauges. If the sending unit is open, the gauge will read past full.

If only one gauge is not functioning, turn the ignition on and remove the sending unit wire from the sending unit. Measure with a voltmeter from the wire connector to ground. If the meter reads less than 1 volt, either the gauge or the wiring is bad.

Remove the gauge from the dash. There are usually three terminals on most gauges. For a three-terminal gauge, with the ignition switched on, one of the terminals will read the ignition voltage. Turn off the ignition, and check for zero resistance to ground on one of the other two terminals. Finally, with the sending unit re-connected, the remaining terminal should read the same resistance to ground as the sending unit. If the sending unit wire is also grounded, the gauge will usually read full scale. If the sending unit is open, the gauge will usually read minimum, except for GM fuel gauges. If power is missing, the gauge will either float above minimum, or read the minimum. Finally, if the ground connection is broken, the gauge may read erratically or full scale.

If your gauges are wired in an instrument cluster, chances are that a printed circuit board connects the gauges to the wiring harness connector. These boards are a common source of problems. If you are experiencing erratic gauge operation, or dash lights that do not work properly, remove the instrument cluster and check the printed circuit board. It is easy to check—use an ohm meter and measure from the wiring harness pin to the end of the trace. Several of the traces will go to multiple destinations, such as the ignition feed, ground, and dash light feed. Check all of the end points to the wiring harness connector. Any high or open reading on the ohm meter indicates a broken trace. The board can be fixed by an experienced electronics technician.

Some vehicles use a regulator for the gauges. This will be mounted near the instrument cluster, and it supplies a lower voltage that remains constant regardless of the vehicle's electrical load. These regulators are usually used with two-terminal gauges. If the regulator is bad, the gauges will not operate. A failed regulator will allow 12 volts to flow through the gauge. The excessive voltage will burn out the coil in the gauge.

Tachometers have four wires connected to them (more if there are indicator lights): the ignition, ground, ignition coil negative, and the dash light feed. If your tachometer is not working, first check for battery voltage at the ignition feed and check that the ground is good. Next, verify that the ignition coil negative is connected. If these check out, the

tachometer is most likely bad. Several companies specialize in the repair of factory gauges. If you don't repair the factory tachometer, you can replace it with a new replacement or aftermarket tachometer.

CHARGING SYSTEM UPGRADES

The first charging system upgrade to consider is a higher-output alternator. Most muscle cars had marginal charging systems at best. Even those with heavy-duty electrical systems only had a 55-amp alternator. This is not enough to support any additional electrical system load. The original charging system will work with stock vehicles. But if you add accessories, such as a better sound system or high-performance lights, a higher-output alternator is a must. You will also need a charging system upgrade in order to accommodate an electric cooling fan, electric fuel pump, or fuel injection.

Several high-output alternators are available in the 80- to 120-amp range. These are internal regulator designs that are simple to install. Just remember, the wire that connects the alternator output to the battery will need to be replaced with a larger wire. For an 80-amp alternator, do not use a wire smaller than 8 gauge. For a 120-amp alternator, use at least a 6-gauge wire. You can use a larger wire (smaller gauge number), but you should never use a smaller one.

Even for one-wire alternators, connect the sense wire to the battery. This allows the regulator to compensate for the voltage drop that will result when the alternator is providing high current levels. You should add a fusible link to protect the charging circuit wire. For high-output alternators, the charge wire should route directly to the battery. If the charge wire is routed to a junction block, then the wire from the junction block back to the battery will also need to be changed to at least the size of the new charging wire.

KEEP YOUR VEHICLE: ADD AN ALARM SYSTEM

The best security measure you can add to your muscle car is an alarm system. Don't install one of those cheap multitone alarms, and make sure that opening the hood as well as the doors triggers the alarm. If you have a motion sensor on your alarm, make sure it is not set too sensitively. You don't want to add to the false alarm problem. If your alarm is set up properly, high winds, thunderstorms, and loud vehicles will not set off your alarm.

Bear in mind that smart car thieves will learn how to deactivate popular alarm systems. Do not help by putting stickers on your car that advertise the brand of your alarm system. A hidden kill switch is also an effective theft deterrent. If the car will not start, a thief is not going to spend the next thirty minutes trying to figure out why.

The ultimate solution is to add an alarm system and a kill switch. Don't use the kill switch provided by the alarm, as the thief may know how to bypass it. Build your own instead. It is easy to do and only you will know how to find it.

To install a kill switch, you will need three automotive relays (refer to the schematic diagram shown on this page). Break the wire that feeds your ignition coil and the wire from the ignition switch to the starter solenoid. With these two wires disconnected, the car will not crank or run. Connect one of the relay coil terminals to a small momentary push-button switch that you have hidden somewhere in reach of the driver's seat. Run another wire from that switch to the fuse block. Connect this wire to a power feed that is hot when the ignition switch is in the on and also the crank position. Pay attention to this; most items in the vehicle are turned off when the key is in the crank position. The gauges and ignition coil are a good bet, as these are on in both the run and crank key positions.

Connect the wire that leads from the ignition switch to one of the relay contact terminals on relay 1. Connect the wire that feeds the coil on relay 1 to the other contact on relay 1. Route a wire from the

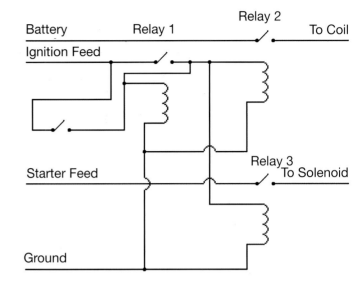

Kill switch schematic. This is the fan speed resistor. The resistance elements are coils of resistance wire. They are always mounted in the airflow from the fan to keep them cool and prevent failure.

ignition switch that originally fed the ignition coil to one of the terminals on relay 2. Connect the ignition coil to the other terminal on relay 2. Connect the coils of relay 3 and relay 2 to the coil of relay 1. Connect the wire from the ignition-switch-to-starter terminal to one of the contacts on relay 3. Connect the wire that leads to the starter solenoid to the other contact of relay 3. For maximum security, hide the relays up high under the dash. The push button should be in reach of the driver, but hidden from view.

If you have access to DPDT relays, your kill circuit can be constructed with two relays. Just make sure that the relays you use are rated for the current that they must handle. The relay that switches the starter solenoid must be rated for 30 amps. Likewise, the relay that switches the ignition coil should be rated for 20 amps. As an added security feature, the three relay terminals can be routed through a high security key switch that opens the ground and disables the vehicle.

CHAPTER 11
TRANSMISSION AND CLUTCH

The typical muscle car was equipped with a heavy-duty transmission from the factory. If you properly enhance the already beefy transmission for the ultimate in performance and reliability, it will be a part of the vehicle that requires only routine maintenance.

Standard equipment on the base model of most muscle cars was a three-speed manual. Four speeds and automatics were optional. But most muscle cars were ordered by dealers with automatics. The odds are good that your muscle car has an automatic transmission. One of the exceptions was the manufacturers' high-end, limited-production models, which typically came equipped with a four-speed manual.

Bear in mind that manual transmission cars usually perform better than those with automatics. The automatic transmission is robbing power due to its increased rotating weight. The torque converter, clutch drums, and planetary gears usually are heavier than the comparable components in a manual transmission. Accelerating that additional weight sucks up horsepower, so the manual transmission–equipped model generally is a bit quicker and seems more powerful.

TRANSMISSION LEAKS

When you have a leak in your manual or automatic transmission, suspect a seal. Both have an input seal, an output seal, seals for the shift linkage, and a seal for the speedometer. Automatics have one seal for the shift linkage and another for the oil pan. Manuals don't have an oil pan seal, but they have more than one shift linkage seal. Manuals also have a seal for the inspection cover, usually on one side of the transmission (except for the Ford top-loader). Automatics have a seal for the pump body, while manuals have a seal for the input shaft bearing. All transmissions have a seal between the transmission body and the tailhousing.

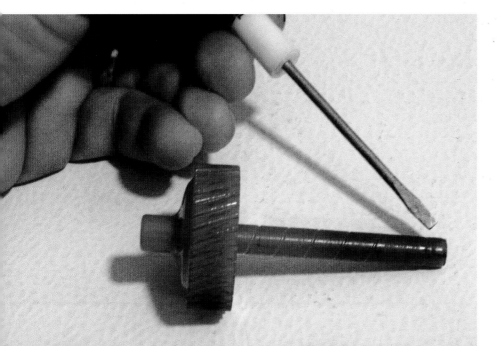

Speedometer gear and gear housing seals. It is hard to see in this picture, but the tan gear is worn and has a groove about a 1/4 inch from the end on the shaft that makes sealing the transmission impossible. The new seal lip will not be effective with this groove in the plastic gear shaft. Transmission fluid will leak into and then from the speedometer cable. Replace the gear when rebuilding the transmission.

Begin the leak inspection process by cleaning the transmission. Next, ensure that the transmission is full of fluid. Make sure it is not overly full, as this can lead to foaming and fluid expulsion through the vent. Drive the vehicle and check for signs of leaking. It may take a couple of days for the leak to show up, especially if it is a subtle one. Be sure to consider the effects of centrifugal force; diagnosing a leak at the input or output shafts can be confusing, since the fluid may be thrown by the rotating shaft.

A leak at the input shaft or the pump body of an automatic or at the input shaft bearing housing for a manual cannot be fixed unless the transmission is separated from the engine. Output shaft seals and extension housing gaskets can be serviced in the vehicle if the driveshaft is removed. Shift lever seals can be changed by first removing the shift lever from the shaft. Extraction tools can be purchased to remove the seal from the transmission.

The speedometer will have two seals, one around the speedometer drive gear housing and one to seal the drive gear shaft. Since the gears are usually plastic, the gear shaft wears down where the seal contacts the shaft as the miles roll by. When the seal fails, the leaking fluid will make the speedometer cable oily without a visible leak. Simply replacing the seal will not correct the problem. Replace the gear when the seal is replaced.

MAINTAINING A MANUAL TRANSMISSION

Manual transmissions are easy to maintain. Change the fluid on a regular basis and adjust the shift linkage and clutch linkage. All muscle car–era manual transmissions used linkage-actuated clutches and linkage-actuated shifters. Check the case for signs of leaking. Inspect the transmission mount for signs of deterioration or looseness.

To change the fluid, remove the drain plug. Be sure you know where the drain and fill plugs are before you remove anything from the transmission case. Several manual transmissions have bolt heads that may appear to be a drain or fill plug, but they hold a shift rod or some other internal component in place. If one of these is removed by mistake, the internal part might let go and require a transmission tear-down to fix.

Once the fluid is drained, install the drain plug and refill the transmission. Use synthetic gear lube. As with engine oil, synthetic will do a much better job. Use the weight recommended by the manual. Most manufacturers used 80W-90 gear oil. You can use an 80W-140 in a box that calls for 80W or 80W-90 gear oil. Don't try to gain a horsepower or two by using engine oil in place of gear lube. This is a popular trick for a drag racer, but these vehicles don't have to cruise down the highway. Also, the thicker gear oil helps to cushion the shock when the gears engage.

SERVICING THE SHIFTER LINKAGE

Check for signs of wear or looseness in the shift linkage. Slop will make adjusting the linkage next to impossible. Also, slop will result in inaccurate and binding shifting.

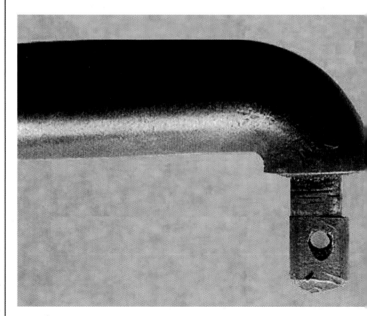

Shifter linkage and clutch linkage rods wear. After 100,000 miles they look like this. All the adjusting in the world will not overcome the slop and looseness that this will cause. Also, when the rods wear down like this, they can break unexpectedly.

The transmission shift levers can be replaced, as can the shift rods and the shifter. After adjusting, verify that the shifter is smooth to operate and that all gears can be engaged cleanly. Don't attempt to adjust out the slop caused by worn rods or shift levers. Replace the worn components. If you are unable to find replacements, a skilled welder can build up the worn areas and then it can be machined back into shape.

Once the transmission lube is replaced, the shift linkage can be adjusted. Check with the manufacturer of your shifter. Several muscle cars came from the factory with Hurst shifters. Most shifters adjust the same way.

Place the shifter in neutral. Next, go under the vehicle and loosen the jam nuts on the shift linkage; they are usually at the shifter. Make sure that each shift lever is in neutral. Insert the appropriately sized pin in the alignment hole on the shifter. Then the shift rods are adjusted so the shift levers on the transmission are exactly centered in their neutral detent position. Tighten the nuts on the shift rods and verify that the pin can be easily removed and inserted into the alignment hole. Remove the pin, start the vehicle, depress the clutch, and check for smooth shifter action. It should go easily in and out of each gear. If not, shut the engine off and recheck the adjustment.

If your vehicle is a 1969 or newer model, it may have a feature that prevents the ignition switch from being turned from off to the locked position unless the transmission is in reverse. If the linkage is not adjusted correctly, it may be impossible to turn the key to the locked position and then remove the ignition key.

To adjust the reverse lock feature, place the shifter in reverse. Locate the back drive rod under the vehicle. This rod will connect the linkage on the steering column with the shift linkage that selects reverse. Loosen the locknut and adjust this rod so that the transmission can be shifted out of and then back into reverse. Verify that the ignition switch can be turned from the locked position and then back to the locked position. This rod is often removed and, unless the steering column linkage is locked in position, the ignition switch may be difficult or impossible to switch to the locked position.

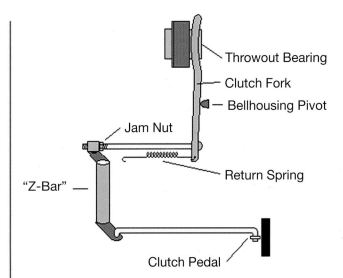

Looking down from the top at the typical mechanical clutch linkage. The common wear points are the rod end-points and the two pivot points on the Z-bar. Replace the clutch rods if they show signs of wear. Replace the Z-bar as well if it shows wear. Don't forget the frame bracket; it can bend or break, resulting in a clutch that is impossible to adjust.

ADJUSTING THE CLUTCH LINKAGE

Adjusting the clutch is straightforward. A properly adjusted clutch should have 1/2 to 1 inch of play at the pedal when released. Just like the shift linkage, check for signs of wear or slop in the linkage. All muscle cars use a fully mechanical linkage setup with a clutch cross-shaft mounted between the frame and the engine block. This should be removed, cleaned, and installed with fresh wheel bearing grease on the ball studs. Check this shaft for wear or looseness, and replace if any signs of trouble are found. Slop in the clutch linkage will make clutch operation loose, and adjustment difficult.

The most accurate way to adjust the linkage is to raise the rear wheels off the ground. Place the transmission in first gear. Have a helper depress and hold the clutch to the floor. Now adjust the linkage so that the rear wheels are just released from the engine and can be turned freely while the clutch is held fully depressed.

Have the assistant release the clutch pedal. Remove the return spring; there should be at least 1/2 inch of slop or free travel at the clutch pedal before the clutch fork places pressure on the throwout bearing. If these two conditions cannot be met, inspect the linkage for signs of excessive wear or for damaged parts. Also, the wrong pressure plate and throwout bearing might have been installed. Re-install the return spring when finished.

If the linkage cannot be adjusted to yield at least 1/2 inch of free play, the throwout bearing will be under constant pressure and will wear out. Also, the clutch might slip. If the clutch linkage pushes the throwout bearing too far past the clutch release point, the pressure plate could be damaged. Going too far can also result in a clutch that hangs disengaged at high rpm.

REPLACING A CLUTCH

If you drive a car with a manual transmission, sooner or later the clutch will need to be replaced. Expect the clutch plate to last from 50,000 to 90,000 miles. And, if the engine's output has been increased, the clutch must also be upgraded.

To remove a clutch, first disconnect the shift linkage from the transmission and remove the shifter. When removing the shift linkage, remove the rod from the transmission but leave them attached to the shifter. From inside the car, remove the shifter handle and the shifter boot. Remove the bolts that hold the shifter to the transmission and remove the shifter. Also remove the speedometer cable from the rear of the transmission. Disconnect any wiring from the transmission, such as the neutral safety switch or the reverse lights.

Next, the clutch linkage can be disconnected from the clutch arm. All muscle cars came with mechanical linkage. Inspect the linkage pivot points for wear. Also, check the return spring and the linkage for signs of damage. Replace any damaged or worn linkage. The return spring keeps the slack out of the linkage.

Mark the rear of the driveshaft and the rear axle driveshaft yoke so that the driveshaft can be installed in the same position it was in before removal. Place a drain pan under the rear of the transmission to catch any fluid that might drain out when the driveshaft is removed.

Here is what is in a typical clutch kit: new pressure plate, friction plate, installation pilot tool, throwout bearing, and pilot bearing.

Remove the nuts or bolts that hold the rear universal joint to the yoke. Push the driveshaft forward and lower the rear of the driveshaft out of the yoke. Now pull the driveshaft out of the transmission. Be careful not to let either end of the driveshaft fall and hit the floor.

Place a jack under the transmission and remove the bolts that hold the transmission mount to the crossmember. Remove the bolts that hold the crossmember to the frame or body and move the crossmember out of the way. Remove the four bolts that hold the transmission to the bellhousing. Leave one bottom bolt loose but in place until you are ready to remove the transmission. Support the transmission and remove the final bolt. Pull the transmission straight back until the shaft clears the clutch assembly. Do not allow the transmission to hang by the input shaft.

Remove the bolts that hold the bellhousing to the engine. On some cars, the starter must be removed first. Pull the bellhousing off and move it out from under the vehicle. Remove the throwout bearing and discard. Check the clutch fork for bent or worn throwout bearing supports. Also check the clutch fork ball and corresponding joint in the fork for signs of excessive wear. If the ball or fork shows signs of wear or damage, replace the fork and ball. Otherwise, clean out the bellhousing and apply grease to the ball and re-install the clutch fork. Now the clutch and flywheel are exposed. Inspect the bellhousing for any signs of cracking or damage. Replace the bellhousing if any fatigue or other damage is found.

To remove the clutch, remove the six bolts that hold the pressure plate to the flywheel. Remove the bolts that hold the flywheel to the engine. Inspect the flywheel for any signs of cracking. Remove the pilot bushing from the flywheel. The flywheel needs to be sent to a machine shop and to be turned.

Clean the flywheel once it is back from the machine shop and install a new pilot bearing or bushing. Pack the pilot bearing or bushing with wheel bearing grease. Install the flywheel using only new bolts. Make sure the bolts are grade 8 or better. Do not reuse the old bolts. Torque the bolts following the manufacturer's recommended sequence. All of the engine's power must pass through this joint; inexpensive bolts or improperly tightened bolts can fail.

Install the new clutch disc and pressure plate. Make sure that the clutch disc is oriented the correct way, but do not tighten the bolts down. Use only new high-quality bolts when installing the pressure plate. Before tightening the pressure plate, insert an alignment tool through the clutch splines and fully into the crankshaft pilot bushing. Tighten the bolts down a little at a time so that the pressure plate is pulled evenly and flat to the flywheel. Torque the bolts to the recommended value, in the order specified by the pressure plate manufacturer. Failure to follow these steps can result in a warped pressure plate.

Install a new throwout bearing on the clutch fork, making sure that the bearing is facing the right way. Install the bellhousing and torque the bolts to the recommended value. Make sure that the bolts are properly torqued, or the bellhousing bolts could come loose. Check the throwout bearing to ensure that it is properly engaged in the pressure plate fingers. Re-connect the clutch linkage.

Clean and inspect the transmission. This is also a good time to replace the front and rear seals, as the transmission must be removed to replace these. They are low-cost and easy to change. Clean and insert the driveshaft slip yoke in the transmission and check for any signs of looseness. The slip yoke rides on a bushing, and if any signs of looseness are detected, remove the tailshaft from the transmission and replace the bushing. A new tailshaft-to-transmission case gasket will be required if the tailshaft is removed.

Replace the transmission fluid when servicing a clutch, as it is easy to do. You don't even have to remove the drain plug—just tip the transmission up and pour the fluid out through the tailshaft. Don't forget to refill the transmission after it is installed in the vehicle.

Remove the pilot tool from the clutch plate. Place the transmission on a jack and roll it under the vehicle. Raise the transmission up so the input shaft is directly in line with the clutch plate. Slide the transmission into the clutch disc, making sure that the splines align. Do not allow the transmission to hang on the input shaft. It may take some jiggling to get the transmission to fully seat, as the input shaft must slide through the clutch disc and the pilot bushing. Install the four bolts that hold the transmission to the bellhousing.

Slide the crossmember back into position and bolt it to the frame. Lower the jack and re-install the bolts that hold the transmission mount to the crossmember. Check the torque settings for the bellhousing bolts, the transmission-to-bellhousing bolts, and the crossmember bolts.

Install the shifter to the transmission and connect the shift linkage. Follow the procedure above to adjust the shift linkage. Install the shift boot and the shift knob inside the vehicle. Reconnect the speedometer cable to the output shaft of the transmission. Any wiring that was disconnected should be connected at this time.

Inspect the universal joints and grease them. Lightly coat the slip yoke with the same gear oil used in the transmission. Next, align the keyway on the slip yoke with the splines on the transmission output shaft. Insert the slip yoke into the transmission. The transmission should be in neutral. Rotate the driveshaft to line up the marks you made before removing it and install the rear universal joint in the rear axle yoke. Install the caps or straps that retain the universal joint and tighten them down evenly. Torque the bolts to the recommended value.

Refill the transmission with synthetic gear oil. Check for smooth shifter operation and clutch pedal feel. Check the clutch adjustment. Now start the engine and test-drive the vehicle.

REBUILDING A MANUAL TRANSMISSION

Manual transmissions are not that difficult to rebuild, and kits are available to replace the common wear items. If your transmission is kicking out of gear (especially when decelerating), leaking fluid, shifting poorly, or grinding, a rebuild is in order.

Kits that contain new seals, bushings, and synchronizer rings are available to rebuild just about any manual transmission. These kits usually do not contain the roller or ball bearings, shift forks, or gears. If these parts are needed, there are companies that specialize in manual transmission parts and service. Bear in mind the fact that gears are usually expensive.

Obtain a factory service manual or a good book that covers how to rebuild your particular transmission. Another good book to read first is *How to Rebuild and Modify Your Manual Transmission* by Robert Bowen. Familiarize yourself with how to take apart and reassemble the transmission before you begin. Any common wear items should be called out in the manual. If the manual suggests that special tools are required, buy or rent the tools before you begin the rebuild.

Before ordering an overhaul kit, verify the model of your transmission. Most factory manual transmissions were available with more than one set of gear ratios.

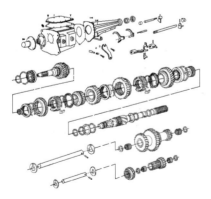

Keep track of how the transmission comes apart. Also, only disassemble one shaft at a time. You will need the factory service manual or a good book that describes how to disassemble and reassemble the transmission properly, including what special tools are required. This is the Ford "Top loader" four-speed.

The gear ratios used in your transmission can make a difference in the parts, especially the synchronizer rings.

To start, drain all of the fluid from the transmission. When disassembling, keep the parts in order. Pay careful attention to the order in which parts are removed, especially any needle bearings. Count the number of needles and their size. Pay careful attention to the order and direction in which the gears are installed on the shafts. Don't mix up the shift rings and shift forks, as these may be different sizes.

Once the transmission is disassembled, clean each part and carefully inspect each one. Gears should be checked for missing teeth, chipped gear teeth, and/or scoring of the gear tooth surface. Also check the shift rings for any signs of damage. Bearing surfaces should be checked for signs of scoring or grooving. Shift forks should be checked for damage and signs of bending. Any damaged parts must be replaced.

When putting the transmission back together, keep the parts and the assembly area clean. Dust and dirt will result in premature wear. Lubricate the parts with gear oil. Also, when installing needle bearings, use a light coating of grease to hold the needles in place.

Once the transmission is assembled, check each gear by manipulating the shift levers. Verify that the input shaft turns smoothly and that the output shaft turns the correct direction at the correct speed. For example, if your transmission has a first gear ratio of 2.4:1, you should have to rotate the input shaft 2.4 times to get the output shaft to turn one complete revolution. For all gears except reverse, the input shaft and output shaft will rotate in the same direction.

AUTOMATIC TRANSMISSION MAINTENANCE

Automatic transmissions are easy to maintain. Most will give 100,000 miles or more of trouble-free performance if properly maintained. The only parts that wear are the bands and clutches. Proper maintenance usually only requires changing the fluid and the filter. On some models, there may be a band adjustment as well.

Basic maintenance includes a filter change. This is a "broiler pan" style of filter. When replacing the filter, pay careful attention to the oil pickup tube and seals. Even a tiny leak here will result in no oil pressure and a nonfunctional transmission.

Here is a B&M deep pan installed on a TH400. This pan has a drain plug, making transmission service easier. This pan has been modified by adding a temperature-sending unit.

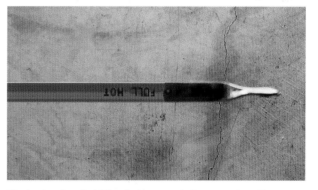

The best and easiest thing that you can do for your automatic transmission is to check the fluid level on a regular basis and keep the transmission properly filled. The fluid should be transparent, and there should not be a "burnt" smell. If the fluid is milky, water has entered the transmission. Check the cooler in the radiator.

Changing the fluid was covered in Chapter 2. Make sure the proper type of transmission fluid is used. Don't skimp and use cheap fluid. Transmission fluid has additives that work with the friction material on your clutch plates and bands. The wrong fluid can result in decreased performance of this friction material, causing increased slippage.

Always keep the transmission fluid level properly filled. Most automatic transmission failures are caused by operation with low fluid. This results in low line pressure and slipping clutches. If the transmission fluid level is low, it may be leaking out. Another cause of low fluid is a damaged vacuum modulator, which causes fluid to be sucked into the intake manifold. To check for this, simply remove the vacuum hose from the modulator valve. It should be dry, with no signs of transmission fluid.

If your automatic transmission is leaking, the source of the leak should be tracked down and fixed. Start by cleaning off the transmission case and pan. Check the pan bolts to make sure they are tight. Start the engine and check the fluid level; make sure that it is full but not overfilled. Drive the car for 5 to 10 miles. Turn the vehicle off and inspect the transmission for signs of leakage.

Check carefully all around the pan. Check around the rear seal where the driveshaft connects. Most transmissions have a removable tailshaft, so inspect around the seam where the tailshaft meets the case for signs of leakage. Check the speedometer gear housing and the governor housing covers for signs of leakage. Check the seals for the modulator valve or shift control cable as well. The shift-shaft seal is also a common leak point. If the fluid appears to be coming from the torque converter cover, remove the cover and look up between the converter and the transmission to see if the front seal is leaking.

All leaks except the front seal can be fixed with the transmission in the car. If the rear seal or tailshaft-to-transmission gasket is leaking, the driveshaft will have to be removed. If the front seal is leaking, the transmission will have to be removed. Several of these seals are simple O-rings, like the modulator valve seals. Electrical connectors that pass through the case are usually sealed with a standard O-ring.

If the fluid appears to be coming from the vent tube located on the side of the case, the transmission was probably overfilled. This will usually cause the fluid to foam up. If the fluid is being forced up and out of the dipstick tube, the vent tube is most likely plugged. The dipstick tube is usually just below the fluid level, so any pressure buildup in the case will force fluid up and out of the dipstick tube.

BASIC AUTOMATIC TRANSMISSION TROUBLESHOOTING

If you have transmission troubles, first determine what is working and what is not. If the transmission will not go into gear, check the shift linkage and the fluid level. If these are OK, then the transmission will need to be rebuilt. Several other problems besides the total failure are also common.

Slipping is always a major concern. If one or more gears are slipping, this needs to be addressed immediately or serious damage and clutch failure will result. Check the fluid level and also sniff the fluid to see if it smells burned. If the fluid level is OK, check the shift linkage to be sure that the transmission is properly in gear. The valve body has a valve that routes fluid to the proper passages to select gear ranges. If this valve is not properly positioned, the result can be improper operation and slippage.

Next, the transmission pan can be removed and the valve body bolts can be checked to make sure they are tight. Loose bolts could result in leakage and low pressure to a clutch that is slipping. If all of these

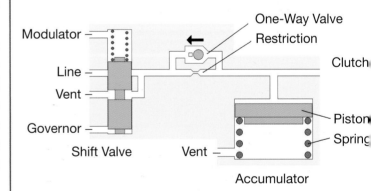

This is how an automatic works. The governor pressure increases as vehicle speed increases and eventually will be high enough to override the modulator pressure that is based on engine loading. When it does, the shift valve moves to allow the line pressure to flow to the clutch (or band servo). The restriction and accumulator soften the application of the clutch or band. Most shift kits work by enlarging the restriction and/or modifying the accumulator to firm up the shifts.

check out OK and the transmission is still slipping, the problem is either a burned or worn-out clutch pack or a damaged seal in the clutch-apply piston. Band-shifted transmissions may have a worn-out band or a damaged seal on the band-apply servo.

Another problem is a whirring sound that changes pitch with engine speed. This is usually caused by the pump. Check the filter and intake pipe. Leaks will cause the pump to suck air and produce noise and slippage. If the pump gears are worn or damaged, the pump will also make noise. The only cure for this is a rebuild.

SHIFTING PROBLEMS

If the transmission is not shifting or is shifting at the wrong time, the problem is most likely with the valve body. Automatic transmissions use governor pressure and throttle pressure to determine when to shift. The governor pressure comes from a spinning governor valve that varies pressure with vehicle speed. The throttle pressure is generated from either a vacuum modulator valve or a throttle cable.

This is a stacked-plate cooler. This cooler also has 1/2-inch NPT fittings as opposed to hose barbs. With a cooler like this, and by using hard line, a cooler can be installed that uses no hose.

Since shifting depends on the governor and modulator (or throttle cable) pressures being correct, start with these. If the vehicle shifts late and hard regardless of how hard you are accelerating, check the throttle cable (on Chryslers, check the downshift linkage). For GM cars, check the vacuum modulator valve and the vacuum line. This is usually a 1/4-inch diameter metal pipe with vacuum hose on each end. If the hose is disconnected, the transmission will think that the vehicle is operating under heavy load and shifts will be late and hard.

For vehicles that use a TV cable (like the GM TH700 R4) or a kick-down linkage (like the Chrysler Torqueflite), the cable sets the modulator pressure and also controls the transmission line pressure. Note that even though the Torqueflite linkage is usually referred to as the kick-down linkage, it is used to signal all loading rather than just wide-open throttle. If the cable or linkage is not connected, the transmission will operate as if the engine is lightly loaded. Besides shifting early, the resulting low line pressure can result in burned clutches or bands.

For vehicles that use a modulator—like the GM TH350 and TH400—a bad modulator valve will cause late and hard shifting, just the same as if the vacuum line were disconnected. The valve may stick in place and simulate a partial engine load, resulting in shifting at only that engine load. This can cause transmission damage if the vehicle is driven under any moderate to heavy load conditions because the line pressure will be low.

Another problem for modulator-equipped vehicles is if the vacuum source is connected to the timed (ported) vacuum source at the carburetor. The vehicle will shift fine while accelerating or maintaining speed, but produce no engine braking when the throttle is released at speeds below 50 to 60 mph. Also, the transmission will be in the wrong gear and will have to shift back into high when resuming from coasting down a hill at moderate speeds (below 50 mph).

If the vehicle goes into reverse and drive correctly but will not shift itself out of low, check the governor.

If this is defective, the transmission will think the vehicle is not moving. One sign of this is that if the throttle is released when in drive at 15 to 20 mph, the engine rpm drops to idle while the car is rolling.

Another governor problem is stuck weights. This results in the transmission thinking that the vehicle is moving at a constant speed. If this happens, the transmission may not have low gear and will start out from a stop in second or third. If the weights are stuck at some intermediate position, the vehicle will shift down under load but will not shift up until the throttle is lifted.

Shifting problems will also result if any valves in the valve body are stuck. This can be caused by dirt or other foreign objects in the valve body. Remove and thoroughly clean the valve body. Only remove one shift valve at a time and lay out the parts in the order in which they were removed.

INSTALLING A TRANSMISSION COOLER

Adding a transmission cooler can double the life of your automatic transmission. Heat is the enemy of an automatic transmission. The seals in the transmission are usually rubber, and the increased heat will harden the seals sooner. Once one of the seals in clutch drum or servo cracks, the transmission will fail. The increased heat will also cause the transmission fluid to oxidize and break down sooner. The goal should be to keep the transmission fluid below 200 degrees Fahrenheit.

A transmission cooler is not an option but rather a must if a high-stall torque converter is used. The increased slippage will result in increased heat. A good cooler will safely dissipate this extra heat.

The cooler should be mounted in front of the radiator and air conditioner condenser. Use the largest size that will fit. There are a couple of options for how to route the transmission lines. For cars that are operated in southern states, the fluid can be routed from the transmission to the cooler and back to the transmission. For northern states, the fluid should be routed from the transmission to the cooler and then through the cooler in the radiator (most

radiators used in automatic transmission vehicles also contained a transmission fluid cooler; it was always installed in the cool side of the radiator, where the water flows back to the engine), then finally back to the transmission. This helps warm up the transmission fluid. Cold transmission fluid is thick and causes slow shifting. When the fluid is cold, it does not disperse between the clutch plates well. This results in insufficient lubrication and protection from burning as the clutch or band is being applied.

A transmission temperature gauge should be installed so the transmission temperature can be monitored. The best place for the sending unit is in the pan, below the fluid level. The location in the pan must be chosen carefully. The sending unit must not interfere with the filter, pickup, or any other part of the transmission that may extend into the pan.

SHIFT KITS

Another way to extend the life of an automatic transmission is to install a shift kit. A shift kit makes the transmission shift quicker and the reduced slippage means longer friction material life. All shift kits come with instructions; follow these to the letter. Below is a rough guide as to what will be done.

Begin by removing the transmission pan and filter. Remove the valve body bolts. Pay attention to which hole each bolt came out of as they may be different lengths. Support the valve body so that it

This is a shift-improvement kit. This kit comes with a new line pressure regulator spring as well as a valve body separator plate. For most automatics, the shift restrictions are in the separator plate. There may be instructions with your kit that allow you to select the desired shift firmness by drilling one or more holes in the separator plate.

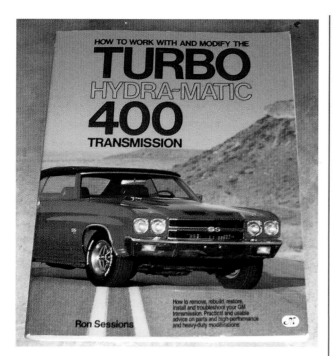

If you plan to perform any serious work on your automatic, get a good reference manual. Don't even consider a rebuild without a factory service manual or the reference manual.

This is a rebuild kit for the Chrysler 727. This kit includes the clutch plates, bands, and the steels. It also has all the internal seals and gaskets.

does not fall off as the bolts are being removed. Note that check balls may fall out as it is removed.

Collect everything and clean the valve body and any check balls. Use lint-free rags, the kind painters use. Do not use standard rags, as the lint fibers can get into the valve body and cause sticking shift valves. Perform any modifications the kit instructions recommend. If drilling is required, carefully deburr the hole and make sure all of the metal shavings are removed.

When installing the valve body, you will find a metal separator plate with two gaskets. Make sure the proper gasket is used on each side of the plate. There will be a case side and a valve body side gasket. Make sure that the gaskets are installed the correct direction.

If check balls need to be installed in the transmission case, use a little grease to hold the check ball in place. I prefer standard chassis grease; use as little as possible. Make sure the check balls are installed in the proper locations.

Once all modifications are complete, replace the filter and the pan. You should use a new filter. Fill the

transmission until the dipstick shows just under full. Start the car and let it idle for 15 to 30 seconds. Check the fluid level with the engine running; it should be above the add mark but below the full mark. Next, apply the brakes and slowly shift through the gear ranges. You should feel the transmission go into gear as the reverse and forward ranges are selected. Place the selector back in park and check the fluid level.

Shift into drive and lightly accelerate, letting the vehicle shift up through second and third (or fourth if it's an overdrive transmission). Make sure that the transmission is working properly and that the shifts are crisp, with no signs of slippage. Start out with light throttle openings, gradually working up as you verify that the transmission is working properly.

DISASSEMBLING AUTOMATIC TRANSMISSIONS

Automatic transmissions are easier to rebuild than an engine. All of the parts that wear are simply replaced and no machining is required.

Several companies sell kits to rebuild automatic transmissions, and these kits come with all the seals, clutch packs, steel plates, and bands that are used for forward gear shifting. Bear in mind the fact that the TH350 and TH400 kits usually do not include bands because they are not used for forward gear shifting. Purchase a good service manual that covers the transmission that you are rebuilding.

Buy a kit that includes the steel plates. These are the metal plates that go between each clutch friction plate. Always install new steel plates with new friction plates. These kits will not include hard parts such as planetary gear sets, clutch drums, one-way clutches and spragues, input shafts, and oil pumps. If any hard parts are damaged, they will need to be purchased separately.

This is a roller style of one-way clutch. The other type that is common is the sprague clutch. Both of these work by allowing motion between the inner and outer elements in one direction while preventing motion or locking the elements together for motion in the other direction.

One tip for removing an automatic transmission: fabricate a strap from a 3/4- or 1-inch-wide piece of steel. It should be around 0.1 inch thick. Drill a hole in one end to fit under a transmission pan bolt and bend the strap and cut it to length so that it will hold the torque converter in place without interfering with the removal process. This strap will prevent the converter from falling out when the transmission is removed.

Before rebuilding the transmission, clean it thoroughly. This will reduce the amount of dirt and debris that can get inside the transmission. It will also make your job much easier; you will not be wrestling with a dirty transmission case. As you disassemble the transmission, keep the parts in order as they come out of the case. Finally, don't disassemble the clutch drums! Wait until you are going to rebuild the drum. Then disassemble and rebuild each drum separately. This helps to prevent parts from getting mixed up.

When the transmission has been disassembled and all parts have been removed from the case, wash the case thoroughly inside and out. Get it clean! Once it is clean, dry it completely, using compressed air to blow out all case passages. Now the case exterior can be painted if desired. Don't get any paint overspray inside the case. The key to a successful transmission rebuild is cleanliness—it can't be too clean. Dirt, lint, and grit will all cause problems. So don't use ordinary rags to wipe down components. Use compressed air and/or lint-free rags.

Next, inspect all components for damage. Make sure the case is not damaged. Look for cracks, broken supports, or other damage. If the case is damaged, replace the case or have an experienced aluminum welder repair it. Inspect the planetary gears for signs of pitting, broken teeth, and loose gears. If any damage is found, these expensive gears must be replaced.

When checking a sprague or roller clutch, look for damage or distortion of the roller cage. Check both the drive and driven races for signs of pitting or scoring. If the roller clutch installs in the case, check the case for signs of damage as well. Spragues can be installed two ways. If the sprague is installed backward, the transmission will not operate because the sprague will be locking rotation in the wrong direction. This is one of the many reasons you must pay attention to how roller clutches, spragues, and other parts were installed during disassembly.

Most rebuild kits also do not contain any valve body parts other than new gaskets. If any modifications or repairs are going to be made to the valve body, these parts will have to be purchased separately. A rebuild is a good time to purchase and install a shift kit.

REBUILDING AUTOMATIC TRANSMISSION CLUTCHES

Rebuild each clutch pack separately to avoid mixing up parts. Begin the rebuild by removing the retaining ring that holds the clutch stack in the clutch drum. Remove the old clutch friction and steel plates, noting in what order they were installed in the clutch drum. Lay out the parts in the same order in which they were removed.

Replace the rubber seals on the clutch pistons. Follow the instructions in the service manual regarding how to disassemble and assemble the clutch. If you don't have a piston installation tool, you can use a feeler gauge to carefully work the piston into the drum. Once the piston is fully seated, install the return springs and the spring retainer. Next, install the spring retainer snap ring.

Once the clutch piston is reassembled, use compressed air and check the clutch for proper operation. Do not use more than 10 psi. Get a rubber-tipped air gun and find the clutch oil feed hole. Press the rubber tip of the air gun up to the feed hole and

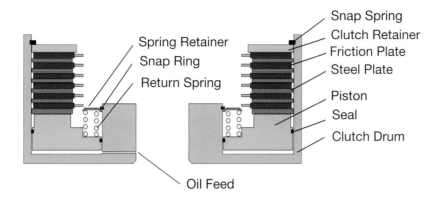

Spring Retainer
Snap Ring
Return Spring

Snap Spring
Clutch Retainer
Friction Plate
Steel Plate
Piston
Seal
Clutch Drum

Oil Feed

This is a cross-section of a clutch drum. Most of these use two seals, one on the inside and the other on the outside of the piston. These are usually rubber, and as the miles and time roll on, the rubber slowly hardens. Once one of these cracks, the clutch will no longer apply.

apply the air. The clutch piston should apply and there should be no sign of air leakage. If there is, check for an exhaust hole; some clutches use these to prevent false clutch application at high rpm. If the clutch drum has an exhaust hole, cover it with your finger and verify that there is no leakage. If there is, identify the cause and fix it, or your transmission will not operate properly.

Take the new friction plates and soak them in automatic transmissin fluid (ATF). Let them sit for several hours. When installing the clutch plates into the clutch, don't dry off the friction plates; take them directly from the ATF and install them in the clutch. The same applies to bands; make sure they are soaked in ATF before installation.

Next, install the clutch plates. There will be a steel plate next to the piston or piston apply ring. The next plate will be a friction plate. Alternate steel and friction until the correct number of plates is installed. After the last friction plate, there will either be a steel plate or the retaining ring will be the last steel. Either way, finish the clutch stackup and install the snap ring.

REASSEMBLING AUTOMATIC TRANSMISSIONS

Wipe down all parts with a lint-free rag to remove any dust. Next, oil the bushings with a thin layer of assembly grease. Install the parts, in the reverse order in which they were removed, from the case.

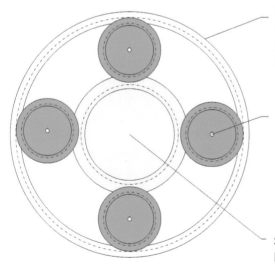

Ring Gear
Power is transmitted directly to the ring gear, either by rotating or holding the gear.

Planet Gear
Power is not normally transmitted directly from gear rotation but instead from the carrier on which the planet gears are mounted. The planet gears are free to rotate on the carrier.

Sun Gear
Power is transmitted directly to the sun gear either by rotating or holding the gear.

All muscle car automatics use planetary gears for shifting.

Pay attention to any special instructions from the reference manual that you are using for the assembly. When indexing parts that seat into a clutch pack, you may have to rotate the driving part to get the splines to fully seat in the clutch pack. Don't force it; steady pressure and rotation back and forth will usually get it to fit.

Pay attention to the orientation of any snap rings or other retaining devices. Some of these are beveled or stepped to support or hold a part in a certain way. The torque specifications for all of the fasteners must be followed.

When installing one-way clutches or sprague clutches, be extremely careful to get the rotation the correct way. If you install the part backward, the car may not move or may slip when the gear that depends on the one-way clutch is selected. Check for signs of brinneling or cracking on the operating surfaces that this type of clutch works against. For a sprague or roller one-way clutch, both surfaces should be smooth and almost polished. If you discover any signs of damage, the parts will need to be replaced.

When installing bands, only install the parts up to where the band is installed. Place the band over the drum and connect it to the case anchor. Next, make sure that the apply pin or lever is properly indexed into the band. Then measure the free play before the band applies. If the band is adjustable, follow the instructions in the service manual. Several transmissions use different lengths of apply pins or levers rather than band adjustments. Follow the instructions in the service manual to verify that the band is being applied with the proper length pin or lever.

Follow the instructions outlined earlier on how to install a shift kit to rebuild the valve body. Make sure that the seal, bushing, or gasket is replaced at every location on the transmission where something passes through the case, such as the shift rod, modulator or shift cable, transmission dipstick tube, and so on. You don't want to complete the rebuild and have a leak.

TABLE 9: COMMON COMBINATIONS OF INPUT AND OUTPUT

Input	Locked	Output	Notes
Sun	Planet	Ring	Ring rotates backward (reverse)
Sun	Ring	Planet	Planet rotates slower than sun
Planet	Sun	Ring	Ring rotates faster (overdrive)
Ring	Sun	Planet	Planet rotates slower than ring

Note that if any two elements are locked together, all three will rotate at the same speed (direct drive).

INSTALLING THE TORQUE CONVERTER

Take the new torque converter and lay it down with the pump-drive tangs up. Pour two quarts of ATF into the torque converter so that the converter will not be dry when the vehicle is first started. Wet the oil pump seal with ATF and place a thin film of assembly lube on the bushing where the oil pump drive of the converter will be riding.

Carefully install the torque converter in the transmission. Slowly rotate the converter while holding the converter parallel to the pump body and gently pushing the converter in. For most transmissions, there will be three clunks as the converter indexes the converter sprague shaft, converter output, and the pump-drive tangs. Once the converter is fully seated, retain the converter in place with a 3/4- to 1-inch-wide strip of thin metal bent to fit under a pan bolt and then wrap around and up to hold the converter in place. Make sure that the retaining strip will not interfere with the flexplate.

INSTALLING AN AUTOMATIC TRANSMISSION

Install the transmission in the vehicle. The retaining strap will help keep the converter fully seated so it does not slip out while you are working the transmission back into place. Install the case-to-engine block bolts first. Properly torque these bolts. A washer is typically used between the bolt head and the transmission case.

If so, use high-quality washers and lock washers. One or more of these bolts may be used to retain other items, such as the dipstick tube. Make sure that these other items are properly installed.

Install a new rear transmission mount. Torque the bolts properly. Install the driveshaft. Before inserting the slip yoke, lightly coat the splines with assembly lube and also coat the outside of the slip yoke with assembly lube as well. Wet the inside lip of the rear seal with ATF. Install the slip yoke into the transmission. It may only fit one way. Go to the other end of the driveshaft and install the U-joint at the rear axle. Be sure to properly torque the caps or straps that hold the U-joint in place. This is a good time to grease the U-joints.

Remove the torque converter retaining strap and rotate the converter so the bolt holes line up with the holes in the flexplate. For Fords, the converter may have studs rather than bolt holes. The procedure is the same—line up the studs with the holes in the flexplate. Move the converter toward the engine. Now install new grade 8 studs (or nuts for Fords). There are usually three. Properly torque these fasteners. You will have to rotate the torque converter to reach all three bolts. Double-check the torque on all fasteners.

Install the transmission cooler lines. If the cooler and lines were not flushed before, do it before connecting the lines to the transmission. Tighten the line fittings, but don't overtighten them. For most cars, these will be 5/16- or 3/8-inch tubes with flare fittings. Make sure the cooler lines are properly routed so they do not interfere with anything. Also make sure they will not vibrate or rub next to something.

Next, connect the shift linkage. Verify that it is properly adjusted. Move the lever through all gears and back to park. Verify that the transmission and the selector match. Next install throttle cables or modulator vacuum lines as well as any electrical connectors.

Lower the vehicle. Fill the transmission with fluid. If the transmission has a mechanical throttle linkage or a throttle cable, follow the adjustment procedure and adjust it. If the shift linkage or cable is improperly adjusted, the transmission may be damaged. Check

the fluid level. It should be slightly over full, but by no more than 1/4 of an inch.

Start the car and listen carefully for any strange sounds. Let the engine run for 10 to 15 seconds at a slow idle. Turn the vehicle off and check the fluid level. Add fluid to get the level up to the full mark and repeat this process until the fluid level does not drop between checks. Don't allow the engine to run for more than 10 to 20 seconds without checking the fluid level, or the pump may be damaged. For vehicles whose fluid level is checked with the engine running, once the fluid level does not drop between the check-run-check sequence, start the engine and check the fluid level. If it does not show on the dipstick, turn the engine off, add more fluid, and repeat the check procedure.

Once the transmission is properly filled, let the engine idle while checking for leaks from the transmission cooler lines. Also check for signs of leakage from under the transmission. There should not be any strange sounds or noises. Verify that the transmission holds the car in place by pushing or pulling on it while in park. Take the vehicle for a test drive. Check that the transmission shifts at the proper time. Start easy and gradually increase acceleration, making sure that the shift points are later and firmer as you accelerate harder.

If they are not, slowly drive the car back and check the throttle cable or shift rod adjustment. The transmission can be damaged if the shift points are early and soft while the vehicle is under any type of load. If the vehicle has a vacuum modulator, check the transmission vacuum line at the modulator and the intake manifold. If the vehicle has a vacuum modulator and the vacuum lines are not properly connected, the vehicle will typically shift late and hard. Cars that use a throttle cable or linkage typically shift early and soft if the cable is not connected or is misadjusted.

OVERDRIVE OPTIONS

Muscle cars were not equipped by the factories with overdrive transmissions. Some of the specialty cars, such as some of the ones modified by Motion Performance, could be had with an overdrive. By contrast, every new car available today has an overdrive transmission. An overdrive transmission can significantly improve fuel economy and increase engine life.

You can now add overdrive capabilities to your muscle car. One option is to install a later-model automatic or manual transmission that has overdrive. You can also add an accessory overdrive transmission behind your current transmission.

OVERDRIVE MANUAL TRANSMISSIONS

A number of kits adapt a five- or six-speed manual transmission to just about any muscle car. Some of these kits include everything you will need for the conversion: the transmission, bellhousing, clutch, hydraulic or manual clutch linkage, and even new clutch and brake pedals! The better kits include a transmission that has been modified so the shifter is in a closer location. Most modern transmissions have the shifter mounted too far back.

Installing one of these kits is similar to installing a manual transmission. Follow the instructions that came with the kit. The driveshaft will typically have to be modified, as the chance that it will be the correct length is slim to none. If you are converting the car from an automatic to a manual transmission, get a kit that is designed for that purpose. The kit will include the clutch pedal, a smaller brake pedal, the flywheel, bellhousing, and a hydraulic clutch master cylinder

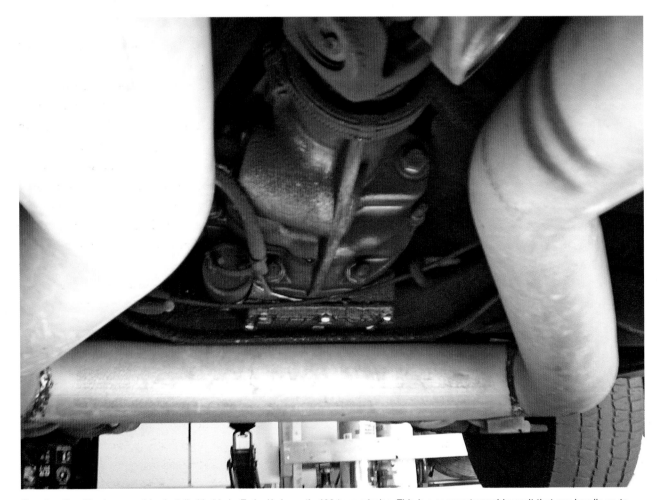

Here is a Gear Vendors overdrive installed behind a Turbo Hydromatic 400 transmission. This is a compact overdrive unit that can handle up to 1,200 horsepower.

with a hydraulic slave cylinder. The kit will also include the fasteners. This will make the job much easier, as you won't have to spend all your time chasing down obscure parts. Several kits even come with a video that shows you how to install the transmission.

Another option for Chrysler vehicles is a conversion for the A-833 transmision that swaps third and fourth gears. The transmission's direct, or 1:1, ratio becomes the third gear and a new gear is cut to become the overdrive fourth gear. Then the 3–4 shift lever linkage is inverted. Chrysler originally came up with this in the late 1970s for the lower-performance economy cars. The aftermarket makes the conversion kit for the high-performance A-833. The advantage to this is that no vehicle modifications are required and the vehicle looks completely stock.

AUTOMATIC OVERDRIVE OPTIONS

You can find electronically and hydraulically controlled automatic overdrive transmissions. Chrysler owners are at an advantage here as the A518 is the four-speed overdrive version of the A727 Torqueflite. This transmission can be built to survive behind your big-block Mopar muscle car. For GM owners, the 4L80E is the modern version of the TH400. You will need to add an electronic control unit in order to retrofit this transmission to your car. This transmission will not operate without the electronic controller.

Several automatic transmissions have overdrive, but be careful. Most of them will not survive behind a big-block powerplant. Remember, it is not the horsepower but the torque that transmissions have to deal with. Talk with a good transmission builder about the expected problem areas and necessary modifications when installing a newer transmission behind a big block. The last thing that you want to do is just bolt one on and see what happens. Also, if the transmission came from, or was designed for, a pickup or SUV, size and weight may be an issue.

INSTALLING AUTOMATIC OVERDRIVES

Installing one of these transmissions may require that new holes be drilled for the transmission crossmember. The driveshaft will probably not fit, and will have to be modified. The output yoke may not match up with the U-joint that is on the driveshaft; check this before you have the driveshaft modified so it can be addressed as well.

The shift linkage is not likely to fit, either. If it does, it may not match the stock gates. You will have to modify your stock shifter or install an aftermarket shifter designed for the overdrive automatic transmission you are installing.

The throttle linkage might require some modification to function properly. If this is wrong, the transmission may not shift properly and could be damaged.

Late-model overdrive automatic transmissions are electronically controlled. You cannot use one without an aftermarket computer that controls the shift points and line pressure. The transmission will not work without the external controller and may even be damaged if it is installed and you attempt to operate the vehicle without the computer.

Also note that modern electronically controlled transmissions are not usually designed to shift under full power. These transmissions are controlled by the same computer that controls the engine. The computer typically reduces engine power during shifts, then restores full power when the shift is complete. Once the shift is complete, full power is restored. This happens quickly and is not noticeable to the driver. If a new electronically controlled transmission is installed in your muscle car, make sure that whoever builds the transmission understands that your application will require full-power shifts.

You also have an assortment of more minor issues to fix. The cooler lines may have metric fittings. The fill tube may not fit properly. The transmission tunnel may have to be modified; if the transmission is longer, the case may hit the tunnel. This can be rectified by either cutting the tunnel and welding it back or by making some room in the tunnel with a hammer.

Modern transmissions usually have lockup torque converters that are usually controlled by an electrical signal to the transmission. There is usually a connector on the case with several connections, as the transmission also informs the computer when it is in the higher gears. You can use the lockup converter, but you will have to identify what each connector is for. You can add a switch that locks the converter when you want it locked. There are companies that make control boxes that will control the lockup converter, making it an automatic.

Most late-model transmissions do not have speedometer drives. This will render your factory mechanical speedometer useless. There are solutions to this problem. For starters, you can use an electronic speedometer. The transmission will have one or two speed sensors. The one at the rear of the case is the one that can be used to drive your electronic speedometer; check with the manufacturer of the speedometer. If the transmission is from an OBD II vehicle, it will have a front speed sensor. This is the input speed sensor, and it is used by the computer to determine transmission slippage.

ADD-ON OVERDRIVE OPTIONS

There are suppliers who sell kits to fit an overdrive to your existing transmission. These kits usually come with everything you need, including detailed instructions. This option works well.

Add-on overdrive kits usually come with a speedometer cable extension, as the speedometer takeoff must be moved to the overdrive unit or the speed will read slow when overdrive is engaged. These extenders may also have an electronic sending unit that allows a small computer to turn the overdrive on and off for you.

The driveshaft will need to be modified to fit. Follow the instructions in the kit. Pay close attention to the driveline angles, or driveshaft vibration may result. If an angle is wrong, shim the transmission or modify the rear mount pad so that the rear of the output is back in line. The crossmember may have to be modified to get the front of the driveshaft back in line.

Finally, the electrical wiring must be connected. All of these auxiliary overdrives use an electric solenoid to engage the overdrive. Follow the instructions that came with the overdrive unit. Use a grommet to protect the wiring where wiring passes through the floor and seal the hole so water cannot enter.

CHAPTER 12
REAR AXLE

Most muscle cars were factory equipped with heavy-duty rear axles. After correcting any inherent weak points, the rear axle should not require more than periodic fluid changes.

Most muscle cars did not come with positive-traction rear axles. This was an option. Most of the high-end muscle cars did have positive traction. Each manufacturer had a separate name for this feature. GM usually called their version a Positraction rear axle or a limited-spin axle. Ford had the Equal Lock and the Traction Lock, and, for high-performance vehicles, the Detroit Locker. Chrysler had the Sure Grip. American Motors called it Twin Grip. Except for the Detroit Locker, all of these devices were friction-plate devices.

No high-torque big block should be driven without a limited-slip rear axle. Besides the obvious

This is a limited-slip carrier. Limited-slip carriers are easy to spot; they have springs that set the preload on the clutch plates or, as in this Auburn unit, the cone clutches.

straight-line traction, they are invaluable when attempting to turn from a side street into moving traffic. Normally, without a limited-slip rear axle, a right turn into traffic results in the passenger side tire going up in smoke and the vehicle not accelerating. With a limited-slip differential, the driver-side tire will take over and accelerate the vehicle. The inside tire will still slip some, but the vehicle will be able to accelerate up to speed.

Another problem is encountered when attempting to accelerate from a standstill on a wet roadway, especially if going uphill in a straight line. Without limited slip, the passenger side tire will spin, even on light acceleration. This is due to the torque of the big block. The result is that you are left holding up traffic as you helplessly spin the passenger side tire on the slippery pavement. With limited slip, you can accelerate with traffic instead of holding it up.

Limited slip does have some drawbacks. The main issue arises when turning. If excessive power is applied, both rear tires will spin and cause oversteer. This can come on suddenly, especially on wet or slippery surfaces. Under brisk acceleration around corners, the inside tire will slip, which can cause increased tire wear.

Limited-slip differentials are not indestructible. You must use some caution in order to prevent excessive wear or damage to the clutches in a limited-slip differential.

If one wheel is on a slippery surface and the other is on dry pavement, use care when accelerating. If you exceed the torque rating of the unit, the wheel on the slippery surface will spin and the wheel with traction will only partially drive the vehicle, with the clutches absorbing the difference in heat. This can cause rapid clutch wear and failure of the limited-slip unit.

Don't believe the stories that more throttle will make the unit "lock up." This is not true.

If you do a burnout at the drag strip, make sure that you are off of the throttle before the rear tires move out of the bleach box and the water. Don't drive out of the bleach box under full throttle with the tires spinning. The sudden shock when one tire hooks up can cause damage to the clutches in the limited-slip differential. A locker or a spool can tolerate this type of abuse, but the axles and the rear gears had better also be up to the task.

One drawback is that clutch-style units will require more frequent fluid changes (usually once a year). These also require that 2 ounces of friction additive be added per quart of rear axle fluid. All original-equipment muscle car limited-slip designs except the Ford Detroit Locker use clutches.

SELECTING THE IDEAL REAR AXLE RATIO

To select the optimum rear axle ratio, consider how the car will be used. Do not install excessively low gears in a daily driver, or you will suffer reduced mileage and the engine rpm during freeway cruising will be excessive. If the car has an overdrive, the rear gear selection can be more aggressive. Don't select a gearset based on what a friend is running or because some car in a magazine is running a certain ratio.

Select the tires and wheels that will be used before selecting a rear gear ratio. For example, a 3.42 rear gear set with 26-inch tires (P245 60R15 or P295 50R15) is almost identical to a 4.11 rear gear set with 31-inch slicks! Take extra care if the vehicle will use different sets of tires for different applications. If it is geared for the bigger-diameter slicks, it will most likely be almost impossible to drive on the highway with the smaller-diameter street tires. Tall slicks will require a stouter gear while the street tires will require a lower ratio gear set.

Select the correct gear ratio so that the car crosses the finish line with the rpm just below the peak horsepower rpm. So if your engine makes 500 horsepower at 5,600 rpm, if the gears are correct, the rpm at the finish line should be around 5,200 to 5,400 rpm. For optimum performance at the drag strip, the following formula will select the correct gears:

$$\text{Gear} = \frac{(\text{tire diameter x RPM})}{(\text{MPH x 336})}$$

RPM is 200 to 400 rpm below the peak horsepower rpm for the engine. This is the point just before horsepower begins to drop off. It is also the ideal shift-point rpm. The rpm at which peak horsepower is attained can be determined from the dynometer chart for the engine. MPH is the trap speed at the end of the quarter-mile. This should be the computed speed for a vehicle with the same weight and horsepower (be honest). For automatic transmission vehicles, subtract 250 from the rpm used in the formula to account for torque converter slippage if the vehicle does not have a lock-up torque converter, or if it has a lock-up converter that is not locked while the engine is under full throttle. Finally, err on the lower side. If the result is a gear ratio that does not exactly match the available gears, always round down to the smaller ratio.

If the vehicle has overdrive, the calculations should be made for the direct-drive gear, usually fourth gear for a 5-speed or the third gear for a 4-speed-overdrive automatic. This gives you the optimum gearing for the strip while maintaining a nice gear for cruising down the highway.

REAR AXLE MAINTENANCE

Working on a rear axle is not that difficult. The key is to get the gears properly aligned. You will need some special tools. A press and a bearing puller will be required, and a dial indicator is mandatory for setting pinion depth. Take your time and get the gears properly installed and the bearing preloads set correctly. Each axle type will have specialized tools that will make the job much easier, such as the bearing preload adjusting wrenches for the Ford 9-inch rear differential.

Rear axle maintenance begins with rear cover removal. Most axles do not have drain plugs, so this is the only way to drain the fluid. This is an "open," or nonlimited, slip rear axle. Also, notice how large the pinion gear is. This is a 2.73 ratio axle.

Get a service manual that covers your rear axle. It will have the details on how to properly service the axle. It will also have all of the much-needed specifications, such as preload, pinion depth, ring and pinion backlash, and the torque specifications for all bolts and fasteners. This information is critical if you perform anything other than a fluid change.

As for preventive maintenance, changing the fluid is about all you have to do. There are no adjustments or service components. Use a good synthetic 85W-140 gear lubricant, and if the rear axle has a clutch-type limited-slip carrier, add the correct amount of limited-slip additive. Typically, the small 2-ounce bottles treat 1 quart. Most rear axles hold between 2 and 3 quarts, so you will need at least 4 ounces. The fluid should be changed every 36,000 miles or once every three years. If you have a clutch-style limited-slip rear axle, the fluid should be changed every 12,000 miles or once a year.

REAR AXLE LEAKS

One of the most common problems with rear axles is leaks. There are three seals and one gasket. This makes leak detection simple. Clean the housing off, top the axle off with fluid, and drive the car for a day or two. You will see where the leak is coming from.

PINION SEAL

If the rear axle's pinion seal is leaking, the driveshaft will have to be removed and the pinion nut will then need to be removed. This is where an extralong breaker bar or an impact gun will be needed. There are special tools that bolt to the U-joint flange so the flange can be held in place while the pinion nut is removed or replaced.

The pinion nut is designed so that it will not loosen. Once it is removed, the nut should be replaced. Also, a crush sleeve maintains bearing preload. Once the pinion nut is removed, this relationship is disturbed and the crush sleeve needs to be replaced. To properly set the bearing preload, the ring gear will have to be removed. If you are going to do this properly, you might as well rebuild the rear axle and replace the pinion and carrier bearings.

Usually when the pinion seal is leaking, the pinion bearing preload has been lost. This can be verified by attempting to move the pinion yoke up and down. If you can move it even just a tiny bit, the rear axle will need to be rebuilt.

Examine the yoke carefully and make sure the area that the seal rides on is smooth. Also check that where the new seal will ride is not covered with corrosion, rust, or scale. Polish the area if it is not smooth, and if the yoke is pitted or grooved, replace the yoke.

If you need to replace the seal but not the bearings, follow the steps that describe how to rebuild the rear axle (but reuse the bearings). Set the pinion rotational torque to 70 percent of the torque drag specification for new bearings. If the specs call for a bearing preload of 14–18 lb-in of rotational drag, tighten the pinion nut to achieve a rotational drag between 10 and 13 lb-in of rotational drag when using good used bearings.

AXLE SEALS

Bad axle seals are a common source of leaks. To change an axle seal, the axle will have to be removed. This is not difficult. There are two types of axle retention schemes: C-clip and bearing retainer. All Chevrolet passenger car axles and later-model Ford passenger car axles (excluding 9-inch) are C-clip. All Chrysler, Ford 9-inch, Pontiac, Buick, and most Oldsmobile axles are retained by a bearing plate (although the GM cars sometimes ended up with Chevy C-clip axles when supplies were tight). This is true for the Oldsmobile version of the GM corporate 8.5 axles as well. While this axle does not use C-clips, all of the internals except the axles and axle bearings will interchange. These were first used on 1971 Oldsmobiles.

To remove the axle, identify the type. If it is a C-clip style, the rear axle cover must be removed. For bearing-plate-retained axles, the cover does not need to be removed. For a C-clip style, remove the differential cover. For all axles, remove the wheel and the brake drum first.

NON-C-CLIP AXLES

Remove the axles by rotating the nuts that hold the retaining plate. These can be accessed by rotating the

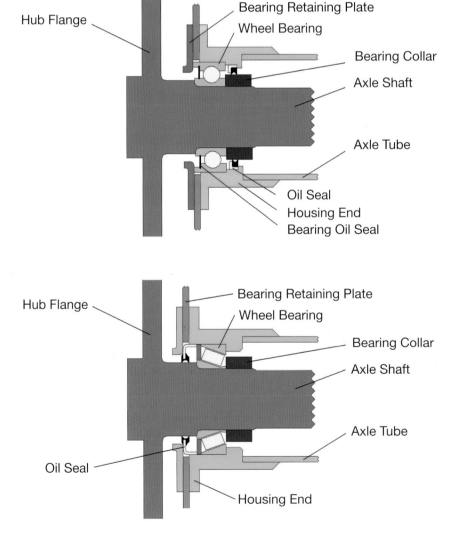

Dry bearing. The axle shaft seal is on the inside of the bearing. The axle shaft fluid does not reach the wheel bearing, and it is lubricated with wheel bearing grease. The seal rides on the bearing collar. This is a retained shaft, not a C-clip axle. The Ford 9-inch uses this style of axle retention. When servicing one of these, it is important that wheel bearing grease be placed between the oil seal and the bearing. Fill this space about one-third to one-half the way up with grease.

Hub Flange — Bearing Retaining Plate — Wheel Bearing — Bearing Collar — Axle Shaft — Axle Tube — Oil Seal — Housing End — Bearing Oil Seal

Wet or axle fluid–lubricated wheel bearing. The axle shaft seal is outside the bearing, allowing axle fluid to reach the wheel bearing. Note the bearing collar that keeps the axle and the bearing from sliding. This is a retained shaft, not a C-clip axle. For this style of axle, the seal can be replaced only by removing the bearing.

Hub Flange — Bearing Retaining Plate — Wheel Bearing — Bearing Collar — Axle Shaft — Axle Tube — Oil Seal — Housing End wheel flange so the hole lines up with the nut. Once all four nuts have been removed, use a slide hammer or re-install the wheel with three lug nuts but leave them loose and pull on the wheel so it slams into the lug nuts. Two to three good tugs will usually pop the axle out of the vehicle.

There are two general types of seals used. Ford 9-inch and early Oldsmobile axles have the seal in the axle tube, riding on the bearing retainer. These axles usually use sealed ball bearings. For this style, the bearing does not have to be removed in order to replace the seal. The other types are the BOP 8.2-inch and the 1971 and later Oldsmobile axle. These use a roller bearing with the seal between the bearing and the wheel flange. These axles require bearing removal in order to replace the seal.

A press is required to press the bearing and the bearing retainer into place. To remove the old bearing, drill a 1/4-inch hole into the retainer, but make absolutely sure you do not go too far and nick or drill into the axle. Use a drill stop or a drill press with the stop set. You only need to drill two-thirds of the way through the retainer. If you use a handheld drill, a piece of 3/8-inch steel tubing works well. Carefully cut it so that when slipped over the drill bit only enough drill bit is exposed to go two-thirds of the way through

The bearing retainer must be split so that it can be removed. Do not attempt to press these off. This is made easier by drilling one or two holes three quarters of the way through the retainer. Do not go too far and nick the axle. These axles went almost 200,000 miles, and the bearings are being replaced as part of a total rear axle overhaul. These are the original "wet" bearings, as they still have the factory stamped steel bearing retainer.

Measure the thickness of the bearing (and seal if the seal is part of the bearing retention system). Slip the bearing and seal onto the axle shaft to help with the measurement. Do not measure the exposed rubber lip seal.

the retainer. Place a chisel across the hole drilled in the retainer and strike the chisel. This should split the retainer. Do not nick or gouge the axle shaft. If you do, it will have to be replaced.

TIPS FOR REPLACING BEARINGS ON NON-C-CLIP AXLES

Before replacing rear wheel bearings on non C-clip axles, it is important to check the thickness of the bearing and, if the seal is part of the retention, the combined thickness of the bearing and the seal. Be careful when measuring the seal; don't include the thickness of the exposed rubber; the retaining plate does not contact the rubber, only the steel edge. To remove the bearing,

you need a guillotine-style bearing puller installed behind the bearing inner cone. Use the press to push the axle down and out of the bearing. Clean the axle shaft and inspect for any signs of damage. This is also a good time to replace the wheel studs.

Then check the depth of the bearing cavity in the axle tube. Hold the brake backing plate up against the housing end, as this also adds to the overall depth of the bearing cavity. The new bearing and seal should be .010 thicker than the cavity. Under no circumstances should the cavity depth measure deeper than the bearing and seal thickness. The result will be a wheel that is loose, which could lead to bearing failure and possible separation from the vehicle.

Check the bearing cavity depth. Make sure that the brake backing plate is held tightly against the axle flange. It must also be included in the depth measurement.

Begin the replacement process on non-C-clip bearings by removing the bearing collar. Do not press the collar off; instead drill two or three quarter-inch holes into the collar. Make absolutely sure you do not drill into the axle. Notice the brass pipe fitting installed over the drill bit—I use this to set the drill bit depth so that as the bit extends past the pipe fitting it will only penetrate three quarters of the way through the collar. Then a chisel can be used to split the collar.

If the size is incorrect, chances are that you have the wrong bearing or seal. This could be caused by a rear axle swap sometime in the vehicle's past. Station wagon rear axles from the same model family will swap in place for most passenger cars rear axles. The station wagon rear axles usually came with larger bearings. There were also manufacturing changes and substitutions as well that could have affected your model year. Check the bearings that were available for the station wagon as well as the surrounding model years.

The replacement bearing should also come with a new bearing retainer. Check the instructions that come with the bearing. Some will have you press the bearing first and the retainer second, while the rest will have you press the bearing and the retainer on at the same time. Make sure the retainer plate is properly installed on the axle before you press on the bearing. Check the seal; some axles have the seal installed in the retainer plate. If this is the case, the seal must be replaced before the bearing is pressed into place.

Before pressing the bearing and retainer into place, measure the inside diameter of the bearing, then measure the axle shaft where the bearing will rest. There should be a .001-inch interference fit. If the bearing is not .001 inch smaller than the shaft, the axle will need to be replaced. Next, check the retainer; it should measure .004 inch smaller than the location on the axle shaft where it will reside. Don't take this lightly. If these measurements don't check out, replace the axle. You don't want to chance a wheel coming off due to a retainer failure. If the bearing is not a press fit, do not use the axle.

Make sure that the bearing is oriented the correct way. On the dry-bearing models, there will be a seal in one side of the bearing to keep in the wheel bearing grease. This side must face out toward the wheel. For the wet style, one side is more open or exposed than the other; the more open side must face out toward the seal.

Press the bearing and retainer into place, following the instructions that came with your bearing. If the bearing uses a separate race, remove the old race from the axle housing and drive in the new race using the appropriate driver. In a pinch, the old race turned around backward can be used as a driver. Depending on your axle, there may be a seal located in the axle tube that rides on the bearing retainer. If so, replace it now. For all the others, the seal rides on the axle shaft, between the bearing and the wheel mounting flange.

Rear axle bearing with retaining collar. This is a press-on axle bearing. The collar is what retains the bearing on the axle shaft.

You should have replaced it before the bearing was pressed into place.

If the seal is in the retaining plate, the bearing is lubricated by the axle fluid. Before installing the axle, pack the bearing with wheel bearing grease and also pack grease in the seal so that the space between the bearing and the seal is two-thirds full of grease. Next, coat the seal lip with wheel bearing grease. If the seal is a dual-lip seal, fill the space between the two lips with wheel bearing grease as well. Slide the axle back in place. It will take a little wiggling and twisting to get the splines to engage the spider gear. Push the axle shaft in as far as it will go.

If your seal resides inside the axle tube so that it rides on the bearing retainer, your bearing is not lubricated by axle fluid. It is critical that you place wheel bearing grease between the seal and the area where the bearing will be, filling about two-thirds of the space. Now you are almost ready to re-install the axle shaft.

For both styles, begin by placing some wheel bearing grease on the axle seal. If the seal is a dual lip style, wipe wheel bearing grease in the V formed by the axle seal. Don't forget this step or the outer seal lip will only last a couple of miles! Properly position the retaining plate— it will usually only line up one way. Line up the brake backing plane and install the retaining hardware. Torque the bolts to the factory's torque specification. It is a good idea to use new bolts on this style of rear end, as these bolts retain the axle. Use only grade 8 hardware.

C-CLIP AXLES

Inspect the axle shaft where the bearing rides. Since this type of axle does not use an inner race, the bearing slowly wears into the axle. If there is a detectable groove where the rollers ride, the axle must be replaced. Remove the oil seal from the axle. Using a slide-hammer-style bearing puller, remove the axle bearing from the axle tube.

Install the new bearing. Using the appropriate bearing driver, tap the new bearing into place. Now coat the bearing with axle fluid. All C-clip-style rear axles use axle fluid to lubricate the bearing. Take the new oil seal and, using the correct size seal driver, tap the seal into position. Lightly coat the seal lip with wheel bearing grease. If the seal is a dual-lip style, fill the V between the two seal surfaces with wheel bearing grease.

Install the axle shafts. It may take a little wiggling to get the splines to line up and engage the differential side gears. Once the axle shaft is installed, push the shaft in as

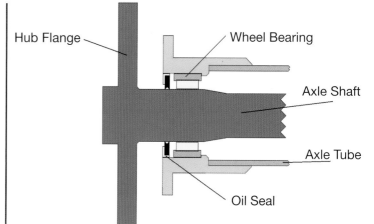

C-clip-style axle bearing. Note that there is not any retaining plate or bearing collar. Also, the bearing has no inner race; it rides directly on the axle shaft. The seal is outside the bearing, and the bearing is lubricated by axle fluid. These always use a roller-style bearing.

far as it will go. Go back under the vehicle and install the C-clip. Now pull out on the axle; it should move very little. Inspect the C-clip to be sure that it is fully seated in the pocket that is in the side gear.

Pressing a new axle bearing and bearing retainer into a non-C-clip-style axle. It is important that the retainer plate, bearing seal, bearing, and retainer are all placed on the axle correctly before pressing the bearing and the retainer. Follow the bearing maker's instructions, this one required that the bearing and the retainer were pressed on the axle as a pair. Always use a press. Never hammer bearings on.

REAR AXLE

207

Inspect the cross-shaft for signs of wear where the axle shafts bump up against the cross-shaft. This is important. If the shaft or axle ends are worn too far, the axle can move in far enough that the C-clip falls off. If this happens, the axle will come out of the vehicle. If there are any signs of wear, replace the cross-shaft.

Install the cross-shaft. Pay attention to how it goes into the carrier. The axle shafts must be back so that the C-clips are fully seated in the pockets that are in the spider gears. Once the cross-shaft is properly oriented, slide it into the carrier and through the spider gears. Install the retention bolt. Torque it to the factory specifications. Replace the rear cover and refill the axle.

REPLACING THE RING AND PINION

Begin the disassembly by removing the rear cover and the axles. Next, remove the driveshaft. For the Chrysler 8 3/4 or the Ford 9-inch there is no rear cover; the gear carrier is removed from the front of the housing. This makes service easy; you set the carrier up on the bench. It also makes swaps easy. You can have two or more carriers set up with different gears; just swap in the carrier that you want. For the rest of us, after removing the rear cover, the ring gear and the carrier must be removed. Remove the bearing caps and remove the carrier. It will not just come out, as there should be pressure from the case loading the carrier bearings.

Carefully pry the carrier out and be sure to catch the shims that are on each side. Don't mix these up. Measure the thickness of the shim stack for each side and record these numbers. Add the two together; this is your total shim thickness for the housing. For Ford 9-inch rear axles and the Mopar 8 3/4 axles with removable center sections, there are no shims. Instead, these use adjuster nuts that set the backlash and the bearing preload. There is a specialty tool that is used to adjust them that makes the job much easier.

Remove the ring gear from the carrier. Several rear axles use left-hand threads on the ring gear bolts. These are grade 8 fasteners. Do not reuse them; they must be replaced if they are removed. Apply thread-

Installing new carrier bearings. Note that the bearing is installed the correct way. Also, don't mix up the bearing race cups. Keep them with their bearing, but do not let them carry any of the press pressure. This will damage the bearings. Note that this is a limited-slip carrier; the springs are the giveaway.

locking compound to the threads when installing new bolts. For most carriers, the bolts are long enough that the new ring gear can be "pulled" onto the carrier by tightening the bolts. To do this, work around the carrier, tightening the bolts one-half of a turn each until the ring gear is fully seated. Tighten the bolts to 25 lb-ft. Remove each bolt one at a time, add high-strength thread-locking compound, and torque the bolt to the recommended torque setting. Mark the head of the bolt and move across to the bolt opposite. Keep going until all of the bolts are thread-locked and properly torqued.

In order to replace the carrier bearings, the old ones will have to be removed with a press. Most axles do not use shims on the inside of the bearings. When installing new bearings, press the bearing in with the taper facing the correct way. In all cases, the smaller diameter faces out, with the wider portion back toward the carrier. Don't mix up the races; each bearing has a race cup that must be kept with its particular bearing. I mark each race with an R or L

Rear axle rebuild kit. These kits come with the pinion and carrier bearings as well as new ring gear bolts and the shims for the carrier and pinion. A new crush sleeve and pinion nut is also included. This kit also has gear marking compound and thread locking compound. Wheel bearings are usually not included and will have to be purchased separately.

that corresponds to the location in the housing into which it will be installed.

With the ring gear out of the way, the pinion can be removed. If the ring and pinion are going to be reused, measure the pinion depth so you can be sure that the pinion is installed to the original depth. Set up a dial indicator to read the depth and record the number. The proper reference point is the depth from the ring gear centerline. Even if a new ring and pinion are going to be installed, it is not a bad idea to measure the pinion depth and make a note of it. This can be used as a comparison when the new pinion is installed.

Remove the pinion yoke nut. Breaking this nut loose requires a lot of torque—use an impact wrench. Use a puller to remove the pinion yoke. A wooden mallet can be used to tap the pinion out if it is stubborn. The front pinion bearing will remain in the case; the rear pinion bearing is pressed onto the pinion and will come out with the pinion. Using a bearing press plate and a press, remove the bearing from the pinion. Don't lose the shims that are between the pinion and the bearing. Measure these as a stack and record the thickness. Remove the pinion seal and drive out the front and rear pinion bearing races.

Clean the housing thoroughly. Install new bearing races for the pinion bearings. Don't install the new pinion seal until the front bearing and crush sleeve are installed. Install new axle bearings. Depending on the type of retention, these are either installed in the housing (C-clip) or on the axle shaft with a press-on retainer (non-C-clip). Install new axle seals.

Begin the reassembly with the pinion. Use the same shims as were originally in the housing as a starting point. This will result in a correct gear installation most of the time. Carefully measure the pinion depth. This number is always referenced from the pinion gear surface to the centerline of the ring gear. For a Ford 9-inch, it is from the flat of the pinion support bearing pilot to the ring gear centerline. If the pinion depth is set correctly and the backlash is adjusted properly, the gear pattern will be right on.

The inner bearing has to be pressed on after the shims are installed. To ease this process, hone out the inside of an old pinion bearing so it just slides on and off the pinion shaft. This makes assembly easier. If the depth is not correct, it is much simpler and faster to change the shims as the bearing does not have to be pressed on and off. Once the correct pinion depth is established, the new bearing can be pressed on.

Ring and pinion. Note the ring gear tooth surface names. The root is the base of the valley between the teeth and the top is the flat at the top of the tooth. The top is also referred to as the face. The heel is the half of the tooth that is by the outside edge, while the toe is the half of the tooth that is near the inside edge.

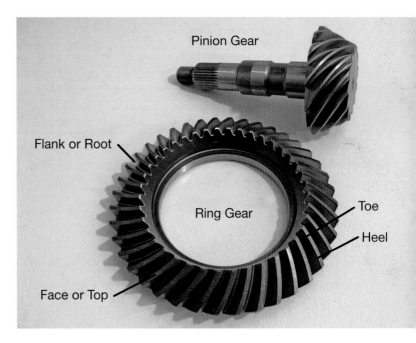

When testing the depth, assemble the pinion in the case with the bearings and the pinion flange. Make sure the bearings are properly lubricated with rear axle lubricant. Do not install the seal in the case and use the old pinion nut. Do not install the crush sleeve, but tighten the pinion nut until the rotational drag is within specs. Be careful—it will not take much torque to reach this point and you are not yet trying to crush the crush sleeve. Next, the pinion depth can be checked.

Aftermarket gears will usually be marked with a true depth number, and it will be in inches. For factory or factory replacement gears, there will either be a correction marking or no markings at all. These gears are set up by measuring the thickness of the pinion head and then subtracting this from

Pinion assembly. This illustration shows how the pinion is assembled. Note that the inner pinion bearing is pressed in place. Also, each time the pinion nut is removed, the crush sleeve must be replaced.

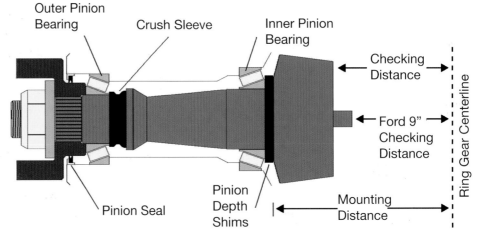

the mounting distance listed in the factory service manual. The resulting number is the pinion depth. If there is a correction number stamped on the pinion, add or subtract this to the calculated pinion depth to get the final depth setting.

Once the proper pinion depth has been established, you have two options. You can assemble the pinion with the new crush sleeve and set the pinion torque. You can also leave the temporary pinion set up and install the ring gear, set the backlash, and take a gear pattern. If you want to take a gear pattern, go to the ring gear and backlash steps in the next section.

There is one other option for setting pinion bearing preload: you can obtain a solid spacer. This is a machined tube that replaces the crush sleeve. These come with shims that allow the proper bearing preload to be established. They have the benefit of holding the proper preload without relaxing over time, as the pinion nut is torqued to 150 to 250 lb-ft with thread-locking compound. If you need to remove the pinion nut in the future, it can be replaced and retorqued without worrying about the pinion bearing preload.

FINAL REAR AXLE ASSEMBLY

Remove the pinion from the case. Lightly lubricate the new front pinion bearing and install it in the case. Install a new pinion seal and run a bead of wheel bearing grease

This dial indicator mounts to the bearing cap mounting point.

around the inside lip of the seal. Press the new inner pinion bearing onto the pinion; be sure to have the correct shims in place. Now slip the new crush sleeve onto the pinion and install the pinion in the case.

Use your finger to help guide the pinion through the outer bearing. Install the pinion yoke and install the pinion nut washer followed by a new pinion nut. Tighten the pinion-yoke-retaining nut until the correct preload is detected. It will usually require at least 150 lb-ft to begin to crush the crush sleeve. Be careful to notice when the bearings begin to tighten up. This is obvious, as the pinion flange will no longer wobble. Stop and check the rotational drag on the pinion. For most axles, 14 to 16 lb-in is the reading you are shooting for. If it is too low, tighten the pinion nut 1/8 of a turn only and check the torque again. Be careful here. If you get the pinion bearing preload too tight, a new crush sleeve will be required.

Pinion bearing and crush sleeve preload are important to ensuring proper gear alignment. As the engine applies torque to the pinion, the pinion will attempt to climb up the ring gear (deflect) and also push forward in the housing. The pressure pushing forward will compress the bearing and relax some of the preload pressure on the front bearing. If the preload is too loose, this could result in a front bearing that is operating with zero preload. As the pinion attempts to climb up the ring gear, the pinion will deflect due to the zero preload on the front bearing. If the preload is too high, the pinion bearings can overheat and could fail.

If the front bearing preload is reduced to zero, there is no pressure on the pinion nut. This can cause the pinion nut to loosen, further aggravating the problem. This is the other reason that a good permanent thread-locking compound must be used on the pinion nut.

The ring gear is installed after the pinion depth is properly set. Begin the assembly by using the factory shim thickness on each side. For Salisbury rear ends, the carrier bearing preload is established by shims being wedged into the case. Some of the

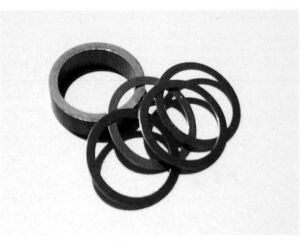

This is a solid spacer that is used to replace a crush sleeve. If you use one of these, save the unused shims; they might be needed the next time you replace a gear set.

factory shims were cast-iron rings; these are not reusable unless you have a case spreader. Attempting to tap them in will usually break them. The factory was able to do this job by using a case spreader to slightly expand the case.

Assemble the ring gear carrier back in the housing using the original factory shim thickness on each side. If the factory shim packs were missing, shim the sides so that the carrier is a snug slip fit into the case and then add an additional .004-inch shim thickness to each side. This additional .004 inch of shims on each side of the carrier bearings sets the case preload. This is important; the preload keeps the ring gear from deflecting away from the pinion when a load is placed on the rear axle. Use a prybar to wedge the gear carrier over or use a case spreader so that the shims can be installed. Install the bearing caps and torque them. Make sure that the caps are installed back into their original position.

Next, set up the dial indicator on a ring gear tooth. With the pinion locked, measure the total amount of backlash on the ring gear. This indicates how much slack is in the gearset. Set the backlash to the gearset manufacturer's specification. Rotate the gearset and check backlash at three to four locations around the gear. It is acceptable to have as much as

.003-inch variance in the backlash measurements. If the backlash is different at various locations, the lowest value must be no less than the minimum value called out in the specifications.

For Ford 9-inch and Chrysler 8 3/4 carriers, the backlash is easy to set: just adjust the carrier spanner nuts. The easiest way to do this is to set the ring gear so that it is just at zero lash. Lock down the driver-side adjuster. Use a case-spread gauge set to measure the deflection of the carrier bearing towers and adjust the passenger side spanner nut so that .008 to .010 inch of preload is added. Follow the factory service manual for recommendations on how to set up the indicator to properly measure the case preload. Next, check the backlash. It should be right on or extremely close. If it is, lock the adjusters down.

READING GEAR CONTACT PATTERNS

Once everything checks out fine, the gear set can be checked for proper gear mesh by taking a pattern. Do not take a gear pattern until you have the backlash adjusted properly. Apply some gear marking compound to several teeth on the ring gear. Rotate the pinion while applying drag pressure to the differential carrier. Rotate the gearset forward and backward. Examine the resulting pattern; it should be a smooth oval shape that is centered between the face (top) and the root (bottom) of the ring gear tooth. It should also be parallel with the tooth. It might not be centered between the toe and the heel. This is OK as long as the pattern fits the guidelines stated above.

If the pattern is too high or too low, you can make corresponding adjustments to correct the problem (depending on how the gears were machined). Determine how your gears were machined; they were either face-hobbed or face-milled. Do this by looking at a tooth on the ring gear. If the tooth is the same width at the toe (inside) edge as the heel (outside) edge, then the gear was machined using the face hobbing method. If the tooth is wider at the heel edge than at the toe edge, the gear was machined using the face-milling method.

See the table for how to read the resulting gear pattern and correct any problems. Regardless of the gear type, you want a contact pattern that has a rounded, bullet-shaped edge at the heel edge on the drive side of the ring gear teeth. If you change either the pinion depth or the backlash, the other will be affected.

Bear in mind that how the housing was machined can also affect the pattern. The pinion shims affect the pinion depth, not the up or down relationship between the pinion and the ring gear. So if the proper up-down relationship between the carrier bearing's centerline and the centerline for the pinion bearings is wrong, no amount of shims will correct it.

TABLE 10: SHIM AND BACKLASH ADJUSTMENTS TO CORRECT PATTERN PROBLEMS

Hobb-Milled Gear Set		Face-Milled Gear Set		Corrective Action
Drive Pattern	Coast Pattern	Drive Pattern	Coast Pattern	
Top toe	Top heel	Top heel	Top toe	Increase pinion shim
Root heel	Root toe	Root toe	Root heel	Decrease pinion shim
Top heel	Top toe	Top heel	Top heel	Decrease backlash
Root toe	Root heel	Root toe	Root toe	Increase backlash

In order to use this table, you must know how your gears were machined. This table will show what change you need to make for each pattern.

Adjust the pinion shims to center the pattern between the face (top) and root (bottom) of the ring gear teeth. If the pattern is located closer to the root, the pinion is too close to the ring gear. If the pattern is too close to the face of the ring gear teeth, the pinion is too far away.

When setting up gears by taking patterns, make changes of .005 to .010 inch at a time until the pattern is close, and then make smaller .002- to .004-inch changes. Usually it is easier to keep making the larger changes until the pattern becomes incorrect, then go

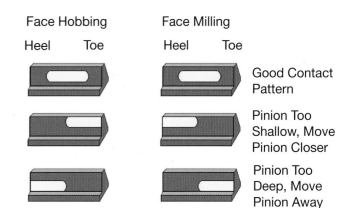

Gear patterns. Note that these are with the backlash set correctly. Always set the backlash to the gear manufacturer's specifications before taking a pattern. Then pay more attention to centering the pattern between the face (top) and the flank (bottom) of the tooth. Pay less attention to the position of the pattern between the toe and the heel.

The factory usually used machined cast-iron rings for setting the side bearing placement and corresponding backlash adjustment. You can try to reuse these, but unless you have a case spreader, there is a good chance that you will break it when you attempt to tap it back in place.

the other way in the smaller increments. For example, if the pinion was too deep, start making your changes .005 to .010 inch at a time and checking until the pattern is too shallow, then back up in .002- to .004-inch changes.

As long as the backlash is set correctly and the contact pattern is centered between the face and the root of the ring gear teeth, the pinion depth is correct even if the pattern is split or favors the heel or toe. Do not attempt to change this by changing the pinion depth. If the housing has several thousand trouble-free miles, it will be OK. You are working to center the contact pressure between the top and bottom of the ring gear teeth, not the inside to outside.

FINAL REAR AXLE ASSEMBLY

Fill the housing with the proper amount of 85W-140 synthetic gear lube. If a clutch-type limited-slip carrier is used, make sure the proper amount of friction additive is included. Add this first, as this way it will fit. If you have an empty container, you can premix the lube and friction additive. Once the housing is full of fluid, install the fill plug. With the wheels off the ground, rotate the wheels several times to lubricate everything.

Your new gears will need to be properly broken in. Drive the vehicle at moderate speeds for 10 to 15 miles to warm up the rear axle, then park the car for 30 minutes or more to let the axle cool completely. Most gear manufacturers will recommend you do this at least twice, allowing a minimum 30-minute cool-down each time. Do not exceed 60 mph or place a heavy load on the rear axle. This is important—how the gears are used for the first few minutes of operation will determine how long the ring and pinion will last. Drive easy the next 50 miles. Do not tow a trailer for the next 200 to 250 miles.

The gears will get hot during the break-in. Let them cool in order to avoid overheating the gears and bearings, which will cause an early rear axle failure. It is recommended that you change the fluid after the first 500 miles to remove any metal particles and shavings that might have come from the gears during the initial break-in.

REAR AXLE PROBLEMS

Rear axles are relatively simple and don't experience a lot of complicated problems. The rear axle will usually last the life of the car. Failures are usually catastrophic, like a broken axle or damaged gears. The spider gears absorb a lot of strain. An engine producing 500 lb-ft of torque with a 2.44 first gear and a 3.50 rear axle ratio will subject these gears to more than 4,200 lb-ft of force!

A common problem is excessive noise caused by worn gears or improper gear setup. If the rear gears are howling, check the gear contact surfaces for signs of wear. The only fix for this is new gears. Also check for worn bearings; play in the pinion bearings will allow the pinion to move and this will disturb the relationship between the gears. This also usually will result in worn and damaged gears. If the gears were installed improperly and the vehicle was driven any distance at all, the gears will be damaged and will have to be replaced.

For trucks or vehicles that do a lot of towing, the ring and pinion can fail. Rear gears generate heat as the gear surfaces slide across each other. As the load is increased, this heat is increased and there is a point at which it results in gear wear and eventual failure.

This is a typical speedometer gear and housing. The gears are changed to match the tire and rear axle ratio. There is an O-ring seal around the outside of the housing that is visible in this picture. There is also a lip-style seal inside that seals the shaft to prevent transmission fluid from leaking into the speedometer cable. This seal is located just back from the speedometer cable attachment point.

Speedometer drive gears. These are just two of the many gears available for the GM TH-400 transmission. You can obtain speedometer drive gears from dealers or over the Internet and from speedometer repair shops or transmission parts suppliers.

This is why trucks have a maximum tow weight. If it is exceeded, the gears can be overstressed and overheated. The same can occur under extended high-speed operation. A rear axle cooler can be used to alleviate the problem and prevent gear failure.

If you find a loose pinion, it is usually due to improper crush sleeve torque or a failed pinion bearing. Bearing wear can cause this. The more likely cause is the crush sleeve slowly loosening and reducing preload to the point that the pinion becomes loose. This is the signal that a rebuild is required. Most rear axles will last 150,000 miles before this happens.

SPEEDOMETER CALIBRATION

The speedometer drive on most muscle cars is located on the transmission tailshaft. Several gears are available with different tooth counts to allow the speedometer to be calibrated to match the rear axle gears. Most modern American cars with a mechanical speedometer use 1,000 rotations per mile as the speedometer-drive ratio. This means that if you drive the vehicle exactly one mile, the speedometer cable will rotate 1,000 times.

If the wheels and tires, transmission, or rear axle ratio have been changed, the speedometer calibration is probably incorrect. The easiest way to correct this is to find a known 5- or 10-mile distance. Some states have speedometer calibration points marked on the highway.

Record the exact odometer reading at the start and then record the odometer reading at the finish. The difference is the error. If you drive 5 miles, but the odometer is indicating 4.6 miles, your speedometer is running at 92 percent and is also slow. This means that the reported speed will also be only 92 percent of the actual speed and the odometer will add only .92 miles for each mile traveled.

This can be corrected by changing the drive gear at the transmission tailshaft. Count the number of teeth on the gear. For our example above, we need a gear with less teeth. You can get replacement gears from the dealership or transmission service shops. You will have to work with them to find out what selection of gears are available and select the gear that will give the closest final result. It is unlikely that you will find a gear that is exactly right. As time goes on, these gears will become less common at new car dealerships, as modern cars do not use mechanical speedometers.

For our example above, if our driven gear has 35 teeth, and it is reading 92 percent slow, then we know that the driven gear needs to turn faster; therefore, it needs less teeth. By multiplying the number of teeth by the error, we can determine how many teeth the replacement gear needs. In this case, .92 x 35 = 32.2, or 32 teeth. Next, check with your local parts counter or one of the many speedometer calibration shops (easily found on the Internet) and see what gears are available.

If the gear size that you calculated is not available, then the drive gear may need to be changed. This is a little tougher to do, as the tailshaft on the transmission will have to be removed. The gear is usually pressed on or retained by a clip to the transmission output shaft. Before removing the tailshaft, count the teeth on the drive gear. If the speedometer is reading slow, the driven gear would need more teeth. If it is reading fast, it needs fewer teeth. The same formula above can be used; just multiply the number of teeth on the driven gear by the inverse of the error.

So for our example, if the driven gear has 17 teeth, then 17 x 1/0.92 = 18.47. This shows that either an 18- or 19- tooth drive gear is needed. This will result in you having to fine-tune with a different driven gear to get the correct result. The same problem can result when calculating driven gears. If you fall between two sizes, then changing to a different drive and driven gear combination should allow you to get closer to a correct ratio. Check with a speedometer calibration shop for your options. Most of these will usually have a good website that shows the various gears available for each particular make of transmission.

Most manufacturers had several different driven gears as well as more than one transmission-drive gear. By selecting the appropriate combination of driven gear and drive gear, you can get close to what you need. The driven gear fits in an offset housing that allows you to install the gear and account for the difference in size between the gears. Watch out—most manufacturers had more than one housing in order to account for the wide range of driven gears. Make sure that your new driven gear will work with your housing.

If your speedometer reading is off more than you can correct for with the drive gear combinations available, all is not lost. You can purchase ratio adapters from speedometer calibration shops. These are small boxes that connect between the speedometer cable and the transmission. These boxes have gears in them and can accommodate up to a 2:1 change in speed. They are sold by the reduction or increase that they provide. One can usually be found to get you in the ballpark, and the fine-tuning can be done with the proper selection of drive and driven gears.

Once the odometer is correctly calibrated, the speedometer can be checked for proper speed indication. It is common for an older speedometer to read the incorrect speed even though the odometer is correctly calibrated. There are three methods you can use. Have someone drive at a set speed—say 60 mph—and follow that person and check the speed on your speedometer.

Another method involves driving for a set distance at a constant speed and noting the time to cover the distance. For example, find a section of highway with mile markers. Using the mile markers to judge your distance, drive 5 miles while maintaining exactly 60 mph on the speedometer. When complete, note how long it took. If you are traveling at exactly 60 mph, then it should have taken exactly 5 minutes. Your true speed can be found by multiplying by 60 the result of dividing the distance traveled by the time it took. For example, if you drove 5 miles in 4 minutes and 45 seconds, then you would first divide 5 by 4.75. Note that 45 seconds is .75 minutes: to convert seconds to a base 10 number, divide 60 into the remainder number of seconds you drove. So the result of our distance divided by the time is 1.05. Next, multiply the result by 60 to convert to miles per hour. In our case, 1.05 times 60 is equal to 63 mph. So our speedometer in this example is reading slow by 5 percent.

The last is to find one of those speed-reporting signs. These are usually found around construction sites or in residential neighborhoods. Be careful as some may have a photographic speed citation camera as well! Drive at a constant speed and note the difference between what your speedometer is showing and how fast the sign says you are going.

You can also use a GPS unit to check speed. They are quite accurate.

Let's say that you have checked your speedometer and the odometer is calibrated correctly but the speed is reading 11 percent fast! This means that when your speedometer reads 70 mph, you are really only going a little faster than 62 mph! You can, of course, opt to just live with the error. You can also replace your speedometer with an aftermarket model; this will not maintain your original look. You can change the transmission speedometer drive gear to correct the speed and have your odometer read incorrectly. The best option is to find a company that specializes in gauge repair. They can repair and recalibrate your speedometer to make it read correctly. Many of these can also restore the face of the gauge as well.

CHAPTER 13
DRIVESHAFT

The driveshaft is perhaps the least appreciated component in the vehicle. It simply transmits power from the transmission to the rear axle. Unless you are having problems with the driveshaft or U-joints, you probably don't even give it any thought.

U-JOINTS

While the driveshaft itself is not appreciated, the U-joints get even less consideration. When was the last time a bench racing session was about U-joints? This is a testament as to how tough they really are. Most people don't even remember to grease them and they will routinely go well over 100,000 miles! Unlike CV joints on front-wheel-drive vehicles, U-joints are simple, reliable, and tough.

The best thing you can do is grease them at regular intervals. If your U-joints do not have grease zerks, the only way to grease them is to remove them and then remove each cap one at a time and add grease. This is most likely not worth the effort, and considering the low cost, the best idea might simply be to replace nongreasable U-joints every 50,000 to 100,000 miles. Note that the greater the operating angle, the shorter the life of the U-joint.

Checking U-joints is simple. With the vehicle on a flat, level surface and with the transmission in neutral, grab the driveshaft right next to a U-joint and try to move the shaft up and down and then side to side. Check for any signs of movement. Also check

1350s-tyle U-joints. These U-joints are retained by external lock rings.

the transmission slip yoke or rear axle pinion for signs of movement. If these move, they need attention. There should be no play or detectable movement between the driveshaft and the other side of the U-joint.

Next, attempt to rotate the driveshaft forward and backward. There should be no movement between the two sides of the U-joint. If the joint fails either of these tests, then the joint is bad and must be replaced. Also, visually inspect the U-joint for any damage. And check the seals between the cup and the cross. If any of the seals show signs of damage, the joint must be replaced. Bad seals are usually what ruin U-joints. The seal cracks, grease escapes, and contaminants enter the joint, all of which are problems that cause accelerated wear.

With the vehicle on a flat, level surface and the engine not running, place the vehicle in neutral and roll the car forward and backward. This test can also be performed with the rear wheels jacked up above the ground by slowly rotating the rear tires forward and backward. Listen for any squeaking sounds. The squeaks are caused by a dry U-joint that needs to be replaced.

REPLACING U-JOINTS

Replacing U-joints is easy. Mark the driveshaft and the transmission slip yoke so the relationship between the driveshaft and the slip yoke can be maintained. To remove the U-joint, simply remove the retaining rings from the cups. U-joints are held together either by C-clips that fit on the inside of the cup, next to the center of the cross, or by snap rings that fit onto the outside face of the cup. A third style combines these two on the same cross.

Once the rings are removed, the cups can be removed. This usually will require a press, as years of service and exposure to the elements will rust the caps in place. Press them in slightly in order to knock the opposite side loose and partially out. Once one side is removed, rotate the shaft 180 degrees. Use a suitably sized pressing tool to press the joint back in to push the cup out. Repeat this procedure for the remaining two cups.

Here is a U-joint with a broken seal. This U-joint needs to be replaced. This is a 1310-style U-joint, and it is retained with an internal clip ring.

Do not hammer or pound on the U-joints. Use a press or a large C-clamp. Do not hold the driveshaft by clamping it in a vice. This will crush the driveshaft and damage it. I simply let it lie on the work surface. When using the press, support the opposite end in such a way that the driveshaft stays level.

Clean the inside surface where the cups reside and check these areas for signs of damage or cracks. Also check the transmission slip yoke for signs of excessive wear; now is the time to replace the slip yoke if it is damaged. Remove the caps from the new U-joint and carefully place them on your workbench. Be careful to not knock any of the needle rollers out of the caps.

If the joint does not have a grease zerk, carefully force a little grease into each cup. Tap one cup just into position from the outside. Do not drive it fully seated as you will not be able to get the cross-shaft into position. If the U-joint has an internal grease passage, you may find that it is easier to use a grease gun and fill the internal passages with grease before installing the U-joint.

Next, place the cross inside the driveshaft. Position the cross shaft so that it begins to go into the one cup that was started. Position the remaining cup on the opposite side. Using a press or a large

DRIVESHAFT

Removing the first U-joint cup by pressing the other side cup and joint down. This will cause the cup on the opposite side to be pressed out. Use a large socket as the support for the yoke; make sure that it is positioned so that the cup can fall clear.

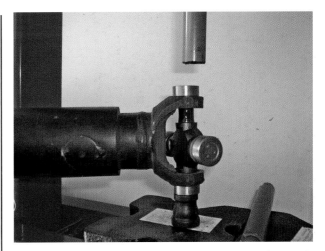

Tap in one cup just so that it will not fall out. Next, position the U-joint in the yoke and be sure that it properly begins to enter the cup. Finally, place the remaining cup into position and then press both cups in. Do not use excessive pressure; this can damage the joint.

Remove the remaining cap by flipping the driveshaft over and then press the U-joint down to push the remaining cup back into the yoke and then out. Use the socket to support the yoke and allow the cup to come out freely.

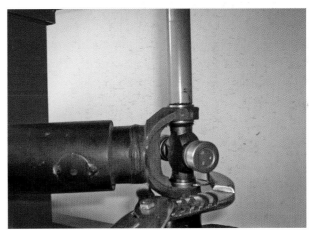

Install the retaining snap rings or locks. For internal snap rings, the first one is easier to install if it is installed before the final cup is pressed the rest of the way.

C-clamp, press the cups into position. Do not use excessive force; use only enough pressure to get the caps into position.

Usually one cup will be fully seated before another. Stop at this point and install the retaining clip for the cup that is fully seated, and then finish pressing the remaining cap into position. Next, install the transmission slip yoke. Make sure the alignment marks are lined back up and install the two cups. Install the locking rings. Verify that the joint moves freely and is not loose. Verify that the locking rings are properly installed.

DRIVESHAFT VIBRATION

Driveline vibration is caused by a misaligned driveline or loose components. Check the U-joints, transmission slip yoke, and the rear axle pinion for looseness. If those are fine and you are still experiencing a vibration, the next step is to verify that the problem is caused by the driveline. Have the wheels balanced. More often than not, a rim or tire out of balance is causing your car to shake. An out-of-balance wheel can either vibrate at a specific speed or begin vibrating at a certain speed and get worse as the speed increases.

Most muscle cars are big and heavy. This should result in a smooth-riding car. Any vibration is an indication that something is wrong. If the wheels are properly balanced, check to see if any part of the exhaust system is in contact with the body. Also check for solid motor mounts. If you or a previous owner installed solid mounts, these can transmit a large amount of vibration into the vehicle.

Don't forget to check the engine and transmission mounts; these should be in good condition and properly installed. They set the angle of the engine and transmission and therefore affect the driveshaft angles. Also verify that they are the proper mounts. Inspect the crossmember; does it look like the correct one for the vehicle? There is a good chance that at some point in the vehicle's past the transmission and engine have been removed, perhaps more than once. If the crossmember was not properly installed or if the wrong mounts were used, the driveline angles might be off.

After verifying that the wheels are properly balanced and all driveline components and their mounts are good, place the vehicle on a lift that supports the vehicle by the wheels. This way, the driveline will be at its normal operating height. The driveline components must be at the same angles when you check them as they are when the vehicle is traveling down the road.

CHECKING DRIVELINE ANGLES

Begin by checking the engine angle. Check this using the starter motor. Do not use the oil pan, as it is most likely not perfectly parallel with the crankshaft centerline. Record this reading; on most vehicles there will be a slight angle down from the front of the engine to the rear. The transmission angle will be the same as the engine angle; usually the engine is easier to check. You should see a 2- to 5- degree angle, with the rear of the engine lower than the front. Do not check the angle on the carburetor mounting surface; this is usually cut at an angle to make the carburetor sit level.

Next, check the rear axle angle. This is checked by recording the angle at the inspection cover surface. If you cannot get to the machined cover mounting surface, measure across two bolts and make sure the tops are both the same distance away from the housing surface. You can use a set of calipers to measure the bolt head height above the machined housing surface and loosen or tighten one of the bolts until the measurement matches. On most vehicles, the front of the housing points down slightly. A common angle is 0.5 to 1.5 degrees down.

Next, measure the driveshaft angle. Make sure the angle-measuring device is placed parallel with the shaft so the reading is accurate.

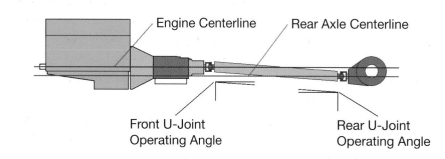

Engine Centerline

Rear Axle Centerline

Front U-Joint
Operating Angle

Rear U-Joint
Operating Angle

Driveshaft operating angles. Note that the centerline of the transmission does not line up with the centerline of the pinion, but that ideally, these two lines would be parallel. This is almost never the case. Most engines are installed with a rear down angle, and most rear axles are installed with the pinion slightly down. What is important is that the vehicle operates with both U-joint angles nearly identical.

Once you have all three angles, you can compute the operating angle of each U-joint. Begin with the front joint. Check the angles of the engine and the driveshaft. If both components are angled the same direction, then subtract the smaller angle from the larger angle to get the operating angle of the U-joint.

If the engine is slanted down, meaning that the rear of the engine is lower than the front, and the driveshaft is also slanting down, with the differential end lower than the transmission, you would subtract the larger angle from the smaller one. For example, if the engine is angled down 4.5 degrees toward the rear and if the driveshaft is angled 1.5 degrees with the rear axle end lower, then both components are angled the same way and we subtract 1.5 from 4.5 for a U-joint operating angle of 3 degrees.

Next, compute the rear U-joint angle. Let's say the rear axle is angled 1 degree, with the pinion down and our driveshaft is angled 1.5 degrees with the rear axle end down. The two components are angled in opposite directions. In this case, add the two numbers to get a 2.5-degree operating angle. Compare the two operating angles. Since they are under 1 degree difference, everything is fine. Also, since the largest angle is 3 degrees, you are not over the 3-degree limit.

The operating angle of the two U-joints would ideally be equal. If they are not within 1 degree of each other, you can suffer driveline vibrations. Besides the annoyance, this can cause the U-joints, transmission output shaft bearing, and differential pinion bearing to fail prematurely. U-joint operating angles of more than 3 degrees increase the likelihood for vibration and driveline shudder, especially when accelerating from a stop.

If the operating angles for a driveshaft with standard U-joints are not opposite and equal, the vehicle will be subject to driveline vibration. This is because when a standard cross U-joint transfers rotation across an angle, there is a speed change across the plane that bisects the angle as the joint rotates. If the input is held fixed at a constant speed, the output will maintain an average speed that is equal to the input speed, but twice per revolution the speed will be more, and twice per revolution the

speed will be less. The amount of this speed-up and slow-down is dependent on the operating angle, with no speed change when operating at zero degrees.

Since neither the engine nor the car can speed up and slow down twice per driveline revolution, the driveline moves on its mounts to compensate and absorb this speed difference. The result of this is vibration, and it can be severe.

CV or constant velocity U-joints don't have this problem. As their name implies, their speed is constant even when operating at nonzero angles. This type of joint is used on front-wheel-drive cars so the wheel can turn without subjecting the vehicle to driveline vibrations. Some trucks use CV joints to overcome steep driveshaft angles.

CV joints work well on trucks with high body or suspension lifts, as the necessary driveshaft angle is too steep for a standard U-joint. To solve the problem, a CV joint is used at the transfer case output and the rear axle is rotated so the pinion centerline is pointed directly at the transfer case output. A conventional U-joint can be used at the rear axle because it operates at a near-zero angle.

CORRECTING DRIVELINE ANGLES

Begin by analyzing the problem. The vehicle did not come from the factory with this problem. Verify that the engine angle is correct. Check that the engine and transmission mounts are the correct ones and that they are properly installed.

Check the pinion angle at the rear axle. Most cars came from the factory with the pinion down by 0.5 to 1.5 degrees. Check the factory service manual for the recommended pinion angle. Changing the rear pinion angle on cars that are running leaf-spring rear suspensions is relatively easy. Vehicles that use a four-link or trailing-arm-style rear axle are more difficult to change; these usually require custom-made or adjustable control arms.

It is not uncommon to find a leaf-spring vehicle with the pinion pointing down 3 to 4 degrees. This is a modification that drag racers make to leaf-spring cars in order to compensate for spring wrap while the vehicle is under full-throttle acceleration. The twisting force of the rear axle distorts the spring, and the excessive nose-down angle of the differential will result in the pinion running near zero. The problem is that this will result in excessive U-joint operating angles during everyday driving, with the corresponding driveline vibration and short U-joint life.

In order to set U-joint angles correctly, begin with the U-joint that is operating at the largest angle. Determine what will have to move and in what direction in order to decrease the angle.

TABLE 11: MAXIMUM DRIVELINE RPM FOR VARIOUS U-JOINT OPERATING ANGLES

Maximum U-joint Operating Angle (degrees)	Maximum Driveline RPM
2.3	7,000
2.7	6,000
3.2	5,000
3.5	4,500
4.0	4,000
4.6	3,500
5.4	3,000
6.5	2,500
8.0	2,000

Note that if the maximum operating angle is kept below 3 degrees, you will not have issues. If you run an overdrive, the driveline rpm will be higher than the engine rpm. This can be found by dividing the engine rpm by the overdrive ratio. This is a linear relationship, i.e., double the speed = half the maximum angle.

For example, if the front U-joint operating angle is 4 degrees and the rear angle is 0.5 degrees, you will begin at the front. Either the front of the engine needs to come down or the rear of the transmission needs to come up. The latter is usually easier, so raise the rear. In this example, a 1-inch increase in the height of the

rear of the transmission results in a 3.1-degree-down engine angle and a 1.5-degree-down driveshaft angle. When coupled with the 0.5-degree nose-down pinion angle, the new U-joint angles come out to 1.6 for the front and 2.0 for the rear. This is actually ideal, as the pinion will twist up as the vehicle accelerates. With the driveshaft rear down and pinion nose down, the rear angle will decrease under acceleration.

As you move one end of the driveshaft up or down (which will happen if the rear of the transmission changed or if the rear axle is rotated), the driveshaft and the U-joint angle on the other end will be affected as well. After any change, check all three angles and compute the new front and rear U-joint operating angles.

Where this gets challenging is if the correction requires that the rear of the transmission be lowered. This usually requires a custom crossmember. The same is true for four-link or trailing-arm rear axle setups; these usually require modification or custom components. In some cases, adjustable arms can be purchased. Always correct the angle at the most severe U-joint. Dialing in more pinion angle to match the front U-joint angle may solve the vibration issue but result in two U-joints operating at steep angles. Even though they are matched, the power and rpm capacity of the U-joints will be reduced.

Don't forget to check the side-to-side angles as well. This is easy. Attach a string to the front of the engine, directly under the centerline at the front of the crankshaft. Stretch it to the rear axle and attach it directly under the center of the pinion. Check if the transmission tailshaft is centered with the string. If not, the transmission centerline and the rear axle centerline are not the same.

This may not be a problem. It is not uncommon to find vehicles with misaligned engine and axle centerlines. What is important is that the engine and rear axle side-by-side centerlines should be parallel. If they are not, the axle mounting points or engine mounts have shifted. This is most often caused by collision damage.

INDEX